Critical Studies of the Asia-Pacific

Series editor
Mark Beeson
Political Science and International Relations
University of Western Australia
Crawley, West Australia, Australia

Critical Studies of the Asia Pacific showcases new research and scholarship on what is arguably the most important region in the world in the twenty-first century. The rise of China and the continuing strategic importance of this dynamic economic area to the United States mean that the Asia-Pacific will remain crucially important to policymakers and scholars alike. The unifying theme of the series is a desire to publish the best theoretically-informed, original research on the region. Titles in the series cover the politics, economics and security of the region, as well as focusing on its institutional processes, individual countries, issues and leaders.

More information about this series at
http://www.springer.com/series/14940

Nicholas Henry

Asylum, Work, and Precarity

Bordering the Asia-Pacific

palgrave
macmillan

Nicholas Henry
Centre for the Study of Globalisation
and Regionalisation
University of Warwick
Coventry, United Kingdom

Critical Studies of the Asia-Pacific
ISBN 978-3-319-60566-1 ISBN 978-3-319-60567-8 (eBook)
DOI 10.1007/978-3-319-60567-8

Library of Congress Control Number: 2017947192

Cover illustration: Anthony Partleton / Alamy Stock Photo

Printed on acid-free paper

This Palgrave Macmillan imprint is published by Springer Nature
The registered company is Springer International Publishing AG
The registered company address is: Gewerbestrasse 11, 6330 Cham, Switzerland

Acknowledgements

Thanks to all the organisations and individuals who generously gave their time for interviews and other assistance during my research for this book: in Bangkok, the staff of the regional and country offices of the United Nations High Commission for Refugees, the International Organisation for Migration, the United Nations Office for Drugs and Crime, the International Labour Organisation, the Regional Support Office to the Bali Process, Asylum Access, Asia Pacific Refugee Rights Network, Arakan Project, Migration Working Group, and the Migrant Worker Resource Centre; in Kuala Lumpur, the staff of the Malaysia Trades Union Congress, Building Workers' International, the All Malaysia Estate Staff Union, CARAM Asia, and the Migrant Worker Resource Centre; in Singapore, the staff of Transient Workers Count Too; and in Jakarta, the staff of SUAKA, Lembaga Bantuan Hukum, the ASEAN Secretariat, the Jesuit Refugee Service (interviewed in Melbourne), and the Human Rights Working Group.

I would like to acknowledge the support for my research provided by the School of Humanities and Social Sciences at Deakin University in Melbourne, including through a research grant that allowed me to visit organisations and conduct interviews in Southeast Asia. Thanks to the efforts of Prof Matthew Clarke as Head of School and all my colleagues in the academic and administrative staff, I enjoyed a collegial and supportive working environment for my research. Thanks in particular to Dr. Belinda Townsend for taking the time to read and provide insightful comments on early drafts, and to Dr. Chengxin Pan for his useful and supportive advice on my research. Thanks also to the staff of the Deakin International Liaison Office in Jakarta for help in facilitating interviews.

I am grateful to everyone in the Centre for the Study of Globalisation and Regionalisation (CSGR) and the Politics and International Studies (PAIS) department at the University of Warwick for hosting me as a Visiting Fellow in 2016. Particular thanks to Dr. Alexandra Homolar, who hosted and supported my visit and seminar presentation through her leadership of the Speaking International Security at Warwick program; Dr. André Broome, who hosted me as a Visiting Fellow in his role as CSGR Director; and Prof Nick Vaughan-Williams who as head of PAIS made me welcome at Warwick and generously made time to discuss our shared research interests.

Thanks, in solidarity, to the members of RISE, Beyond Borders, Anarchist Affinity, and xBorder in Melbourne, for the intellectual rigour and principled commitment of your work challenging carceral border regimes, from which I had the privilege of learning.

I would like to acknowledge all the friends and family I have learnt from and been supported by in the process of writing this book. Thanks to Alexandra Homolar and André Broome for your friendship and generous hospitality; Belinda Townsend and Tris Galloway for your encouragement; and my parents John Henry and Tricia Glensor for all your support.

Above all, my acknowledgement and thanks to Meredith Harris for your constant support and encouragement in the process of writing this book, for all the enlightening conversations, and your insightful comments on drafts.

Contents

List of Tables

CHAPTER 1

Introduction

This book explores the regional coordination and impact of state responses to irregular migration in Southeast Asia and the Pacific. The main argument is that regional and international trends of securitisation and criminalisation of irregular migration—often associated with framing the issue in terms of migrant smuggling and human trafficking—have intensified carceral border regimes and produced greater precarity for migrants. Bilateral and multilateral processes of regional coordination at multiple levels of government are analysed with a focus on the impact on asylum seekers and migrant workers arriving or staying in major destination and transit countries—including Malaysia, Thailand, Singapore, Indonesia and Australia.

When I began work on the research for this book, I was based in Melbourne, Australia, where I witnessed the steady escalation of political discourse framing the movement of asylum seekers by sea as an international security and criminal threat. The two major parties of government, Labor and Liberal, appeared locked into a battle of competitive xenophobia in their public statements about both asylum seekers and migrant workers, and shared bipartisan commitments to policies of restrictive labour migration and deterrence of asylum seekers. Policies of asylum deterrence backed by both major parties are based on arbitrary enforcement of migration borders through intercepting and turning back boats at sea, mandatory and indefinite detention of asylum seekers, and deportation without due process.

N. Henry, *Asylum, Work, and Precarity*, Critical Studies of the Asia-Pacific, DOI 10.1007/978-3-319-60567-8_1

The externalisation of Australia's border to deter and prevent the arrival of asylum seekers has created what Hyndman and Mountz (2008, 253) describe, borrowing Gregory's (2004) phrase, as an 'architecture of enmity, framed as protection'. The 'architecture of enmity' refers to the institutional framing of criminalisation and securitisation, together with the carceral responses and production of precarity covered in subsequent chapters. That these policies can continue to be 'framed as protection' owes much to the ambiguity of the shared discourse of Liberal Humanitarianism, with claims on both sides of parliamentary politics to be 'saving lives at sea' by 'disrupting the people smugglers' business model'. Dauvergne (2005) calls this shared, though ambiguous, discourse the 'humanitarian consensus' of migration debates, and draws attention to its roots in appeals to nationalist identity.

Nationalist identity is at the core of debates over migration policy. From the nationalist perspective of opponents of migration, the national identity is seen as threatened by the arrival of those marked as foreign and other to the imagined cultural identity of the nation. On the other hand, for the mainstream liberal advocates of increased openness to migration and protection for refugees, it is a mark of national identity to be generous in extending hospitality to those similarly marked as foreign and other. In the words of a poster campaign that appeared around Melbourne in 2015, advocating greater openness to refugees, 'Real Australians Say Welcome'. As Verma (2015) observes, there is something jarring in seeing white anti-racist activists claiming the right to welcome others to the land of a settler colonial nation, with no acknowledgement of the sovereign rights of Aboriginal owners over that land. In taking up the position of welcoming others, white liberal humanitarians valorise themselves as the inheritors of the settler-colonial mandate to control territory and migration while showing their willingness to conditionally open membership to others as an act of generosity, or what Verma calls 'pretended largesse'.

The convergence of carceral and humanitarian discourses of migration border management around national identity is matched by a convergence in practice of carceral and humanitarian border work. In a comparative study of carceral border regimes of Europe and Australia, Vaughan-Williams and Little (2016) draw attention to the ambiguous roles of humanitarian organisations and discourses. In a research note based on their fieldwork with unaccompanied minors among refugees and asylum seekers recently arrived in Europe, Sigona and Allsopp (2016) reported that children and young adults who wanted to continue their journeys into Europe—and avoid detention in so-called care facilities—had learnt to run from volunteers and staff of humanitarian NGOs conducting outreach work. In Australia's regime of migration detention in the Pacific states of Nauru and Papua New Guinea, the integration of humanitarian and carceral border work is even starker as humanitarian NGOs, including the Salvation Army and Save the Children, have accepted government contracts to operate in the detention camps.

The insular and nationalistic nature of public and parliamentary debates around policy responses to asylum seekers and migrant workers in Australia leave little room for consideration of how these issues fit into a broader regional context. Having spent some time learning about conditions for refugees and migrant workers in Southeast Asia, including through previous research with trade unions and other community based organisations from Myanmar and the Philippines, I knew that the regional context was important for understanding how and why asylum seekers and migrant workers arrive in Australia, as well as for putting into a more appropriate context some of the exaggerated claims about the difficulty of managing the arrival of relatively small numbers of asylum seekers by sea. I decided that the best way for me to contribute to public and academic debates around migration border governance was to undertake a detailed study of the regional institutions and processes of inter-state cooperation that I saw as playing a significant role in shaping responses to irregular migration in the region, although with relatively little public attention or scrutiny.

As I completed the manuscript for the book in 2017, the inauguration of Donald Trump as US President seemed to guarantee that carceral and restrictive approaches to migration border management would remain in the news for the foreseeable future. Based on the findings of the research in this book I have two responses to the initial policy announcements of the Trump administration. First, the arbitrary enforcement of migration borders targeting undocumented migrants for arrest, detention and deportation, together with the restriction of asylum and refugee resettlement, represents an escalation of existing trends in the US rather than new developments, and in many ways mirrors the status quo in Australia's carceral migration border regime. Second, the lack of an evidence base for claims by the Trump administration that migrants with irregular status and refugees constitute criminal and security threats reinforces the argument in this book that carceral border regimes are produced by securitisation and criminalisation of irregular migration, but are independent of trends in the form or scale of migration itself. Unlike in the European Union, where an escalation of carceral responses and arbitrary enforcement of migration borders from 2015 has coincided with increases in the arrival of asylum seekers at the Mediterranean borders of the EU, similar developments in the framing and enforcement of carceral migration borders in Southeast Asia and the Pacific have developed in the absence of such movements or in response to much smaller numbers of migrants with irregular status travelling by sea. For this reason, the Melbourne-based organisation Refugees, Survivors, and Ex-Detainees (RISE 2015) rejects the label 'refugee crisis', arguing instead that 'it is a crisis of state abuse and hyper-militarisation for which the abused are blamed'. A staff member at the UNHCR's regional office for the Asia-Pacific made a similar argument, although in different terms, in explaining that UNHCR also rejected the term 'refugee crisis' to describe the stranding of several thousand Rohingya asylum seekers and Bangladeshi migrant workers in the Andaman sea in May 2015. It was pointed out that the approximately 5000 people on the boats represented 'no more than arrive in a single day in Europe', and that the crisis was caused by state responses rather than by the movement of asylum seekers and other migrants.

In the process of interviewing staff with responsibilities related to irregular migration and border management in a range of regional organisations, I was struck by the prevalence of a shared set of liberal humanitarian values and aims that these staff saw as guiding their work, including at organisations such as UNODC, IOM and the Regional Support Office to the Bali Process with active commitments to promoting cooperation on law enforcement responses to irregular migration. These professionals generally framed their work in humanitarian terms as contributing to the protection of migrants, despite, or perhaps connected to, the fact that many of these regional organisation staff were engaged in projects explicitly connected to the criminalisation of people smuggling and trafficking in persons, which I connect in Chap. 4 to the securitisation of carceral border regimes, or in the promotion of cooperation between states to prevent and deter irregular migration more generally.

This apparent consensus around liberal humanitarian values was certainly in stark contrast to my brief experience of engaging with officials at the Australian Embassy in Jakarta on the issue of irregular migration. While visiting the embassy, accompanying a group of students, I had raised a question in the discussion about whether the embassy saw potential to cooperate with advocacy organisations working with asylum seekers on developing safe alternatives to dangerous sea journeys. The junior diplomat briefing our group had previously worked on the embassy's counter-smuggling projects, but responded defensively and refused to comment. Later, at an embassy function, she explained her view that asylum seekers in Indonesia were not genuine, because she had heard that some held parties with their friends before boarding boats to Australia. 'Is that how genuine refugees would behave?' she asked me rhetorically. Pickering (2014) has documented similar attitudes among frontline officers in Australia's border enforcement attitudes, who made negative inferences when asylum seekers did not conform to their gendered and racialised expectations about the correct behaviour for genuine refugees.

I expected to find some similar level of prejudice among staff of regional organisations towards asylum seekers and other migrants with irregular status—or at least a wider range of views than the almost unanimous commitment to liberal humanitarian values I encountered. I had previously associated a liberal humanitarian perspective with support for legal protection mechanisms for refugees and migrant workers, but was surprised to hear similar values and commitments expressed so universally (although admittedly among a very small sample) among those I perceived to be working to restrict irregular migration. This prompted me to become more curious about the role and function of liberal humanitarian discourse, including in helping to legitimise aspects of carceral border regimes.

Structure of the Book

I begin Chap. 2, Border Spaces, with an explanation of the approach of this book to conceptualising borders as techniques of state power, producing political spaces and regimes of governance that extend across and beyond state territories. My focus is on the development and distribution of techniques of state power—including through inter-state and regional co-ordination—as the basis for the evolution of national and regional border regimes. This differentiates my approach from theories of regime formation in the International Relations literature that prioritise the role of international norms. While international norms, including those of humanitarian protection, do have a role and function in regimes of border management, I argue that this is often as post hoc justifications for regimes formed by the selective adoption by states of techniques of border management.

I make use of Deleuze's concept of the fold to describe the political spaces of the border formed by techniques of governance that make strategic use of obscurity and ambiguity in the sites and processes of migration processing. Using examples from Australia's responses to the maritime arrival of asylum seekers transformations, I describe the folds of location, legality, logistics and legibility in the political space of contemporary migration border regimes.

In situating the study of border regimes within the regional context of Southeast Asia and the Pacific, I draw on Walia's (2013) concept of border imperialism to understand the role of Australia in perpetuating the power dynamics established through settler colonialism. The legacies of settler colonialism are visible in the techniques of contemporary border management in Western states, in the ways that populations are racialised and defined as risks, and in the ways that borders are externalised through unequal relations with neighbouring states.

Finally, I discuss the particular context of Southeast Asia with reference to the ongoing processes of ASEAN integration. The formation of the ASEAN Economic Community from 2015 is an ongoing and open-ended process which has already produced substantial integration of markets and production through the free movement of goods, services, investment, and skilled labour among the 10 ASEAN member states. This economic integration produces a tension with the lack of adequate mechanisms for the free movement of people, including migrant workers and asylum seekers. The institutions and processes of ASEAN integration will continue to be central to the regional dynamics of Southeast Asia and the Pacific, although developments in the area of migration border management may be produced as much by contradictions and gaps in ASEAN integration as by the organisation's initiatives.

In Chap. 3, Leaving Home, I give a detailed overview of the patterns and trends of migration in Southeast Asia and the Pacific, focusing on key source and destination countries for migrant workers and asylum seekers. Using close engagement with statistics on asylum seekers and migrant workers based on UNHCR figures and World Bank estimates, I present a fine-grained analysis of the patterns of collective decisions to depart, and choices of destination and mode of travel made by migrants. By relating these patterns in official statistics on migration to trends in economic growth and employment, persecution and conflict, as well as evidence of irregular migration, I demonstrate that in the aggregate, the relationship between regular and irregular migration owes most to decisions made by policy makers rather than migrants. The decisions that individual migrants make are generally rational responses to the relative availability of opportunities for regular and irregular movement and status, and the phenomenon of irregular migration is produced by the failure of opportunities for regular migration to keep pace with economic demand for migrant workers and the protection needs of asylum seekers.

One of the main patterns evident across the region is the tendency for rates of labour migration to rise as the country of origin reaches middle-income status, before tailing off at higher stages of economic development. Within this broad trend, significant variation between states of both origin and destination at similar levels of development can be partly attributed to differences in state policies facilitating migration. Migration patterns are also highly path dependant, with contemporary rates and routes of movement influenced strongly by the social and economic networks established by past migration. The main outlier in the region is Myanmar, which has significantly higher rates of labour migration than other low-income states such as Lao PDR and Cambodia. I argue that this is due to the higher prevalence of persecution and conflict in Myanmar, especially in border areas. In addition to being by far the largest source country for refugees and asylum seekers in the region, Myanmar has become a significant source of migrant workers, in part because migrants seek safety from persecution and conflict as well as economic opportunity, and in doing so establish the patterns of ongoing migration.

In making these arguments, I point out that while the administrative categories of asylum seeker and migrant worker are distinct, in practice the separation breaks down as migrant workers can be motivated in part by the need to escape persecution and conflict in their home areas, and refugees and asylum seekers need to seek work to support themselves and their families. In discussing the overlapping situations of asylum seekers and migrant workers, I suggest that all migrants exercise agency and make choices about their journeys, although not in circumstances of their choosing. In making these observations, I also argue against the liberal humanitarian tendency to predicate the acceptance of protection obligations on assumptions about the abject victimhood of asylum seekers. Humanitarian approaches that base limited exceptions to restrictive migration borders on an absolute distinction between migrant workers and asylum seekers owe more to moral tropes of the deserving and undeserving poor than to any necessary or descriptive validity of the categorical division between the two groups. To the extent that the labels of worker and asylum seeker describe different groups of migrants, I argue that this difference is produced by the administrative categories of border management that define the limited freedom to enter and remain within the territory of states.

In Chap. 4, Framing Threats, I describe the criminalisation and securitisation of irregular migration in terms of the process of institutional framing centred on the categories of migrant smuggling and trafficking in persons. By institutional framing, I mean the selection and definition of policy problems and governance approaches through which the jurisdiction, mandate and management techniques of organisations are contested and established. Trafficking and smuggling are *institutional* frames because they are not only ways of talking about the phenomenon of irregular migration, they also establish the responsibilities and techniques for managing it. While there are important differences in the institutional framing of trafficking in persons and migrant smuggling, they share a prioritisation of responses by criminal law enforcement agencies through carceral techniques of border management.

To understand the effects of institutional framing in the criminalisation and securitisation of irregular migration, I review the global history of counter-trafficking and counter-smuggling lobbies and their influence on international and national legal frameworks since the definition of trafficking and smuggling as crimes under the Palermo Protocols to the UN Convention on Transnational Crime in 2000. Framing the intersection of irregular migration and exploitation as a crime of trafficking, as opposed to an issue of forced labour, tends to involve a disproportionate focus on the sex industry together with narratives of abject victimhood, and a reliance on law enforcement responses. Similarly, framing the intersection of irregular migration and dangerous journeys as a problem of smuggling, rather than of a lack of access to safe and regular modes of travel, shifts the institutional focus onto targeting and criminalising smugglers.

In the context of Southeast Asia and the Pacific, institutional framing of irregular migration as threats of trafficking and smuggling is produced by the intersection of the mandates of international organisations and the interests of states in gaining support for criminal and border enforcement capacity. States in the region have been persuaded to adopt policies criminalising trafficking in persons and migrant smuggling through the provision of policy templates, cooperation and data-sharing between border agencies, support for training and capacity building, and the strategic use of financial incentives and sanctions.

Chapter 5, Screening Migrants, deals with the mechanisms of coordinated control of migration borders across Southeast Asia and the Pacific. I show that even as states disagree on normative frameworks for responding to irregular migration, there is convergence in practice around cooperation on techniques of border control. For instance, even as cooperation between the governments of Australia and Indonesia on maritime border governance appeared to stall at the diplomatic level from 2013, routine cooperation between agencies of both states continued through the Regional Support Office to the Bali Process. Building networks of multilevel cooperation between government officials and civil servants, as well as military and police officers, is a key part of the processes I describe as soft multilateralism, by which states and institutions in Southeast Asia and the Pacific promote policy convergence and cooperation while preserving the independence and sovereignty of states.

Despite the prevalence of a liberal humanitarian consensus among international agencies coordinating migration border governance in the region—emphasising the benefits of formal management—the adoption of liberal norms and policy proposals has been uneven and selective. Using the case study of the regional response to the events of May 2015, when boats full of Rohingya and Bangladeshi migrants—including refugees and asylum seekers—were abandoned by smugglers and pushed back to sea by border enforcement agencies from Thailand, Malaysia and Indonesia, I show that coordination between border agencies has proceeded unevenly and prioritises deterrence over protection.

Migration border controls across the region display varying combinations of formal management, informal tolerance of irregular migration, and arbitrary enforcement. While the promotion and incentivisation of policy change on the part of international organisations and Western governments has tended to promote a shift from informal tolerance to formal management, arbitrary enforcement has remained a feature of migration border regimes and has been strengthened by inter-state cooperation and capacity building.

Chapter 6, Carceral Responses, focuses on the enforcement of the categories of migration status created by borders. Enforcement of migration border regulations is arbitrary in two senses: first, when it is applied unevenly and selectively, often due to discriminatory risk profiling, policies of deterrence, or to create public spectacle; and second, when it is applied without independent limit and due process, including the presumption of liberty and rights of appeal. Although migration border regimes vary in formality and capacity across Southeast Asia and the Pacific, they are similar in their arbitrary use of enforcement powers to arrest, detain and deport migrants with irregular status.

The political priority that Australian governments have placed on deterring the arrival of asylum seekers by boat is not shared elsewhere in the region, but overlaps with the interests of states in Southeast Asia and the Pacific to expand the capacity of border regimes to manage movements of migrant workers, as well as to guard against terrorism and other potential cross-border security threats.

Chapter 7, Producing Precarity, considers the effect of migration border regimes in exacerbating the personal, social and economic insecurity of migrants. Migrant lives are made precarious by techniques of border enforcement that block or withdraw access to legal and social protection while increasing vulnerability to exploitation and abuse. The structural conditions of precarity for migrants are backed by the arbitrary enforcement of carceral border regimes, but have a greater reach, affecting migrants with regular status as well as those without, and affecting the lives of those who manage to evade carceral mechanisms of enforcement. By withdrawing access to regular status and legal protection at the same time as escalating policing and punishment of migrants with irregular status, states create conditions of enforced precarity for migrants, as well as the conditions for others to profit from the precarity of migrant populations.

Asylum seekers in Southeast Asia and the Pacific remain in extended conditions of precarity as a consequence of delays in status determination, in addition to the fact that even recognition of refugee status often does not offer substantial protection or improvement in circumstances. For both asylum seekers and migrant workers without regular status, exposure to arbitrary enforcement in most states of Southeast Asia involves daily risk of violence and extortion of bribes from police and other government agencies. Immigration enforcement actions are also used to discipline workers and to deter protests, industrial action and organising activities. Migrant workers are also deprived of protection from exploitation and abuse through specific exemptions or lack of enforcement of labour legislation and minimum standards, and exclusion from membership of trade unions. Nevertheless, where migrants have been able to organise through informal channels and community based organisations, including through relationships of solidarity with national and regional organisations, there is potential to partially mitigate the effects of precarity and organise against its structural causes.

Bibliography

Dauvergne, Catherine. 2005. *Humanitarianism, Identity, and Nation: Migration Laws of Australia and Canada*. Vancouver: UBC Press.

Gregory, Derek. 2004. *The Colonial Present: Afghanistan, Palestine, Iraq*. Malden: Blackwell.

Hyndman, Jennifer, and Alison Mountz. 2008. Another Brick in the Wall? Neo-Refoulement and the Externalization of Asylum by Australia and Europe. *Government and Opposition* 43 (2): 249–269.

Pickering, Sharon. 2014. Floating Carceral Spaces: Border Enforcement and Gender on the High Seas. *Punishment & Society 16* (2): 187–205.

RISE—Refugees, Survivors and Ex-Detainees. 2015. Twitter Post, 3 September 2015. https://twitter.com/riserefugee/status/639597818559098880

Sigona, Nando, and Jennifer Allsopp. 2016. Mind the Gap: Why are Unaccompanied Children Disappearing in their Thousands? *Open Democracy*. https://www.opendemocracy.net/5050/nando-sigona-and-jennifer-allsopp/mind-gap-why-are-unaccompanied-children-disappearing-in-thous

Vaughan-Williams, Nick, and Adrian Little. 2016. Stopping Boats, Saving Lives, Securing Subjects: Humanitarian Borders in Europe and Australia. *European Journal of International Relations*: 1–24.

Verma, Sanmati. 2015. Why Were Most of the Anti-Reclaim Protestors White? *New Matilda*. https://newmatilda.com/2015/04/19/why-were-most-anti-reclaim-protestors-white/

Walia, Harsha. 2013. *Undoing Border Imperialism*. Oakland: AK Press.

CHAPTER 2

Border Spaces

Border regimes define the limits and conditions of the freedom to move and to remain in a territory. As such, borders are not only ubiquitous to contemporary states but also exert fundamental influence over political life. As Hannah Arendt (1995, 9) wrote in her acceptance speech for the 1959 Lessing Prize:

> Being able to depart for where we will is the prototypal gesture of being free, as limitation of freedom of movement has from time immemorial been the precondition for enslavement.

As Hirschman (1978) argued, the freedom to leave the state of one's nationality ('exit') is as fundamental a political freedom as the freedom to participate in processes of governance and contestation ('voice'). And, as Arendt saw clearly, the freedom to leave is conditional upon the freedom to arrive. The freedom to depart is abstract and useless to the extent that it is not a freedom to 'depart for where we will'.

Borders are composed of techniques of state power, producing regimes and spaces of governance that are distributed within and across national territories rather than limited to the boundary lines between territories. Alongside their geopolitical function as territorial demarcation, borders act on bodies along a continuum of interventions that aim to control movements across state territories. This approach to the political space of the border draws on studies of borderscapes (Rajaram and

N. Henry, *Asylum, Work, and Precarity*, Critical Studies of the Asia-Pacific, DOI 10.1007/978-3-319-60567-8_2

Grundy-Warr 2007) and borderzones (Squire 2010), as well as critical approaches that emphasise the biopolitical practices of border regimes (Vaughan-Williams 2009).

Rajaram and Grundy-Warr (2007, xxxi) identify the political role of territorial borders as a self-legitimising function of the nation-state, filtering norms and exceptions, belonging and non-belonging, through practices of inclusion and exclusion that reinforce the power of sovereign decision. The discourse of territorial borders reinforces the moral and political claims of state power by authorising a 'curtailed conception of justice' based on the 'utopic unity' of a political community within a defined physical space (Rajaram and Grundy-Warr 2007, ix). These authors propose disrupting the hegemonic view of the border as the stable limit of a political community by studying the activity of what they term 'borderscapes'—the zones in which borders are reproduced and contested.

It is widely accepted that international borders should be understood as interconnected parts of a global assemblage or regime. Joly (2002, 2) observed an increasing global interconnectedness of border regimes accompanied by convergence of humanitarian norms under the leadership of international organisations, although with the convergence driven more by the search for technocratic solutions to the 'problem' of refugees than by any increase in shared commitments to norms of protection and asylum. The international system of migration borders remains heterogeneous and unstable in the opportunities it provides for both asylum and labour migration. Rather than a convergence of norms, the interconnectedness of national and regional border regimes manifests in a convergence of techniques. While international organisations have increased their role in the management of border regimes, this has not resulted in substantial convergence around either humanitarian norms or solutions, but rather in the international proliferation of techniques of migration control. This is largely because the assistance that international organisations can offer is filtered by what states will accept.

Regional cooperation for border control and against the irregular movement of migrants in the Asia-Pacific, built through the soft multilateralism of layered networking between officials at multiple levels across state agencies in the region, constitutes a different kind of regime from the traditional model of international relations theory. By soft multilateralism I refer to the form of non-binding dialogue and coordination typically favoured by Southeast Asian states, exemplified by the ASEAN system, and distinct from the hard multilateralism of binding international agreements that seek to establish supranational legal norms and organisations (Caouette and Cote 2011). Through soft multilateralism, states are able to coordinate activities to shore up the core Realist goals of sovereignty and security without compromising the concomitant principle of self-reliance and the Realist suspicion of pooling or delegating sovereign powers to international agencies, as is the case with the hard multilateralism of European Union institutions such as FRONTEX. Rather than a top-down regime of norms codified by a supranational peak body and disseminated down the hierarchy to local implementation, the growth of a regional border regime in Southeast Asia and the Pacific has been characterised by the horizontal dissemination of *techniques* of border management between states.

This dynamic of a decentralised regime of techniques differs from the model of international regimes proposed by Krasner (1982) and associated theorists, based on a hierarchy of norms, principles, rules and procedures, with the assumption that regime institutionalisation tended to proceed downwards from the normative peak of the regime pyramid to the procedural base. This assumption of top-down norm diffusion has been shared by constructivist theorists of international institutionalisation processes.

Both Constructivist and Liberal institutionalist theorists of international regimes have tended to take a structuralist approach to political agency and international norms, assuming that both operate primarily at the level of an international normative structure (Ruggie 1982; Finnemore and Sikkink 1998, 403). While political actors, usually states, are seen by regime theorists as having a role in constructing norms through processes of interaction, the regime is identified with the resulting structure of international norms and is seen as the intervening force through which actors are able to act on others. For Krasner the regime is the 'intervening variable', while Reus-Smit argues that 'constitutional structures' can be discerned at the foundation of international society, 'comprising the constitutive values that define legitimate statehood and rightful state action' (1997, 558). For Reus-Smit, these normative structures are formed through relational processes, in that the values that define norms, such as sovereignty, political legitimacy and procedural justice, are negotiated in a Habermasian process of communicative action. However, once established as norms by states at the international level, these norms are seen as taking on a structural role. The role of relational processes within and between states, including the role of non-state actors, is therefore restricted to the original establishment of an international normative structure, while political change is explained by a 'trickle down' theory of norm diffusion from the international to the domestic levels of politics.

For both Liberal institutionalist and mainstream Constructivist scholars, the solutions to problems of global governance are expected to be found through the negotiation and institutional embedding of new international norms. The mechanism of action for both the negotiation and the implementation of norms is expected to be multilateral diplomacy by states. Liberal institutionalists in particular put their faith in existing institutions of the international system, perhaps with certain proposals to reform or extend their mandate and structures, to facilitate this process of normative change (Weiss and Thakur 2010, 10–12, 42–43).

Liberal institutionalist responses to international migration border regimes tend to frame the problem as one of insufficient institution building, resulting in an underdeveloped regime for protection of refugees and other migrants. Since Bimal Ghosh's (2000) work for the IOM on a proposed New International Regime for Orderly Movements of People (NIROMP), it has been common to suggest there is a 'missing regime' (Hollifield 2000; Ghosh 2005) for the international governance of migration. Ghosh traces the impetus for his call for an international migration regime to an earlier report he prepared for the 1993 Commission on Global Governance and a report in the same year by the Trilateral Commission, calling for a 'viable international framework within which to manage migration pressures effectively' (cited in Ghosh 2000, 2).

Citing Ghosh's report for the IOM and the similar conclusions reached by Doyle (2000) for the UN Migration Working Group, Koslowski (2011, 3–4) suggests there is 'relatively little cooperation' between states on migration compared to other issues. Koslowski cites the relatively low rate of ratifications of the International Labour Organisation (ILO) Convention on Migrant Workers as an example of the reluctance of states to make binding commitments to international norms in the area of migration. However, this analysis of migration regimes as underdeveloped ignores the growing international cooperation on restrictions to migration and carceral responses that run counter to liberal norms and human rights protection mechanisms. For Liberal institutionalist scholars such as Ghosh, Hollifield and Koslowski, the institutionalisation of an international migration regime has been seen as lacking in comparison to the progress in global trade governance associated with the founding of the World Trade Organisation in 1994 and the coming into force of new global trade agreements such as the General Agreement on Trade in Services (GATS). While GATS contained some limited provisions on temporary migration to facilitate in-country provision of services by foreign firms, the progress of liberal economic globalisation was seen by these scholars as requiring an associated liberalisation of global migration, to be managed by new international organisations. While the IOM has increasingly defined its role in these terms as promoting the smooth management and facilitation of global migration, it relies on partnership with cooperative states rather than acting under a substantial mandate from international treaties.

Rather than describing international coordination of migration borders as an insufficiently institutionalised regime, other authors have emphasised the influence of multiple intersecting trends, including increased mobility related to economic globalisation combined with increased securitisation and restriction of labour migration (Andrijasevic and Walters 2010). For these authors, the persistence of restrictions on international labour mobility and general migration in contrast to the liberalisation of cross-border trade and capital flows does not result from the lack of an institutionalised regime of international migration, but rather is reflective of the collective preferences of states to utilise borders as filtering mechanisms of a 'gated globalisation'. The targets for filtering at the migration border are defined by racialised national demarcations, which aim to block the free movement of the poor working class across international borders while selectively facilitating the movement of migrant workers into temporary and precarious labour.

Mitropoulos (2016) argues that a key economic effect of migration border enforcement is the lowering of the price of migrant labour. This form of labour arbitrage, deriving profit from the differential market value of labour across different populations, is an effect of border enforcement rather than migration as such. This is because it is border enforcement that creates migrants with irregular status as a precarious and therefore exploitable population through the constant threat of arrest, detention, and deportation. At the same time, even migrants with regular status through temporary work visas are subject to restrictions and precarity that limit their ability to effectively bargain or access legal protection of their conditions of work. More fundamentally, it is the existence of borders as boundaries to citizenship that creates the possibility of labour arbitrage in the first place, by marking the labour of workers as of variable worth depending on the passport they carry. On a global scale, labour arbitrage is produced by the disjunction of the relatively free movement of capital, goods, and services, combined with restrictions placed on the movement of labour.

Mitropoulos (2012, 50) describes migration border governance as a form of 'oikonomia'—or household management—on a national scale, in which 'geopolitical demarcations come to assume the character of a domestic space (as in the familial concept of the nation, or as with the term "domestic economy").' Mitropoulos' theory of borders turns on a tension between the evolution of the law of contracts, as the foundational basis of the household—and of all modern corporate structures up to and including the nation-state—and the persistent threat of 'contagion' in the form of uninsurable risk. In arguing that modern nation-states and their borders rely on the law of contracts, Mitropoulos is not invoking the abstract Liberal analogy of the 'social contract' but, rather, dealing in material terms with contracts as 'infrastructures that seek to crystallise the allocation of relational risk' (Mitropoulos 2012, 116). The application of this analysis to the evolving infrastructure of offshore detention in Australia's extended border regime, and its dependence on a network of contracts and contractors, is dealt with specifically in Chap. 6. In this chapter and the subsequent chapters dealing with the framing of threats and screening mechanisms, the focus is on how states use border regimes to define and manage risk, as well as to define the territory and population in need of protection.

In a speech to the Lowy Institute announcing the creation of the Australian Border Force, Minister for Immigration and Border Protection Scott Morrison (2014) emphasised the importance of the border in defining the social territory of the nation: 'Our border is not just a line on a map. Our border is a national asset. It holds economic, social and strategic value for our nation.' Morrison went on to argue that borders define the sovereign space of the nation as the necessary conditions for democracy, the rule of law, free markets, commerce and property rights, civil society, cultural expression, freedom and liberty: 'Our border creates the space for us to be who we are and to become everything we can be as a nation.' This list of defining features of national aspiration is recognisably liberal, although with an emphasis on the neo-liberal values of property rights and market freedom over social-liberal values of equality and inclusion. In appealing to the border as protective of liberal social space, Morrison echoes communitarian liberal arguments for the importance of national political community against cosmopolitan liberal appeals to more international affiliations.

The idea that borders are a national asset was echoed by the Department Secretary of Immigration and Border Protection, Michael Pezzullo in a 2014 speech to the Australian Strategic Policy Institute. The speech is extraordinary for its explicit and ideological celebration of the state—and the institutions of border management in particular—as the sole defence against 'the evils' of the world. To fulfil this protective role, the institutions of the border need to be 'connected and networked' to cover and extend beyond the territory of the state:

> in the age of global interdependence, rather than being seen exclusively as a territorial barrier, we should see the border as a *space* where sovereign states control the *flow* of people and goods in to and out of their dominion. (Pezzullo 2014, 4. Emphasis in original)

Much of the speech deals with the role of the newly combined Department of Immigration and Border Protection in filtering these flows in order to facilitate movements defined as desirable while detecting and intercepting those profiled as presenting security risks. This viewpoint, which is echoed and expanded upon in Departmental strategy documents, is examined in more detail in Chap. 4. In comparison to official documents, Pezzullo expands further on his views of the source of threats to the state embedded in the networks of globalisation.

> As the planet continues to urbanise, as populations continue to grow and centralise in coastal cities, and as international connectivity enables globalised communications and the global movement of people and goods, the transnational criminal threat will only increase. Critically, while some of these cities suffer from a lack of good public governance and the enforcement of laws, they are connected to the global network through airports, seaports, communications cables and financial centres. In these environments, non-state groups such as drug cartels, street gangs and local warlords draw their strength from local populations, and hide amongst them. They embed themselves into legitimate networks of commerce and adopt a laundered face, which they present to the global network of trade and travel. (Pezzullo 2014, 5)

In this view of world affairs, states are the enablers and facilitators of economic globalisation, bringing prosperity and opportunity to their national economies but, in the process, creating networks of flows that are open to the threat of contagion by hostile and obscure non-state actors. The representation of this threat is remarkable for its echoes of the frustration of the colonial administrator, or for that matter, the Vietnam-era military strategist, unable to reliably distinguish categories of friendly and hostile among the subaltern population ('the laundered face'). This is a story in which the career bureaucrat casts himself in the role of world-historical hero, defender of civilisation against hostile populations, presiding over a Department that will 'stand the test of time' and achieve recognition as a 'policy powerhouse', while in the process demonstrating the grand claim that 'alongside military power and statecraft, borders are the third leg of the trinity of state power which underpins and ensures state sovereignty'.

In describing borders alongside military power and statecraft, Pezzullo is both valorising border management as a vocation and presenting it as an international power of states, as a means of geopolitical power projection. Just as the use or potential use of military power secures the sovereignty and control of the state within its territory as well as in relation to other states, the institutions of the border function to control and manage populations profiled as bearers of risk within and beyond the territory of the state. Seeming to borrow from the language of Castells' (2010) theory of the network society to describe borders as a 'space' of 'flows', Pezzullo's account of the Australian border suggests a mobile and adaptable set of institutions that facilitate as much as inhibit cross-border movements, dependent on real-time assessments of risk profiles.

Pezzullo's justification of the necessity of these developments in border institutions in relation to the growth of post-Fordist global networks of production speaks to the shift to post-disciplinary institutions of government anticipated by Foucault's (2008) analysis of biopolitics and Deleuze's (1992) *Postscript on the Societies of Control.* That is, a shift from disciplinary power located within fixed institutions (school, workplace, prison) to more diffused and mobile systems of surveillance and control. Mitropoulos (2015) argues with regard to Australia's Pacific detention network that the transition towards the institutional forms of layered and mobile border control has evolved in response to perceptions of uncertain and uninsurable forms of risk introduced by movements of migrants that resist and evade the traditional forms of enclosure and control of territorial borders. The key dynamic in the evolution of the carceral network has been the development of an expanding network of private contracts and contractors, with associated networks of physical infrastructure and logistics.

This shift in the operation of border management has occurred throughout the developed world and bears more than a passing resemblance to the previously defined Revolution in Military Affairs (see for instance Cohen 1996) with its emphasis on technology-enabled real-time analysis of risk across a broad territory, dispersed beyond traditional understandings of the field of battle. For instance, the UK border strategy document *Secure Borders, Safe Haven*, released in 2002, outlined a 'high-tech, integrated, and flexible approach to the UK border' (Vaughan-Williams 2009, 1072) distributed across and beyond the territory of the UK, as well as at points of entry.

Responding to these developments, Parker and Vaughan-Williams et al. (2009) outline an agenda for a Critical Border Studies in terms of shifts in the epistemology, ontology, topography, and temporality of our concepts of the border. Epistemologically, the authors draw attention to the foundational assumptions of fixed and essentialised nation-state borders in Western academic disciplines that prevent us from seeing both the contingency and violence of contemporary borders. Alternative epistemologies of the border could include theorisation of the border as sets of practices and experiences that remain open to radical contingency and the possibility of transformation. Ontologically, the Critical Border Studies agenda invites attention to the processes of establishment and maintenance of borders, rather than description as finished products or natural forms, and suggests the creative use of dynamic concepts of spaces and thresholds, of the fold and the in-between, and the events and practices of bordering. For the authors, this requires transformation of the habitual topologies and temporalities of the border to avoid foreclosing the possibility of resistance, including the ways that transgression of borders contributes to the constitution of what borders are and what they mean.

Political Space of the Border: The Fold

In the context of the regional migration border regime in Southeast Asia and the Pacific, a central dynamic of transformation has been the series of changes in Australia's border governance practice that have introduced functional obscurities in the location, legality, logistics, and legibility of the Australian border. In the discussion below I suggest that these changes can usefully be described in terms of the folding of political space.

I am concerned here with interrogating the political space of the border; the geographies of power that map onto physical space in the ways that actors are enabled or constrained to act and interact. In undertaking this exercise of political mapping we need to bear in mind the ways that political space may be constructed in different ways to physical space. In the governance of border regimes, the relative abstraction of political from physical space is an important factor in determining the freedom of movement of actors within the space.

Here, the concepts of territorialisation and deterritorialisation can help to make sense of the ways that borders may be detached, repositioned and reattached to conceptions of the physical frontiers of nation-states and regions. In addition, we need to consider ways in which the particular character of political space can be understood, including the tensions introduced by relative abstraction under conditions of continuing connection to physical spaces. Concepts of folding and unfolding may be usefully applied to understand the complexities of action enabled and constrained by the articulations of physical and political spaces in the governance of Australia's migration border.

Successive Australian governments since 2001 have responded to the arrival of asylum seekers by making fundamental changes to the border regime. The political space defined by Australia's border regime has become characterised by frequent change, radical uncertainty and systematic ambiguity. The uncertainties and ambiguities of sovereign jurisdiction and action in the border space are not accidental but are inherent to what the border has become as a space of enclosure that operates to defer and disrupt the establishment of any stable political ground for those caught within its folds. While my focus is on the articulations and manipulations of political space carried out through the activities of sovereign governance, I argue that especially in the migration space, these activities can only be understood in relation to efforts to contain and control practices of resistance and evasion.

The concept of a folded political space is drawn from Deleuze, who illustrates the topological dynamic of folding with the example of Koch's curve, a fractal shape constructed so that it has no tangent:

> It envelops an infinitely cavernous or porous world, constituting more than a line and less than a surface. (Deleuze 1992, 17)

A model of the border as a folded space, 'more than a line and less than a surface', would be one that operates in a different spatial mode than geopolitical territory (the 'surface') and demarcation (the 'line'), as an interstitial space, a folding of the demarcating line that creates space within itself to hold bodies outside of territorial political space or jurisdiction, and which confronts unwanted movement of bodies with a deferment of the border line, rather than a confrontation with a clearly defined limit. The border folds around the migrant and follows their body into and beyond the territory of the state. The border folds onto and into itself to create political spaces of indeterminate jurisdiction and deferred administrative decision around the geographical places of migrant detention. The forms of political space introduced by the multiplication of administrative folds evoke images of labyrinthine forms of folded walls and enclosed spaces.[1]

Calvino described the labyrinth as a form of 'premeditated chaos' producing a 'game of orientation and disorientation' (Pilz 2005, 98–99), both being phrases that could be directly transposed to describe contemporary border regimes. Barthes (2012, 62) describes labyrinths as spaces of 'active enclosure' producing: '[e]ndless, futile efforts expended on finding the way out. In the subject's efforts to find the exit, he only exacerbates his own imprisonment.' This function of the labyrinth to exhaust effort by turning movement back on itself will be familiar to those who have experienced or studied the administration of contemporary migration borders. Another description by Detienne explores the temptation and frustration of movement within the labyrinth in more detail:

> A labyrinth cries out for exegesis, but the network of its crossroads and ramified passages irresistibly draws the interpreter into a thousand and one detours… it is at once a trail that leads nowhere and the longest path possible enclosed in the smallest space possible. (Detienne 2002, 92)

Here we have a quite precise description of the characteristics of folded space defined in terms of the form of action—or the degrees of freedom of movement—produced. Folded spaces produce detours that simultaneously lengthen the journey of bodies passing through them, confine the space of action, and defer the possibility of reaching a destination. The production of the 'longest path' in the 'smallest space' is a spatial image of the Kafkaesque bureaucratic process in which asylum seekers are caught, with all its attendant frustration and claustrophobia.

In applying this model of folded political space to the analysis of border management, using the example of Australia, I consider four such foldings in the location, legality, logistics, and legibility of the border. Each of these processes by which political space is folded on itself by the operation of Australia's contemporary border management are expanded upon in subsequent chapters, and summarised below.

Location: Definition of the Border

In May 2013, the Australian government passed legislation that was widely reported as having the effect of excising the mainland territory of Australia from its own migration zone (see for instance Wilson 2013). In fact, the legislation as passed (Parliament of Australia 2013) replaced a classification of excluded territory (excised places) created by previous amendments with a classification of an excluded population (irregular maritime arrivals). Under previous legislation, the Australian parliament had voted to excise the territory of certain islands from Australia's migration zone. The effect of this was that persons arriving at the excised territory would not be considered to have entered Australia for the purpose of the Migration Act, removing the requirement to consider claims for asylum under Australian law. The legislation passed in May 2013 extended this effect to the entire territory of Australia by defining a category of persons—those arriving by boat without a valid visa—to whom the migration zone would not be considered to apply. For the members of this group, even if they stepped foot on Australian soil or were brought to Australia for processing and transfer to offshore detention, they would not be considered to have arrived in Australia for the purposes of the Migration Act. The effect of the legislation follows the migrant, so that even in the case that an asylum seeker is detained at an offshore location and subsequently brought to Australia for medical treatment, they are precluded from lodging a claim for asylum. The Migration Act as amended now functions to fold a personal border around the body of every migrant who fits the definition of irregular maritime arrival, so that even if they are physically present in Australian territory, they are considered for the purposes of migration law not to be there and to never have arrived. From the perspective of refugees and asylum seekers who arrive in Australia by boat, the effect of the legislation is as it was reported in the Australian media, as if the possibility of arriving on the continent had been excised—along with the promise of relative safety and protection it had represented as a destination.

Legality: Ambiguity of Jurisdiction

The policy of offshore detention for asylum seekers arriving in Australia by boat, introduced by the Howard Coalition government in 2001 and reintroduced by the Gillard Labour Government in 2012, created a deliberate and functional ambiguity in the jurisdiction over the places of detention on Nauru and on Manus Island in Papua New Guinea (PNG). As will be discussed in Chap. 6, the detention centres are under the effective control of the Australian government and its contractors while remaining, at least nominally, under the sovereignty of Nauru and PNG. The status of the camps is therefore similar to that of foreign military bases, and Australia's use of the centres for internment of asylum seekers is similar in its functional ambiguity of jurisdiction to the use of the Guantanamo Bay Naval Base in

Cuba by the United States as an immigration processing centre for Cuban refugees (separate to its function as a military holding prison in the 'War on Terror' but used for the same reason: the territory lies outside the jurisdiction of domestic US law). In both cases, the operation of offshore detention has the effect of folding the space of the border into the territory of another state. The fold in political space introduced at the boundaries of Australia's Pacific detention camps allows the administrators to switch between jurisdictions opportunistically. When the detention of refugees and asylum seekers on Manus Island was declared illegal by the Supreme Court of Papua New Guinea in 2016, Australia's Immigration Minister Peter Dutton claimed that the government of Australia was not bound by the decision. Conversely, in defending against legal challenges to the regime of offshore detention in the Australian courts, and in responding to questions from Senate enquiries, the Department of Immigration and Border Protection (DIBP) has consistently claimed that the detention centres are operated by the governments of Nauru and PNG and that the department only provides technical support and funding.

Logistics: Supply-Chain and Contractual Complexity

The lines of responsibility for providing the 'services' involved in running Australia's carceral network in the Pacific are further folded on themselves by the proliferation of contractual relationships involved (Mitropoulos 2015). Asylum seekers or their representatives seeking to make a request or complaint are confronted with a labyrinthine and obscure chain of command between multiple subcontractors and government agencies.

For instance, detainees requiring medical treatment that cannot be provided in the limited camp facilities have to first submit requests through health contractor International Health and Medical Services (IHMS), who then seek permission from DIBP in Canberra to transfer the detainee to public hospitals in Nauru or PNG. Despite the severe limitations of public health facilities in these countries, only rare cases are approved for medical evacuation to Australia. The coroner's inquest into the death of one asylum seeker, Hamid Khazaei, who died in Brisbane after extensive delays to his medical evacuation for treatment of sepsis, heard testimony that medical requests for a transfer to Australia were initially denied because a visa could not be obtained for the patient (Rebgetz 2016). Approval was required from every level of the DIBP hierarchy before the evacuation was granted, and over the course of 13 days, Khazaei died of a treatable leg infection while email requests and queries were forwarded through the department (Thompson et al. 2016). Similar difficulties have been faced in many cases by detained refugees and asylum seekers trying to access medical care in PNG and Nauru, including cases of women requiring access to abortions and treatment for complications of pregnancy, not available on Nauru. In contrast to a well-functioning health system where clear lines of clinical decision-making are required to provide timely and appropriate care, the system of decision-making applied to the healthcare of those detained in Australia's Pacific detention network is subject to multiple folds of obscurity, as lines of decision-making cross between different jurisdictions and agencies.

While clearly detrimental to the wellbeing and interests of detainees, the folded space of decision-making introduced by the contractual and logistical complexity of the detention network functions to insulate the Australian government from the perceived risks of bringing refugees and asylum seekers to Australia. These risks include that refugees and asylum seekers could embarrass the government by gaining access to supporters and media outlets and could challenge the terms of their detention through access to Australian lawyers and courts. By utilising obscure contractual relationships and processes of decision-making to defer and deter asylum seekers and refugees from navigating the administrative systems of control governing detention arrangements, including in order to access medical care in Australia, the logistical folds of the detention system function to reinforce the folds of location, legality and legibility that maintain layers of functional obscurity around the detention network.

Legibility: Obscurity of Information

Under Operation Sovereign Borders, launched by the Abbott Coalition government in 2013, a general policy of refusing comment on so-called on-water operational matters imposed an effective media blackout on the interception and turning-back of boats carrying asylum seekers to Australia, the detention and processing of asylum seekers at sea, and transfers to offshore detention sites. Additional layers of obscurity and secrecy were introduced in 2015, with the provisions of the Border Force Act prohibiting any staff employed by DIBP or its contractors from commenting to the media about the operation of offshore detention. When asked to comment on the operation of the detention centres, it was common practice for the Minister of Immigration and senior DIBP officials to refer questions to the governments of Nauru and PNG, who would generally refuse to comment or refer questions back to Australian officials. The difficulty of reporting on conditions in the detention centre on Nauru in particular was exacerbated by the general refusal of the government of Nauru to issue visas to journalists.[2] Each of these limitations on the movement of information is enabled by previously introduced folds in the political space of border governance so that folds in the location, legality and logistics of the border contribute to the folds in legibility that obscure the border processes.

Liberal Humanitarianism

Critical border studies theorists have drawn attention to the role of liberal humanitarian discourses and practices in both challenging and constituting contemporary border regimes (Vaughan-Williams 2015; Squire 2015).

Reid-Henry (2014, 418) describes humanitarianism as a liberal diagnostic, meaning, 'a recursive moral practice that helps constitute a liberal politics as much as it projects that politics onto other people and places'. In particular, humanitarianism practices aim to govern precarity by extending 'biopolitical claims over vulnerable life' as part of the management of social risks, often on behalf of the state (Reid-Henry 2014, 419). In making this claim, Reid-Henry draws on Fassin's (2012) *Humanitarian Reason* to describe liberal humanitarianism as a moral economy constitutive of governmentality through the distribution of technologies of care. Humanitarian work thrives in the liminal zones of the power of liberal democratic states and functions in part to extend the power and reach of liberal institutions. As Reid-Henry (2014, 422) points out, there is a long history of liberal humanitarianism filling this function in multiple scales and settings, including the role of missionary work in colonial expansion. More recently, humanitarian NGOs have taken up significant roles in extending the capacity of institutions of 'global governance', including through contracts with states. Arguing against perspectives that describe the growth of global humanitarian 'civil society' as diminishing the power of states, Sending and Neumann (2006) analyse this development as an extension of liberal 'governmentality' that involves both states and non-state actors in new modes of global governing.

The transformation of border governance in the context of globalisation is an example of how states and non-state actors both compete and combine in the constitution of humanitarian discourses and associated sets of practices that both transform and extend existing powers of government. As Waters argues (138), the phenomenon of the humanitarian border emerges to govern the situation in which border crossing becomes a matter of life and death, itself a product of the securitised carceral border regimes that coexist with the humanitarian border, so that humanitarian border work both ameliorates and morally justifies the regime of migration control. Humanitarian border practices comprise the actions of a combination of state and non-state actors and are emerging unevenly, constituting a network spreading out from the physical intersections of rich and poor worlds, such as along the US-Mexico border, at the Mediterranean borders of the EU and at Australia's Northern maritime border and the sites of offshore detention maintained by the Australian government.

Humanitarian border work contributes to the constitution of new forms of border space and territoriality, even as humanitarian actors and agencies frequently aim to work against existing definitions of territoriality. Although humanitarian border work may claim, or be seen, to operate in ways that challenge state-centric territoriality, including by promoting viewpoints and practices that are 'global' or 'without borders', humanitarian work operates as much to re-territorialise the border as a space of governance, including through the contested introduction of humanitarian norms. This point is addressed in Chap. 7, with regard to the specific involvement of humanitarian NGOs in providing services to detained refugees and asylum seekers under contract to the Australian government, including in offshore detention sites in Nauru and Papua New Guinea.

For Dauvergne (2005), humanitarianism is the point of convergence in liberal debates between those who advocate for open borders, closed borders and pragmatic interventions in existing border policies. The foundation of the 'humanitarian consensus' at the heart of liberal debates around migration is a self-regarding narrative of national self-image, rather than any fundamental duty or obligation to outsiders. The discourse of humanitarianism is about 'applauding ourselves' for doing more than we were obliged to do, while contributing to reinforcing and policing the boundaries of obligation in a way that 'enshrines inequality and circumvents justice' (Dauvergne 2005, 73–74). The difference that makes the relations of humanitarianism possible is the material inequality that humanitarianism both ameliorates and reinforces, including by deciding on the exceptions to be made. In the specific case of humanitarian borders, debates over the numbers and criteria for humanitarian migration programmes, including refugee resettlement, reinforce the moral legitimacy of the general powers of migration control exercised by the state. At the same time, because humanitarianism operates as the point of consensus in liberal debates, it is frequently the most strategic way for actors to frame appeals to reform migration border governance to be 'more open or more responsive to those in need' (Dauvergne 2005, 74).

Border Imperialism

To understand the emergence and expansion of Australia's migration border regime and its relation to border regimes in Southeast Asia and the Pacific—as well as to analyse the expansion of the Australian border regime into the region—requires a historical perspective that takes account of the ways that imperialism and settler colonialism have shaped the borders of Australia, New Zealand and the broader region.

Walia (2013, 5) uses the term 'border imperialism' to distinguish her object of study from the traditional view of borders as 'lines demarcating territory', explaining that

> an analysis of border imperialism interrogates the modes and networks of governance that determine how bodies will be included within the nation-state, and how territory will be controlled. (Walia 2013, 6)

This understanding of border imperialism encompasses the critical border studies approach to borders as comprising modes of governance concerned with population and territory within and beyond the territorial boundaries of the state. In addition, Walia's work draws attention to the continuities of contemporary bordering practices with colonial histories of the establishment and maintenance of control over territories and populations or, in other words, the histories of imperialism. This includes the important reminder that the historical and functional foundations of the modes and networks of border governance include 'the circulations of capital and labor stratifications in the global economy, narratives of empire, and hierarchies of race, class, and gender within state building' (Walia 2013, 39). The analytical framework of border imperialism also draws attention to the fact that the same 'Western' developed states that are most active in building border regimes to deter and prevent the movement of displaced populations into their territories are also actively involved in the conflicts, interventions, and associated extractive economies that give rise to much of this displacement. As Walia (2013, 40–52) argues, the global hotspots of mass displacement in the Middle East and North Africa can be traced directly or indirectly to the interventions of Western powers and their regional allies from 2001 onward, in the invasions of Afghanistan and Iraq and the subsequent and ongoing interventions throughout the region under the broad designation of the 'war on terror'. Other sources of mass displacement associated with conflict and persecution, including in Central and East Africa, and in Latin America, are also linked to regimes and local actors that benefit from resource extraction financed and directed by Western-based global corporations—with the complicity of Western governments. In summary, the mass displacements and consequent irregular migrations that Western governments seek to defend against with the securitisation of migration borders are produced in large part due to the global structures of imperialism on which the power and prosperity of Western states are founded.

A benefit of Walia's approach to border imperialism is that it bridges what might otherwise be seen as a contradiction or gap between migrant solidarity work and the perspectives and political priorities of indigenous peoples in settler societies. Writing from her perspective as a founding organiser of the No One is Illegal (NOII) network of activist collectives in Canada, Walia argues that the commitment of NOII activists to migrant justice includes an analysis of their movement as 'linked and interwoven in a web of movements' for causes 'rooted in anticolonial, anti-capitalist, ecological justice, Indigenous self-determination, anti-occupation, and antioppressive communities' (Walia 2013, 98).

The connections that Walia draws between border imperialism and settler colonialism in the Canadian and broader North American context translate well to similar issues and histories in Australia and New Zealand. In 'settler societies' (Stasiulis and Yuval-Davis 1995) such as Canada, Australia and New Zealand, the dominant narratives of border security and migration management are based on a cultural and institutional hegemony formed in the process of settlement. As Nethery (2010) argues, the institutions and practices of administrative detention used to control migrants defined as security risks to Australia were first used against indigenous people in the process of colonisation.

Regional Integration in Southeast Asia and the Pacific

In Southeast Asia and the Pacific, the political spaces defined by regimes of border governance, including migration border governance, are undergoing rapid changes based on coordinated, though uneven, processes of regional integration. Regional integration centred on Southeast Asia is proceeding through multiple overlapping processes in different areas of policy, largely coordinated by or related to ASEAN forums, and variously including partnerships and dialogue with states in East Asia and the Pacific. Since the end of the Cold War, ASEAN has cast off its previous identity as a common front of anti-communist states, although the organisation had always been inhibited in this role by the strong preference of the United States to provide support to anti-communist states through a 'hub and spoke' system of bilateral alliances, rather than dealing with ASEAN as a multilateral body. ASEAN now includes all ten states in Southeast Asia and, in addition to annual meetings of heads of state, coordinates a constant process of multi-level dialogue across all areas of government activity. A large number of these multi-level dialogue processes are conducted under the ASEAN Plus Three process, including government officials and civil servants from Japan, South Korea, and China. Less frequent high-level dialogues include a wider range of partners, including India, Australia, New Zealand, the USA, and the EU.

Since the Bali declaration of 2003, ASEAN's programme of policy coordination has centred around three pillars of regional integration: the ASEAN Economic Community (AEC); the ASEAN Political-Security Community; and the ASEAN Socio-Cultural Community. Declared in effect at the end of 2015, the AEC comprises freedom of movement for goods, services, investment, and skilled labour across the region. Noticeably absent from the AEC framework is agreement on free movement for migrant workers, or freer migration more generally. While the ASEAN (2015) Integration Report refers to progress towards the 'freer flow of capital,' there is no corresponding commitment to freer migration, with skilled migration grouped under the general heading of trade in services.

Conclusion

Scholarship on borders has become increasingly aware of the function of border governance regimes in constituting political spaces that extend beyond the lines of demarcation between state territories. Contemporary regimes of migration border governance are composed of multiple layers of interventions by states in movements of people before, during and after their entry to the territory of the state. Transformations of migration border governance—of the kind undertaken by successive Australian governments since 2001—amount to a fundamental rearticulation of the political space of the national territory as it presents to asylum seekers, which I have argued can be understood as a series of folds in the location, legality, logistics and legibility of the border. The dynamics and contradictions of Australia's efforts to extend these transformations in border governance into the wider region can be understood through the overlapping influence of liberal humanitarianism, which I have argued is increasingly articulated in terms of an accommodation with carceral practices, and border imperialism, including the continuing influence of the institutions and practices of settler colonialism in Australia and New Zealand. As states in Southeast Asia pursue their own processes of regional integration, the results of efforts to influence migration borders in the region will continue to be shaped by the selective adoption of techniques and processes of governance according to state and regional priorities.

Notes

1. Deleuze links the spatial forms of complex folds to the imagery and architecture of the Baroque period, suggesting that these forms correspond to the Baroque 'image of thought' found, for instance, in Leibniz's philosophy.
2. One of the few exceptions to this general rule was the granting of a journalist visa in 2016 to Chris Kenny of *The Australian*, known for his strong editorial line in support of the Australian government's policies on migration border management, including offshore detention.

Bibliography

Andrijasevic, Rutvica, and William Walters. 2010. The International Organization for Migration and the International Government of Borders. *Environment and Planning D: Society and Space 28* (6): 977–999.

Arendt, Hannah. 1995. *Men in Dark Times*. New York: Harvest.

ASEAN—Association of Southeast Asian Nations Secretariat. 2015. *ASEAN Integration Report 2015*. ASEAN. http://www.miti.gov.my/miti/resources/ASEAN_Integration_Report_20151.pdf?mid=431

Barthes, Roland. 2012. *How to Live Together: Novelistic Simulations of Some Everyday Spaces*. New York: Columbia University Press.

Caouette, Dominique, and Denis Cote. 2011. Ripe for A New Asian Multilateralism? Asean and Contemporary Regional Dynamics. *European journal of East Asian studies 10* (1): 5–36.

Castells, Manuel. 2010. *The Network Society*. Hoboken: Wiley.

Cohen, Eliot A. 1996. A Revolution in Warfare. *Foreign Affairs 75* (2): *37–54*.

Dauvergne, Catherine. 2005. *Humanitarianism, Identity, and Nation: Migration Laws of Australia and Canada*. Vancouver: UBC Press.

Deleuze, Gilles. 1992. Postscript on the Societies of Control. *October* 59: 3–7.

Detienne, Marcel. 2002. *The Writing of Orpheus: Greek Myth in Cultural Context*. Trans. Janet Lloyd. Baltimore: Johns Hopkins University Press.

Fassin, Didier. 2012. *Humanitarian Reason: A Moral History of the Present.* Berkeley: University of California Press.

Finnemore, Martha, and Kathryn Sikkink. 1998. International Norm Dynamics and Political Change. *International Organization* 52 (04): 887–917.

Foucualt, Michel. 2008. *The Birth of Biopolitics: Lectures at the Collège de France, 1978–1979.* Basingstoke: Palgrave Macmillan.

Ghosh, Bimal, ed. 2000. *Managing Migration: Time for a New International Regime?* Oxford: Oxford University Press.

———. 2005. Managing Migration: Whither the Missing Regime? UNESCO. http://unesdoc.unesco.org/images/0013/001391/139149e.pdf

Hirschman, Albert O. 1978. Exit, Voice, and the State. *World Politics 31* (1): 90–107.

Hollifield, James F. 2000. Migration and the 'New' International Order: The Missing Regime. In *Managing Migration: Time for a New International Regime?* ed. Bimal Ghosh. Oxford: Oxford University Press.

Koslowski, Rey. 2011. Global Mobility Regimes: A Conceptual Framework. In *Global Mobility Regimes*, ed. Rey Koslowski. New York: Palgrave.

Krasner, Stephen D. 1982. Structural Causes and Regime Consequences: Regimes as Intervening Variables. *International Organization* 36 (2): 185–205.

Joly, Danièle. 2002. Introduction. In *Global Changes in Asylum Regimes*, ed. Danièle Joly. Palgrave Macmillan.

Mitropoulos, Angela. 2012. *Contract and Contagion: From Biopolitics to Oikonomia*. New York: Minor Compositions.

———. 2015. Archipelago of Risk: Uncertainty, Borders and Migration Detention Systems. *New Formations* 84 (85): 163–183.

———. 2016. On Borders / Race / Fascism / Labour / Precarity / Feminism / etc. *Base* 30 (1). http://www.basepublication.org/?p=107

Morrisson, Scott. 2014. A New Force Protecting Australia's Borders. Address to the Lowy Institute for International Policy, Sydney. Friday, 9 May 2014. https://www.lowyinstitute.org/news-and-media/multimedia/audio/podcast-future-border-protection-scott-morrison-mp

Nethery, Amy. 2010. *Immigration Detention in Australia*. PhD Thesis, Deakin University. https://dro.deakin.edu.au/eserv/DU:30032385/netheryimmigrationdetention-2010A.pdf

Parker, Noel, Nick Vaughan-Williams, et al. 2009. Lines in the Sand? Towards an Agenda for Critical Border Studies. *Geopolitics 14* (3): 582–587.

Parliament of Australia. 2013. Migration Amendment (Unauthorised Maritime Arrivals and Other Measures) Act 2013. https://www.comlaw.gov.au/Details/C2013A00035

Pezzullo, Michael. 2014. Sovereignty in an Age of Global Interdependency: The Role of Borders. Speech to Australian Strategic Policy Institute, 4 December 2014. https://www.border.gov.au/newsandmedia/Documents/sovereignty-age-interdependency-04122014.pdf

Pilz, Kerstin. 2005. *Mapping Complexity: Literature and Science in the Works of Italo Calvino*. Leicester: Troubador.

Rajaram, Prem Kumar, and Carl Grundy-Warr, eds. 2007. *Borderscapes: Hidden Geographies and Politics at Territory's Edge*. Vol. 29. Minneapolis: University of Minnesota Press.

Rebgetz, Louisa. 2016. Inadequate Care, Communication Failures in Lead-up to Asylum Seeker's Death, Court Hears. *ABC News*, 10 June 2016. http://www.abc.net.au/news/2016-06-10/khazaei-coronial-inquest-inadequate-care-in-lead-up-to-death/7501106

Reid-Henry, S.M. 2014. Humanitarianism as Liberal Diagnostic: Humanitarian Reason and the Political Rationalities of the Liberal Will-to-Care. *Transactions of the Institute of British Geographers 39*: 418–431.

Reus-Smit, Christian. 1997. The Constitutional Structure of International Society and the Nature of Fundamental Institutions. *International Organization* 51 (4): 555–589.

Ruggie, John G. 1982. International Regimes, Transactions, and Change: Embedded Liberalism in the Postwar Economic Order. *International Organization 36* (2): 379–415.

Sending, Ole Jacob, and Iver B. Neumann. 2006. Governance to Governmentality: Analyzing NGOs, States, and Power. *International Studies Quarterly* 50 (3): 651–672.

Squire, Vicki, ed. 2010. *The Contested Politics of Mobility: Borderzones and Irregularity*. London: Routledge.

———. 2015. *Post/Humanitarian Border Politics between Mexico and the US: People, Places, Things*. Basingstoke: Palgrave Macmillan.

Stasiulis, Daiva, and Nira Yuval-Davis, eds. 1995. *Unsettling Settler Societies: Articulations of Gender, Race, Ethnicity and Class*. Thousand Oaks, CA: Sage.

Thompson, Geoff, Joel Tozer, and Wayne Harley. 2016. Manus Island: 'Pathetic' Bureaucratic Response Blamed for Asylum Seeker Hamid Khazaei's Death. *ABC News*, 26 April 2016. http://www.abc.net.au/news/2016-04-25/manus-island-blunder-blamed-for-asylum-seeker-death/7355858

Vaughan-Williams, Nick. 2009. The Generalised Bio-political Border? Re-conceptualising the Limits of Sovereign Power. *Review of International Studies* 35 (4): 729–749.

———. 2015. *Europe's Border Crisis: Biopolitical Security and Beyond*. Oxford: Oxford University Press.

Walia, Harsha. 2013. *Undoing Border Imperialism*. Oakland: AK Press.

Weiss, Thomas, and Ramesh Thakur. 2010. *Global Governance and the UN: An Unfinished Journey*. Bloomington: University of Indiana Press.

Wilson, Lauren. 2013. Senate Passes Amendment to Excise Mainland from Migration Zone. *The Australian*, 16 May 2013.

CHAPTER 3

Leaving Home

This chapter seeks to understand how and why people cross borders in Southeast Asia and the Pacific, whether or not they have permission. The focus is on identifying and explaining trends of irregular migration in the broader regional and international context of labour migration and asylum-seeking into, out of, and within the region. To build an understanding of irregular migration in the region, the chapter situates the issue within the dynamics of both forced and voluntary migration.

There is considerable overlap between the categories of asylum and labour migration, for a number of reasons. First, it should be noted that the categorisation of asylum seekers, migrant workers, and others such as international students or even tourists, is an administrative process controlled by states, rather than an identification of clearly bounded social groups. The motivations and expectations of migrant workers are conditioned and limited by state policies that restrict their movement and status, which are reviewed in more detail in subsequent chapters. An individual may fit into one or more migration categories at a certain time or for a part of their journey and a different category at a later time. It is also entirely possible and in fact very common for a person to be both an asylum seeker and a migrant worker. They may seek work to temporarily support themselves during their journey or while waiting for refugee status determination, or they may be seeking refuge in a country where they can settle and work to support themselves and their family.

N. Henry, *Asylum, Work, and Precarity*, Critical Studies of the Asia-Pacific, DOI 10.1007/978-3-319-60567-8_3

There are important distinctions to be made between asylum-seeking and labour migration. But the approach taken in this chapter starts from the assumption that these different categories of movement across borders are primarily the result of categorisation by border regimes, including the influence of international agreements. The distinctions between forced and economic migration are produced by contingent political processes of categorisation, rather than neutral or natural definitions. This chapter therefore treats both labour migration and asylum-seeking within the context of international migration, understood in the broadest sense as human movement across borders. This allows for an analysis that is sensitive to the common struggles of refugees and migrant workers, as well as the differences between these categories.

Discussion of commonality between refugees and migrant workers can be politically sensitive, since one of the ways that hostility towards refugees is sometimes expressed is through suggestions that asylum seekers are 'economic migrants' not 'genuine refugees'. It is also politically fraught to discuss the elements of choice and agency exercised by asylum seekers, since liberal humanitarian narratives tend to base sympathy for refugees on viewing them as passive and abject victims of forces beyond their control. For those who maintain a belief in the moral legitimacy of border controls on migration while making exceptions for refugees because their movement is seen as involuntary, the basis for the exception can be seen as undermined by the idea that refugees make choices in their journeys. The argument that refugees exercise agency in seeking a better life for themselves and their families has largely been captured in public debates by right-wing conservative standpoints that seek to undermine the liberal argument that refugees are morally deserving of protection due to the forced rather than voluntary nature of their migration.

The point of departure for the approach taken in this book is the assumption that all migrants, including both asylum seekers and workers, make choices and exercise agency within the range of options available to them. To paraphrase Marx's famous statement in *The Eighteenth Brumaire of Louis Bonaparte*, migrants make their own journeys, but not in circumstances of their choosing. This argument has both a descriptive and a normative component. Descriptively, I suggest that the evolution of regimes of border governance can only be understood by acknowledging the impact of the collective agency of migrants in shaping the social phenomena of human movement that states seek to manage and control. Normatively,

I maintain that there is no morally consistent reason to discriminate between migrants, including in their access to legal protection, on the basis of their documentation or mode of travel.

Migration Trends in Southeast Asia and the Pacific

Migrants from ASEAN countries living outside the region, estimated at 21.3 million in 2015, greatly outnumber the estimated 3.4 million from outside ASEAN living in Southeast Asia. In addition, the majority of immigration in ASEAN is intraregional, with the World Bank estimating there were 10.2 million international migrants in the region in 2015, of whom 6.8 million were from another ASEAN country (ILO 2015).

While migration statistics are indicative of broad dynamics, they can be unreliable for more precise comparisons between specific countries. Data provided by national governments are compiled by the UN Department of Economic and Social Affairs (UNDESA), with the World Bank maintaining a separate dataset based on multiple sources, including government data and staff estimates. An analysis of both datasets for the ASEAN region by the ILO (2015) shows significant disparities between statistics from different sources. For instance, bilateral emigration and immigration data which should match are often wildly different. A World Bank (2016, x) analysis indicates immigration data are generally more reliable than emigration data, suggesting that states take greater care in monitoring who is entering their borders than who is leaving. The World Bank (2016, xiii) also acknowledges that irregular migration contributes to underestimation of migration.[1]

A 2010 study by the IOM and Asia Development Bank (ADB) surveyed migration experts in the region together with a review of trends of demographic and economic growth to predict migration trends within the Greater Mekong Subregion (GMS).[2] The study predicted continued growth in labour migration within the subregion over the following decade, based on the differences between demographic and economic growth trends. For instance, whereas Thailand was likely to experience continued high levels of economic and employment growth, the demographic trends were towards an ageing and slowly growing population. Job growth in Thailand was predicted to match labour force growth in the period 2007–11 as a result of economic slowdown, potentially reducing the demand for migrant workers. However, job growth was predicted to increase from 2012 to 2016, producing 3.6 million jobs, of which only 0.9 million could be filled from labour-force growth, leaving a surplus of 2.5 million jobs to be filled by migration (Lewis et al. 2010, 31). Predictions of continuing growth in demand for migrant labour were repeated in a 2012 report by Thailand's Office of the National Economic and Social Development Board (cited in IOM et al. 2013, 1).

The combination of slowing demographic growth and high economic growth, which Thailand had experienced since the 1970s, was matched in Vietnam since the 1990s. High rates of population growth were starting to fall in Cambodia and Lao PDR, while remaining high in Myanmar. While other GMS countries, such as Vietnam, were seen as likely to follow Thailand's growth model over the long term, the continued growth in the cohort of young people joining the workforce over the following decade would stimulate continued migration within the region, especially to Thailand.

Deciding to Depart

Patterns of labour migration across the region of Southeast Asia and the Pacific can be partially explained in terms of large-scale economic and demographic trends, but are also path-dependent, reflecting the histories of transnational social and cultural relations across borders, including previous migration. Castles (2013) identifies the combination of uneven rates of economic development and rapid demographic transitions as key drivers of labour migration, both of which are found across Southeast Asia and the Pacific. However, as de Haas (2010) emphasises, the relationship between economic development and migration is non-linear, with rates of migration tending to increase in populations reaching middle-income status. Social networks are also important for sharing experiences and information on migration opportunities, including access to informal intermediaries to facilitate travel and employment.

Patterns of asylum seeker movements are episodic and related to events and trends causing loss of human security, including persecution, conflict and political instability. Analysis of the country cases below shows that where there is correlation between economic and asylum migration, this is likely to be a result of migrants motivated by insecurity and persecution taking opportunities for labour migration.

Seeking Livelihoods—Migrant Workers

Migrant workers who do not formally seek asylum or refugee status may also nonetheless be motivated to migrate by conditions of persecution and generalised insecurity similar to those experienced by asylum seekers. These conditions are often intrinsically linked to economic motivations for migration, since the lack of opportunities for migrant workers to earn a living in their home countries is very often linked to more general experiences of insecurity and precarity.

The Philippines

The Philippines is the largest source country for labour migration in ASEAN, with 6,001,696 migrants from the Philippines living throughout the world in 2015, according to World Bank (2016) estimates. Labour migration began to Hawaii and the Continental United States after the Philippines became a US colony in 1895. Since 1974, migration has been actively promoted under the government's 'labour export' policy, contributing to what Asis (2006) describes as a 'culture of migration'. The largest destination for migrants from the Philippines is the United States, with a population of 1,998,932 in 2015. Most Filipino migrants travel outside the Asia-Pacific region, many to the Middle East, with 700,000 in the United Arab Emirates and 670,000 in Saudi Arabia. The largest ASEAN destination for migrants from the Philippines is Malaysia, with a population of 410,149.

Government figures from the Commission on Filipinos Overseas (2014) cite a higher number of 10.2 million migrants from the Philippines living abroad in 2013, including 3.2 million in the United States, although these statistics include migrants of Philippine origin who have become permanent residents and naturalised citizens of foreign states and are less likely to be included in World Bank estimates. In addition, the Philippines government registered 367,166 Filipino workers as international seafarers in 2013.

The longstanding government policy of facilitating labour export from the Philippines has been successful in establishing the country as the primary source of migrant labour in the Asia-Pacific region. Remittances from migrant workers make a substantial contribution to foreign exchange revenues and cash incomes for the Philippines, totalling an estimated 28 billion US dollars in 2015, according to the World Bank (2016). The largest sources were the US with 9.6 billion dollars, the United Arab Emirates with 3.6 billion dollars and Saudi Arabia with 3.2 billion dollars. Within ASEAN, the largest source was Malaysia, where migrants from the Philippines sent home 1.7 billion dollars of remittances in 2015.

However, the labour export policy has also been criticised for failing to substantially contribute to the development of the Philippines' economy. Social movement organisations affiliated to the left-wing BAYAN network have been particularly vocal in their criticism of labour export policies. Interviewed by the author in 2008, the leader of the Anakbayan youth network claimed that 'the few educated youth tend to go abroad to secure employment, while the majority of our youth will find themselves at a loss of how to get employment, whether locally or abroad'. The problem of domestic unemployment and outward labour migration was blamed squarely on the government, which was seen as unconcerned with creating local employment and solely focused on how to 'facilitate the movement of the young people from here to other countries' in order to increase the volume of foreign exchange the country receives from remittances. The government's labour export policy was also criticised by the Secretary-General of the KMU union federation, who described the policy in a 2008 interview with the author as part of the government's neoliberal economic policies of trade liberalisation, privatisation, and deregulation. According to the KMU, the majority of migrant workers under the government's labour export scheme are actually educated professionals, yet were often assigned to domestic or menial work.

These claims are supported by statistics from the Commission on Filipinos Overseas (2014, 26–30) showing migrant workers tend to be young, well-educated women. The population of migrants from the Philippines is weighted toward the under-30s, with an average age of 31. The majority are women, outnumbering male migrants by a ratio of 100 women to every 67 men. The most common level of education for migrants between 2005 and 2014 was a university degree. More than 30% of migrants had graduated university and a further 17% had studied at the university level. Most female migrant workers are employed as domestic workers, while the most common occupations recorded prior to migration were 'student,' 'housewife,' and 'professional'.

Myanmar

Myanmar is a significant source country for outward migration, with the World Bank (2016) estimating 3,139,596 migrants of Myanmar origin living outside the country in 2015 (see Table 3.1). Apart from a relatively small population in Malaysia, the vast majority of migrants from Myanmar in the ASEAN region are based in Thailand, with a total of 1,892,480 migrants with regular status in 2015. After Thailand, the most significant

Table 3.1 Bilateral Estimates of Migrant Stocks for selected countries in Southeast Asia and the Pacific, 2015

Source	*Destination*												
	Brunei Darussalam[a]	*Cambodia*	*Indonesia*	*Lao PDR*	*Malaysia*	*Myanmar*	*Philippines*	*Singapore*	*Thailand*	*Vietnam*	*Australia*	*New Zealand*	*World*
Brunei Darussalam	–	0	0	0	976	0	82	0	0	121	3556	0	43,118
Cambodia	0	–	0	1201	17,226	0	40	0	750,109	2485	33,616	6570	1,118,878
Indonesia	352	108	–	0	1,074,737	0	3325	152,681	2952	7671	78,744	4914	4,116,587
Lao PDR	0	265	0	–	0	0	0	0	926,427	4284	12,016	0	1,294,218
Malaysia	643	175	1979	0	–	0	798	1,044,994	8199	0	145,227	16,353	1,683,132
Myanmar	0	53	0	282	79,691	–	424	0	1,892,480	9783	23,742	2118	3,139,596
Philippines	3468	156	3517	0	410,149	0	–	14,176	17,581	292	189,969	37,299	6,001,696
Singapore	2285	125	19,681	0	42,474	0	825	–	2962	466	63,077	5370	282,213
Thailand	25,451	31,472	19,681	1652	93,635	0	342	17,644	–	512	57,176	7722	1,007,294
Vietnam	0	37,225	0	11,447	28,223	0	416	0	17,663	–	225,749	6153	2,592,233
Australia	934	119	9476	17	3518	0	4018	9267	11,298	205	–	62,712	487,275
New Zealand	150[b]	0	0	0	5847	0	387	3604	1779	0	582,761	–	763,731
World	**206,173**	**75,566**	**295,433**	**21,801**	**2,408,329**	**103,117**	**213,150**	**2,323,252**	**4,490,941**	**68,290**	**6,468,640**	**1,261,215**	**247,245,059**

Source: World Bank Migration and Remittances Factbook 2016 (www.worldbank.org/prospects/migrationandremittances)

[a]Estimates for Brunei appear to be based on government figures, which seem inaccurate in identifying country of origin

[b]Source: NZ Ministry of Foreign Affairs and Trade. The World Bank figure of 25,363 appears to be an error

destinations for migrants from Myanmar are Saudi Arabia, with a registered population of 600,000, followed by Bangladesh with 197,625, the United States with 116,775 and Pakistan with 93,057 (World Bank 2016). In addition, a significant number of Myanmar nationals work as seafarers and are effectively migrant workers, although they are not resident in a foreign state. In 2014, there were 98,000 Myanmar seafarers registered with Myanmar's Department of Marine Administration, of whom approximately 30,000 were deployed at sea at any time (Shwegu Thitsar 2014). Also not included in these statistics are the significant populations of refugees from Myanmar living without stable official status in camps and informal settlements in the border areas of Thailand, Bangladesh and Northern India.

Considering Myanmar's low level of economic development, migrant remittances are a significant source of foreign exchange cash incomes for the country, with the World Bank (2016) estimating migrant workers sent over 3.2 billion US dollars home to the country in 2015. The largest sources of migrant remittances were migrants in Thailand, who sent 1.7 billion US dollars home, and those in Saudi Arabia who sent 881 million US dollars in 2015.

The large number of workers who have migrated from Myanmar to Thailand in the last two decades have also sought to escape conditions of absolute poverty as well as military and political oppression in their home areas. Migration routes and networks to Thailand have become particularly well established from border areas of Myanmar, where conditions caused by the military presence have been severe and where Thai industrial towns located near the border provide proximate opportunities for escape. Studies of migrant workers' motivations for leaving home in these border areas have found that a large number, even a majority, have suffered displacement due to persecution and conflict (IRC 2012, 9–10). The differences between refugees and migrant workers from Myanmar on the Thai border were found to be largely based on where and how people crossed the border and where they settled on arrival, rather than fundamental differences in their conditions at home or reasons for departure. A survey of migrant workers from Myanmar in Thailand, conducted in 2013 by IOM and researchers at Chulalongkorn University, found that of the 5027 migrant workers from Myanmar surveyed across seven provinces in Thailand, 21% had been unemployed prior to migration, 32% had been self-employed farmers, 8% were merchants and 39% were employed as wage workers. The majority (64%) came from rural areas, and 23% reported their previous living standards as bad or very bad (IOM 2013, 9).

Vietnam

Vietnam is a significant source of outward migration, with 2,592,233 people born in the country estimated to be living abroad in 2015 (World Bank 2016). By far the majority of these migrants are based in developed countries, with the largest populations being in the US with 1,381,076 and Australia with 225,749. This reflects the continuing significance of former refugees from Vietnam who were resettled in Western states under the Comprehensive Plan of Action, as well as further migration encouraged by ties to established migrant populations in these states. Vietnamese migrants sent 13 billion US dollars in remittances back to the country in 2015, according to World Bank (2016) estimates. The most significant sources of migrant remittances to Vietnam were all developed countries, with the largest sources being the US with 7.3 billion dollars and Australia with 1.1 billion dollars.

More Vietnamese migrants are registered in East Asia than in Southeast Asia, with the largest number of migrants from Vietnam in the Asia-Pacific in South Korea, with a population of 122,449. In Southeast Asia, smaller but still relatively significant populations of Vietnamese migrants are found in Cambodia with 37,225, Malaysia with 28,223 and Thailand with 17,663.

Indonesia

Indonesia is a major source of outward labour migration, with 4,116,587 migrants abroad in 2015. Like the Philippines, Indonesia has a longstanding policy of encouraging labour migration as a strategy to reduce urban unemployment and to boost foreign exchange earnings through remittances. The World Bank (2016) estimates that Indonesia received 9.6 billion US dollars in remittances from migrant workers in 2015.

The largest destination for labour migration from Indonesia is Saudi Arabia, with an estimated 1.5 million migrant workers in 2015. Together, these workers sent home around 3.7 billion US dollars in remittances in 2015, according to World Bank estimates. The second most popular destination for migrants from Indonesia is Malaysia, with an estimated 1,074,737 registered in 2015, sending home around 2.3 billion US dollars in remittances (World Bank 2016). However, the ease of crossing the Indonesia-Malaysia border—with or without a visa—means that a large number of Malaysia's millions of undocumented migrant workers come from Indonesia, according to trade union and labour support organisation staff interviewed in 2015. If the unknown number of Indonesian migrant workers with irregular status were included, it is likely that Malaysia would exceed Saudi Arabia as the primary destination for Indonesian workers.

Other States in Southeast Asia

The countries in ASEAN that do not represent significant sources of labour migration are those with particularly high and particularly low per-capita incomes: Cambodia, Lao PDR, Singapore and Brunei. The outlier in this regard is Myanmar which combines low economic development with high levels of emigration. In this case, as noted above, labour migration from Myanmar to Thailand can be considered as an extension of mass displacement as a result of conflict and repression. This correlation of middle-income development with higher migration fits the general pattern worldwide, being that the majority of migration is from middle-income countries to richer countries (UNDESA 2016, 14). Although it is sometimes claimed that poverty is a 'push' factor for migration, in fact, rates of outward migration tend to rise as a country develops to middle-income status, as more people gain access to the resources needed to migrate (Clemens 2014).

Pacific States

The legacy of colonial relationships continues to shape the migration patterns of states in the Pacific region. Some territories in the Pacific remain formally incorporated into the colonising state, as is the case for Hawaii as a State of the US, and New Caledonia and French Polynesia as Collectivities of France.[3] Other parts of the Pacific are unincorporated territories under the sovereignty of foreign states, as is the case in American Samoa, Guam and Palau in relation to the US, and Tokelau in relation to New Zealand. As part of transitions—or partial transitions—to self-government, other Pacific states have negotiated access to joint citizenship or preferential migration with colonial powers, including the United States, Australia, and New Zealand.

The majority of emigrants from Fiji are of Indian ethnicity, estimated at 90% of migrants—motivated by a combination of economic and political uncertainty and opportunities for work in Australia and New Zealand. Australia is the most common destination for migrants from Fiji, with a population of 67,233, followed by New Zealand with 52,755. In addition, a large number of Fijian soldiers have served as UN peacekeepers, another source of foreign exchange revenue for the government, and veterans are in global demand as private security contractors (Firth 2007, 123).

New Zealand is also the largest destination for migrants from Samoa, with a population of 50,661 in the country, as well as from Tonga, with a population in New Zealand of 22,416.

For most of the Pacific, economic opportunity is the main motivation for migration. Remittances from migrant workers are the largest source of foreign exchange revenue for many Pacific Islands, including Samoa, Tonga and Fiji. Remittances to Tonga were 118 million US dollars in 2015 according to World Bank (2016) estimates, largely from the US, New Zealand and Australia. Figures from 2004 showed remittances made up 22% of cash incomes across Tonga, and up to 50% in some villages (Small and Dixon 2004). Samoa received 154 million US dollars, of which 70 million dollars came from New Zealand and the balance from Australia, the US and American Samoa. Fiji received 235 million US dollars in remittances in 2015 from migrants in Western countries, including 79 million dollars from Australia and 59 million from New Zealand.

Forced Displacement—Refugees and Asylum Seekers

The distinction between refugees and other migrants is first and foremost an administrative one, created by the different categories and channels of migration defined by states. Research on asylum seekers who arrived in industrialised countries without regular visas shows that for the overwhelming majority, the primary factor explaining their decision to depart was to seek protection from persecution (Castles and Loughna 2005, 60). Any other motivations, including economic opportunities, were secondary and insufficient to motivate irregular migration as an asylum seeker.

Myanmar

Myanmar is by far the largest source of refugee movement of any country in Southeast Asia, and accounts for a significant proportion of refugees in the region. UNHCR (2015a) estimates for 2015 showed over half a million refugees and asylum seekers originating from Myanmar (458,381 refugees and 55,639 asylum seekers). In addition, UNHCR recognises over 400,000 Internally Displaced Persons (IDPs) within Myanmar as a result of ongoing civil conflict and persecution, particularly in the states of Kachin and Rakhine. The scale of internal displacement in Myanmar is of international concern, as it indicates the country will continue to be a significant source of refugee movements for some time—until durable solutions are found to the root causes of displacement within the country.

Successive regimes in Myanmar have been blamed for creating what the International Committee of the Red Cross described in 2007 as 'a climate of constant fear among the population' (Brees 2008, 4). Although the political situation in Central Myanmar has improved since the change of government in 2011, the situation in the border areas is very different, and exposes the deeply entrenched patterns of dysfunctional civil-military relations produced by decades of conflict.

The largest group of refugees from Myanmar are the Rohingya minority from Rakhine. Bangladesh hosts over 230,000 Myanmar Rohingya who are recognised as persons of concern to UNHCR, with many more in informal camps or integrated with the local population (UNHCR 2015b; Arakan Project Interview 2015). An estimated 950,000 Rohingya are internally displaced within Myanmar, some effectively held prisoner in state-run camps, as a result of communal violence and state persecution (UNHCR 2015b). Legal persecution of Rohingya is centred around the 1982 Citizenship Law, which restricts Myanmar citizenship to members of 'national races' and those who can prove their ancestors settled in the country prior to the first British annexation in 1823. UNHCR identifies the conditions of statelessness and lack of documentation experienced by Rohingya as the single greatest driver of irregular migration in the Asia-Pacific region (UNHCR staff interview 2015). In addition to routine police persecution and restrictions on movement, state violence against Rohingya in Rakhine has escalated since the launch of a military counter-insurgency operation in 2015. The operation, ostensibly in response to an isolated incident in which a police station was attacked in a Rohingya area, has followed the pattern established in other Myanmar military operations of indiscriminately targeting civilian populations as a means of attacking the support base for insurgent groups.

The continued displacement of refugees from Myanmar's border areas needs to be understood in the context of the ongoing complex conflicts and generalised lack of security centred on the deeply antagonistic relationship between the armed forces (Tatmadaw) and local populations. Although outbreaks of open conflict have been common as a proximate cause of refugee movement across the Thai-Myanmar border, explaining the scale and protracted nature of the displacement requires attention to a broader range of conditions affecting life in the border areas over the longer term.

Patterns of displacement from Kayin (Karen) and Kayah (Karenni) States in Eastern Myanmar shifted dramatically in the mid-1990s as rebel groups lost territory to Tatmadaw offensives. Conflict between the Tatmadaw and ethnic minority armed groups had been causing displacement of civilians since at least the 1960s, but the intensification of offensives and loss of territory held by the rebel groups in the 1990s led to worsening conditions for IDPs and escalating cross-border movements of refugees. Displacement of civilians was part of a deliberate Tatmadaw strategy to deprive insurgent groups of a base of operations in government-controlled areas.[4] While insurgent groups held secure territory they could offer shelter to civilians displaced from government-controlled areas, including students and other democracy activists who fled central Burma after the 1988 Coup, but this became increasingly difficult in the 1990s and 2000s. As rebel groups lost territory on the Burma side of the border, displaced people were forced to move further towards the border and to cross into Thailand. The most dramatic shift occurred in 1995, after disaffected Buddhist members of the Christian-dominated Karen National Liberation Army split to form the Democratic Karen Buddhist Army (DKBA) and joined with the Tatmadaw to overrun the KNU headquarters at Manerplaw, leading to a major loss of territory. DKBA attacks even crossed the border into Thailand to target refugee camps in 1995 and again in 1997.

In each of the conflict zones on Myanmar's borders, displacement has been driven by a consistent range of abuses against civilians living in the vicinity of army bases, including in areas under formal ceasefire agreements. Representatives of Mon opposition groups interviewed in 2006 emphasised that human rights violations by the army had continued despite a 1995 ceasefire agreement between the SPDC regime and the New Mon State Party (NMSP). Those interviewed reported systemic abuses such as rape by soldiers, land confiscation, and forced relocation of villages in the area. The Karen Women's Organisation has also documented what they describe as the systematic use of rape as a 'weapon of war' by soldiers given impunity to abuse the local population, even during ceasefire agreements.

Leaders of the Karen National Union interviewed in 2006 and 2011 reported the systematic destruction of villages and crops, with villagers confined to their homes or forcibly relocated and cut off from their fields and food supplies. The Border Consortium (TBC) (2016) estimated in 2010 that 3700 civilian settlements in the region had been destroyed by the Tatmadaw and allied forces since 1996. The practice of forced relocation of villages in Myanmar has operated as part of a counter-insurgency program similar to the British policy of 'strategic hamletting' applied on a large scale in Malaya during the 1948 insurgency and later used by American forces in Vietnam (Nagl 2005, 129). Village relocation in Myanmar has also facilitated state-led development schemes that largely benefited military-owned entities or associated interests. In 2010, over 28,000 people from Karen communities were forcibly displaced from areas affected by the Kyauk Na Ga dam project, which flooded large areas in Kayin State and Eastern Bago Region (TBBC 2011, 18). In the context of generalised insecurity, this loss of land and livelihood as a result of confiscation and state-led development projects has contributed to further displacement within South-East Myanmar and across the Thai-Myanmar border.

Major infrastructure projects undertaken by the military regime and in partnership with transnational corporations, such as the construction of the Yadana gas pipeline, made systematic use of forced labour. The Tatmadaw has also regularly taken people from villages and from urban prisons to act as forced 'porters' on military campaigns in which many were killed by landmines, exhaustion and abuse. These longstanding practices were frequently cited by both refugees and migrant workers interviewed in 2006 and 2011 as reasons for leaving their home areas.

With the change of government in 2011, conditions in some parts of Myanmar have improved. Relaxation of restrictions on political activity and expression have allowed some exiled activists to return to the country (Henry 2015). The government has held talks with armed opposition groups with the aim of establishing a nationwide ceasefire. Local ceasefire arrangements in parts of Karen have become secure enough for small numbers of refugees to start returning under a pilot scheme supported by UNHCR. However, in other parts of the country, conditions have deteriorated rapidly. In addition to the increased persecution of Rohingya in Rakhine, repeated outbreaks of conflict in Kachin have produced new sources of mass displacement since 2011.

Other Sources of Displacement in Southeast Asia and the Pacific

Vietnam is the second largest source of refugees originating in Southeast Asia, according to UNHCR statistics. However, in contrast to Myanmar, this is not due to an ongoing crisis in Vietnam, but rather reflects the status of the ethnic Chinese or Hoa refugees who fled from Vietnam to China between 1979 and 1982. Like Vietnamese refugees who resettled in Western countries, the Indochinese refugees in China have integrated into local communities and received recognition and effective protection from the government. Unlike their counterparts in Western countries, however, refugees from Vietnam in China have not been granted citizenship, and so remain listed as refugees of concern to UNHCR (2007a, b; Ministry of Foreign Affairs of the PRC 2014).

A small but growing number of asylum seekers from Malaysia have sought refuge in Australia. These asylum seekers are predominantly either non-Malay ethnic minorities or non-Muslim religious minorities, claiming persecution on the basis of intensifying racial and religious discrimination and the actions of state agencies—including the religious morality police (Burton-Bradley 2016). In 2015, UNHCR (2017) recorded 2549 asylum seekers from Malaysia in Australia, compared to only 741 the previous year.[5]

Conflict in other countries of Southeast Asia has tended to produce more internal displacement than international movements of refugees and asylum seekers. This is the case in the Philippines, where conflict between central government forces and those of the Communist New Peoples' Army—as well as Moro groups in the South of the country—have created significant internal displacement. Civil conflicts in Indonesia have also created mass displacements, which have at times created international movements of refugees, from the former Indonesian territory of East Timor prior to that country's independence, and from the province of Aceh prior to the agreed autonomy that followed the devastation of the 2006 Tsunami.

Current conflicts and state repression in the Indonesian territory of West Papua have produced similar displacements, with a significant number of West Papuan refugees crossing the border into Papua New Guinea, and a few seeking asylum in other states, including Australia and New Zealand. In 2015, UNHCR (2017) recorded 9368 asylum seekers from Indonesia in Papua New Guinea, all of whom are likely to be from neighbouring West Papua. A long history of documented abuses by Indonesian police and military in the province of Papua involves a similar pattern to that of Myanmar, with collective punishment of indigenous Papuan communities used as part of a campaign of repression targeting the movement for West Papuan independence and self-determination (Brundige et al. 2004). In 2017, a number of Pacific states raised concerns at the UN Human Rights Council that widespread abuses of civilians as well as targeted political repression was continuing in West Papua (Radio New Zealand 2017).

The history and legacy of forced displacement in Southeast Asia and the Pacific is strongly connected to the use of slavery and forced labour by colonial states in the region. For instance, the use of forced porters by the armed forces in Myanmar described above is a practice directly carried over from the British army in Burma. Throughout the nineteenth century and into the early twentieth century, Pacific islanders were kidnapped, or otherwise coerced and deceived, into indentured labour in slavery-like conditions on British plantations in Fiji and Queensland. The practice continued despite the abolition of slavery in the British Empire from 1834, and was only abolished in 1908 in Queensland and 1911 in Fiji (Phillips 2000, 21). Indentured labourers were also brought from India to work on British plantations in Southeast Asia and the Pacific, under conditions that would now be described as forced labour or human trafficking, with the descendants of these labourers forming the core of the contemporary Fijian-Indian population.

A new threat of mass displacement now threatens several Pacific states affected by rising sea levels and extreme weather related to climate change. For states whose territory is composed of low-lying atolls, such as Tuvalu and Kiribati, the prospect of even moderate rises in sea-level represents an existential threat that could displace the entire population. In the wider Asia-Pacific region, the same threat of sea-level related displacement is faced in the Maldives and in large areas of Bangladesh. Given the climate-related risks of mass displacement, some such as Williams (2008) have called for new international or regional multilateral treaties to create protection regimes for climate-related forced migrants, modelled on existing refugee protection regimes. However, others including McAdam (2011) have questioned the utility of a multi-lateral protection-focussed approach to climate displacement. As McAdam points out, unlike other events or crises that provoke sudden and desperate movement of refugees, migration and displacement related to climate change will have a gradual onset and has already begun. Governments need to plan and cooperate to respond to this category of migration, but this is not necessarily best done through seeking multilateral commitments to protection mechanisms that apply after the fact of displacement, even if such a system could be successfully agreed and implemented. Leaders and representatives of Pacific states likely to be affected by climate related displacement have also criticised responses that frame their citizens as likely 'climate refugees', rejecting the fatalism of assuming climate change and mass displacements are inevitable, as well as the implied assumption that Pacific peoples will be passive victims of these processes (McNamara and Gibson 2009).

Refugees from Outside the Region

Refugees and asylum seekers arrive in Southeast Asia from all over the world, with many hoping to travel onward to Australia or to apply for resettlement through UNHCR. The largest numbers of refugees and asylum seekers arriving in Southeast Asia and the Pacific from outside the region in 2015 were predominantly from South Asia and the Middle East. As Table 3.2 shows, the largest group of refugees and asylum seekers from outside the region in 2015 was from Afghanistan, with a combined total of more than 16,500 refugees and asylum seekers registered with UNHCR, followed by Pakistan with more than 11,800, Sri Lanka with more than 9000, Iran with at least 8300 and Iraq with at least 6900.

Deciding Where to Go

The major destination countries for labour migration into and within ASEAN are three of the four states with the highest level of economic development: Malaysia, Thailand, Brunei and Singapore. Despite a similarly high level of GDP per capita as Singapore, Brunei has relatively lower levels of migration, although as a proportion of the workforce, the ratio of migrant workers in Brunei is similar to that of Thailand and Malaysia. As ILO (2015) analysis suggests, the major drivers of labour migration within the ASEAN region are the significant disparities in GDP per capita and poverty levels, reflecting the uneven economic development of the region. However, in choosing between destinations, migrants consider a range of factors, including proximity and ease of travel, cultural and religious affinity, and the existence of established networks. For instance, Malaysia is preferred by Muslim migrant workers from Pakistan and Bangladesh, as well as by Rohingya and other Muslim groups from Myanmar. Government policies also play a significant role as an intermediating factor, affecting the extent to which migration is able to respond to economic growth as a drawcard, as well as which countries are favoured as sources. As the country analysis below shows, the approach to government regulation is a significant factor affecting the migration and work status of migrant workers, and can have a major impact—both positive and negative—on outcomes for migrants.

Thailand and Malaysia are heavily reliant on migrant labour in primary and basic manufacturing industries, as well as for construction, domestic labour and informal sectors. In both countries, demand for labour exceeds the number of registered migrant workers, and the gap is filled by large

Table 3.2 Refugees and Asylum seekers in selected countries in Southeast Asia and the Pacific, registered with UNHCR in 2015

Source	*Destination*								
	Indonesia	*Malaysia*	*Thailand*	*Philippines*	*Australia*	*Australia, held in Nauru*	*Australia, held in Papua New Guinea*	*Papua New Guinea (not including Manus)*	*New Zealand*
Myanmar		142,235	107,976	6	564				22
Afghanistan	6681	509	63	5	9207	48	34		45
Pakistan		1415	5266	68	4938	77	26		61
Indonesia								9368	
Sri Lanka		3073	305	17	5729	39			103
Iran	8	484	166	64	6750	372	362		177
Iraq	657	1305	306	40	4242	32	59		285
China	32	47	232	6	5133				147
Malaysia					2672				
Syria	359	1302	340	76	434				52
Somalia		1398	495	29	125	60	11		21
Stateless					2370	106	21		
All sources	13,508	154,486	116,468	404	57,362	757	558	9368	1372

Source: UNHCR Population Statistics Database

numbers of migrants with irregular status. In Singapore, employment is weighted more towards service sectors, and although almost all workers enter the country through regular channels, a significant number lapse into irregular employment status. In the broader region, Australia and New Zealand are also destination countries, although like Singapore they have restrictive border regimes that tend to prevent irregular arrivals. Workers with irregular status in these countries may have stayed past the term of their entry visa, or may have regular immigration status but lack a work permit.

The choice of destination and mode of travel for both refugees and migrant workers is significantly influenced by intermediaries who help to facilitate travel and other needs on arrival. As Ambrosini (2016) shows, the role of intermediaries is especially important for irregular migrants, who lack formal or legal channels to find work, housing and welfare assistance. The assistance that intermediaries provide to migrants may be motivated by family ties, broader community solidarities, profit—or some combination of these—and there are often no fixed or clear lines between altruistic and self-interested motivations or between helpful and exploitative actions by intermediaries. The existence of networks of intermediaries willing to help migrants travel to a new country and to access work and shelter on arrival can be a powerful motivation for migrants in selecting their destination. Indeed, research on decision-making by asylum seekers in Europe has shown that the existence of personal networks can outweigh a lack of legal opportunities for settlement and integration, including where restrictions have been introduced in attempts to deter irregular migration (Neumayer 2004, 176).

UNHCR (2017) figures for 2015 show a total of 355,558 asylum seekers and refugees registered as persons of concern in the region of Southeast Asia and the Pacific. Source and destination countries for significant populations of refugees and asylum seekers in the region are shown in Table 3.2.

Malaysia

Statistics kept by the Ministry of Immigration (2015) show a total of 2,139,474 migrants with work permits in Malaysia as of October 2015. The World Bank estimate for the total number of migrants in Malaysia in 2015 is slightly higher, at 2,408,329 (see Table 3.1). The number of unregistered migrant workers in Malaysia is unknown, but in meetings with the MTUC, top officials including former Prime Minister Dr. Mahathir

Mohammed have estimated the number at 7 million. This figure is at the high end of commonly cited estimates and is likely to be somewhat exaggerated. One estimate from the Malaysian Employers Federation, cited by Ah Lek (2016), suggested there were twice as many undocumented as documented migrants, putting the number with irregular status at more than 4 million. Whatever the exact figure, it is generally assumed that there are significantly more migrants working in Malaysia without permits than there are with formal status.

According to World Bank estimates, Indonesia is the most common country of origin for migrant workers in Malaysia, with 1,074,737 Indonesian migrants registered in 2015 out of a total registered migrant population of 2.4 million. The next largest group of migrants is from the Philippines, with 410,149 migrants registered. The significant population of migrants of Thai origin (93,635) is driven in part by persecution of Muslims in Southern Thailand, although this group is more likely to take opportunities to migrate across the border for work in Penang than they are to seek asylum. Although low numbers of migrants from South Asia are listed in World Bank estimates for Malaysia, representatives of trade unions and labour support organisations interviewed in 2015 reported working with large numbers of migrant workers from Nepal, Pakistan, India and Bangladesh—indicating that these populations may be more likely to be working with irregular status.

Malaysia hosted 154,547 refugees and asylum seekers identified as persons of concern to UNHCR (2017) in 2015. The majority of these, 142,235 were from Myanmar, of whom Rohingya were the largest single group.

Thailand

Government figures reported the total number of international migrants in Thailand in 2013 as 3,721,735 (UNDESA 2013). World Bank estimates for 2015 are significantly higher, suggesting a population of 4,490,941 migrants with regular status in Thailand. Of these, 3.25 million are employed with work permits, the majority of whom (2.7 million) are from the neighbouring countries: Cambodia, Laos and Myanmar (Huguet 2014, xiv). Over 1.3 million migrant workers from Cambodia, Laos and Myanmar already in Thailand without legal status have registered under the Nationality Verification process since 2009 to acquire regular immigration status. The number of undocumented workers remaining in

Thailand is unknown, but widely assumed to be more than a million (Huguet 2014, xix). Thailand's 2012–16 national economic planning strategy noted that 1.3 million migrant workers entered Thailand in 2010, of whom only 28% acquired legal work and migration status, with 72% remaining undocumented or partially documented (National Economic and Social Development Board 2011, 9). The document emphasised Thailand's continuing need for labour migration, due to economic development and an aging population.

In addition, Thailand hosts a substantial population of refugees and asylum seekers, primarily from neighbouring Myanmar. UNHCR (2017) recorded a total of 116,923 refugee and asylum-seeking persons of concern in 2015, of whom 107,976 originated in Myanmar. Refugees and asylum seekers from Myanmar are housed in camps on the Thai-Myanmar border, while those from other countries are more likely to be based in urban areas in Thailand. These urban asylum seekers numbered 8947 in 2015, of whom the largest group was from Pakistan—with a population of 5266.

The majority of refugees living in camps on the Thai-Myanmar border are ethnic Karen and Karenni displaced by conflict and military activity in their home areas in the states of Kayin and Kayah. The total population of nine camps on the border was 102,607 in December 2016, with 79% identifying as Karen and 10% as Karenni (The Border Consortium 2016). This is the population remaining after more than 100,000 refugees were resettled to third countries through UNHCR since 2005. The protracted refugee situation of the border camps has its origins in Tatmadaw (Myanmar Military) offensives since 1984 against territory held by separatist ethnic minority organisations, primarily the Karen National Union (KNU). One group of 1100 Karen refugees who crossed the border in 1984 to escape a Tatmadaw offensive against nearby KNU territory established a settlement that would become the location for Mae La camp, the largest and oldest of the refugee camps on the border. In the 1980s and early 1990s, refugee settlements were constructed along the border in an ad hoc manner, resembling villages more than formal camps. Although they lacked legal status in Thailand, there were few restrictions in practice on refugees' freedom of movement within the immediate border area at this time. With the Burma side of the border controlled by rebel groups, including the KNU and others such as the Karenni National Progressive Party (KNPP) and New Mon State Party (NMSP), refugees were also relatively free to move to and from Thailand. In response to new threats to the security of refugee settlements after the KNU's loss of border territory in 1995, and to regain control over the border and the growing refugee population, Thai authorities moved to consolidate the refugee settlements into larger more formal camps and introduced stricter regulation of movement between the camps and other areas on the border.

In addition to fleeing persecution in their home areas, refugee families have been motivated to seek shelter in the Thai camps to access education for their children. Myanmar's education system is chronically under-resourced and disrupted by conflict in border areas. In addition, the state education system heavily privileges the Myanmar language and restricts opportunities to learn minority languages. Interviews conducted with refugees in two camps on Thailand's border in 2006, and further interviews with support organisations in 2011, revealed the high value placed on education by refugees from Myanmar. The low quality of education in Myanmar was a frequent grievance and a number of those interviewed cited opportunities to further their own education or that of their children as a motivation to migrate to Thailand as refugees. During fieldwork in Mae La camp in 2006, I learned that the newest students enrolled in the school were three sisters, all less than ten years old, who had crossed the border unaccompanied, walking across mountainous terrain for several days to reach the camp school.

Indonesia

Overall international migration to Indonesia is low, with the total migrant population in the country in 2015 estimated by the World Bank to be 295,433 (see Table 3.1). The largest single group of migrants by country of origin is from China, with a population of 63,172 in 2015. This group of migrants are more likely to operate small and medium-size businesses or work in professional occupations than to be employed as low-skilled workers. The number of Chinese migrants in Indonesia is similar to that in other ASEAN countries, but is relatively higher than other groups due to the relative lack of labour migration to Indonesia. Like other rapidly developing countries with large populations of rural poor, Indonesia draws most of its urban workforce from internal migration. Some of these internal migrant workers face similar conditions of precarity, discussed further in Chap. 7, as international migrant workers in other countries. This is particularly the case for female domestic workers who move from provincial areas to Indonesia's main cities. Apart from fisheries workers on foreign fleets in Indonesian waters, the largest group of undocumented migrants in Indonesia are asylum seekers.

Asylum seekers arriving in Indonesia often do not regard the country as their final destination, with many planning to continue on to Australia. Increasingly though, asylum seekers who may have intended to make the onward journey to Australia are spending significant periods of time in Indonesia, where some have built more settled lives (Sampson, Gifford and Taylor 2016). However, as described in Chap. 7, refugees face significant barriers to establishing secure livelihoods and legal status in the country. Indonesia is not a signatory to the 1951 Refugee Convention and has no formal process for legal recognition or protection for refugees. This means there are few ways for refugees to attain legal status or opportunities for settlement and livelihood. However, Indonesia is relatively accessible on a visitor's visa for citizens of most countries. This allows asylum seekers to travel by regular routes to the country in the hope of being recognised as a refugee by UNHCR and resettled to a third country.

There were 14,134 Refugees and Asylum seekers recognised as persons of concern to UNHCR in Indonesia in 2015, up from around 11,000 in 2014. The largest group originated from Afghanistan, making up 47% of the total, followed by 13% from Myanmar and 8% from Somalia. Of the population in 2015, 590 had been accepted for resettlement, 569 to the United States and 21 to New Zealand. None had been accepted to Australia as a result of a change of government policy to no longer take in refugees from Indonesia. Detention of refugees is common in Indonesia, with 4620 refugees and asylum seekers held in 14 detention facilities and locations across the country, including 1187 children. In 2015, 730 refugees and asylum seekers were released to IOM community housing, while a further 744 surrendered to authorities in order to access IOM assistance. As of August 2015, UNHCR had registered 950 Rohingya (including 521 children) who arrived since 10 May[6] (UNHCR 2017; SUAKA 2015).

Singapore

Singapore is a major migration destination, with a total migrant population of 2,323,252 in the country in 2015 according to World Bank (2016) estimates. Of these, 1,404,700 were migrant workers holding work permits issued by Singapore's Ministry of Manpower (2016a, b, c) as of June 2016. The majority of these workers were in low-skilled jobs, with 1,009,300 on general work permits, allowing them to earn no more than

2200 Singapore Dollars per month. An additional 326,700 workers had permits to work in construction, while 237,100 were employed as domestic workers.

The largest population of migrants in Singapore is from Malaysia, with 1,044,994 registered in 2015 according to World Bank estimates. There is also a large population of 380,766 migrants from China. The next most common countries of origin for migrants are Indonesia with 152,681, India with 138,177, Pakistan with 118,765 and Bangladesh with 74,074.

Singapore does not accept applications for asylum or refugee resettlement. This, combined with the lack of opportunities for irregular migration and harsh punishments for overstaying temporary visas, means that Singapore has no known population of refugees or asylum seekers. If asylum seekers pass through Singapore, they would do so as part of regular travel in transit to another country.

Brunei

Brunei hosts a significant number of migrant workers relative to the size of the population, with 206,173 migrants living in the country in 2015, according to World Bank (2016) estimates. World Bank estimates for Brunei appear to be based directly on government statistics provided to UNDESA, and do not seem to accurately identify the country of origin of migrants. For instance, official figures suggesting large numbers of migrants from New Zealand and Japan, and small numbers from Indonesia, are contradicted by other sources. Statistics collected by the Brunei government based on residency status recorded 85,900 migrants with temporary visas in 2011, of whom 67,700 were employed (ILO 2015). The majority of migrant workers in Brunei are from Southeast Asia and South Asia. Significant numbers of female migrant workers from Indonesia and Philippines are employed as domestic workers, while male migrant workers from South Asia, especially Bangladesh, are employed in the construction and petroleum industries. Although smaller than the migrant population in other states in Southeast Asia, including Indonesia and Philippines, the number of migrants is significant—given that Brunei has a population of 393,400 and a workforce of 202,500. In recent years, the government of Brunei has taken steps to limit labour migration in the service sectors and imposed levies on employment of migrant workers in an attempt to promote the employment of local workers (*The Borneo Post* 2014).

Australia

Although no longer restricted in explicitly racial terms, the largest sources of migration to Australia follow the pattern established under the White Australia policy from 1901 to 1973. The most common country of origin for migrants to Australia is the United Kingdom, with a population of 1,277,474. The next largest group is from New Zealand, with 582,761 migrants taking advantage of free movement between the two countries under the Closer Economic Relations agreement (World Bank 2016). However, the significant diversification of migration to Australia is demonstrated by the next largest populations of migrants by origin being from China with 447,407, and India with 364,764. Substantial migrant populations are drawn from a range of countries in Europe, Asia, the Middle East and the Pacific. The largest group of migrants from an ASEAN country in Australia are from Vietnam, with a population of 225,749 first-generation migrants reflecting the continuing impact of refugee resettlement under the Comprehensive Plan of Action. Significant numbers of migrants from the Philippines, with a population of 189,969, and Malaysia with 145,227, show the continuing importance of migrant labour to the Australian economy, both in professional occupations such as nursing and in lower-skilled employment, especially in agriculture.

There were 736,124 temporary migrant workers with work permits in Australia in 2014, including skilled migrants on temporary work (subclass 457) visas, international students, working holiday makers and workers in the Seasonal Workers Programme (UNSW Human Rights Clinic 2015, iv). In addition, 582,761 New Zealanders lived in Australia in 2015, with access to Special Category Visas on arrival, which include the right to work. Of the 98,571 subclass 457 visas granted in the 2013–14 financial year, 65% were granted to migrants already in the country on student, working holiday and other visas (DIBP 2015a, b, 53). There were also 190,000 new permanent migrants to Australia, of which 128,550 were accepted under the skilled migrant category, with a further 61,112 applying as family members. Just over half of successful applications for permanent residence in Australia were made onshore by those on student and temporary work visas (DIBP 2015a, b, 22).

Compared to other countries in the region, there are very few undocumented migrant workers in Australia. The total number of migrants classified by the Australian government as 'Unlawful Non-Citizens'—representing migrants who have stayed in the country longer than permitted by their visa class—was 62,100 in 2013–14 (DIBP 2015a, b, 69). Other workers on temporary visas such as student visas may hold valid immigration status but be working outside the terms of their visa. A report provided to a government enquiry in 2010 estimated a total of around 100,000 migrants were working in Australia without regular status (Howells, cited in UNSW Human Rights Clinic 2015, iv).

UNHCR records 57,362 refugees and asylum seekers as persons of concern in Australia in 2015, in addition to 757 persons held on Nauru and 558 in Papua New Guinea who are considered by UNHCR to be the responsibility of the Australian government. As shown in Table 3.2, the largest group of refugees and asylum seekers in Australia in 2015 were from Pakistan, with a combined total of 9207, followed by Iran with 6750, and Sri Lanka with 5729.

Research commissioned by the Australian government on the motivations of refugees who had travelled by boat to Australia found that seeking protection from persecution was the primary but not sole motivation (McAulife 2013). In addition to meeting their protection needs, asylum seekers were motivated to escape corruption and poverty in their home countries and hoped to be able to find employment, housing, and access to education and health services in Australia. Additional reasons for choosing Australia over other possible destinations included geography and links to family and community already in the country. Similar research commissioned by the UK government (Robinson and Segrott 2002) also found that the primary motivation of asylum seekers was to seek a place of safety, while the choice of destination was secondary, based primarily on the cost and availability of the means to travel, including facilitation by smugglers and other agents. Significantly, the UK study found that asylum seekers lacked a detailed knowledge of immigration or asylum processes, or the availability of government benefits or work rights, and concluded that these were not significant factors in the choice of destination.

New Zealand

The largest group of migrants to New Zealand by country of origin is from the United Kingdom, as is also the case for Australia, reflecting the continuing influence of British colonisation of Australia and New Zealand in the nineteenth century. The next largest groups of migrants to New Zealand are from China, with a population of 98,109, and India, with 67,176 (World Bank 2016). Australian migration to New Zealand is not as significant as the reverse, with 62,712 Australian migrants in the country in 2015. The population of 54,276 migrants from South Africa mainly reflects the exodus of middle-class white South Africans after the end of Apartheid, combined with New Zealand's openness to English-speaking migrants with wealth to invest. Many migrant workers in New Zealand are from the Pacific, including 52,755 from Fiji and 50,661 from Samoa. The largest group of migrants from ASEAN are from the Philippines, with 37,299 migrants.

UNHCR recorded 1491 refugees and asylum seekers as persons of concern in New Zealand in 2015, including approximately 100 asylum seekers with pending applications. The majority of the remainder of the population were accepted by New Zealand through UNHCR's resettlement population and would normally qualify for New Zealand citizenship after three years of residency.

Deciding How to Travel

Of all the choices that migrants make in their journeys, mode of travel can be one of the most limited in the options available. As detailed in Chap. 5, the introduction of carrier sanctions, punishing transport operators that allow passengers to travel without authorisation—combined with the introduction of improved identity documentation and checking systems including biometric passports—has dramatically reduced the ability of asylum seekers and migrant workers to travel by conventional means without visas or other documentation of regular status.

A substantial number of the asylum applications made in Australia each year are lodged by travellers who arrive in the country with valid visas and travel documents, generally travelling by air. This has generally been the way that most asylum seekers arrive in the country. In the 2012–13 financial year, 8480 applications for asylum (5817 principal applicants and 2683 dependants) were made by people arriving in Australia by regular means, or already present in the country with a valid visa (DIBP 2014). The largest groups of applicants were international students and people in Australia on working holiday visas (DIBP 2013). The following year, 2013–14, 9646 applications were made by 6699 primary applicants and 2947 dependants. In both years, the top three countries of origin for these asylum seekers were China, India and Iran. In 2013–14, 19% of applicants were from China, 13% from India and 10% from Pakistan. However, although applicants from China and India were the largest groups of asylum seekers in this category, both groups had low rates of acceptance, with only 21% of applicants from China and 13% of applicants from India being granted asylum in Australia in 2013–14 (DIBP 2014).

2012 was the first year that a sharp rise in maritime arrivals of asylum seekers with irregular status outnumbered applications by those already in the country with regular migration status. In the 2012–13 financial year, 18,365 applications for asylum were made by people arriving in Australia by sea without visas. A further 8383 applications were made in the September quarter of 2013–14, before the numbers dramatically declined, making a total of 9072 for the year. As DIBP (2014) suggests, the decline in arrivals and subsequent applications was due to the news filtering back to asylum seekers of the Australian government's policy change of July 2013 requiring mandatory offshore detention for asylum seekers arriving by boat without a visa, with all new arrivals in Australia being sent to the detention centres on Manus and Nauru.

Australian government research (McAulife 2013, 26), based on a survey of asylum seekers who arrived by boat and were accepted as refugees, reported 'a high degree of risk, fear and uncertainty' associated with the journey to Australia, which involved 'crossing multiple borders, spending time in countries with no legal status and relying on strangers to progress the next stage of their journey'. These conditions are common for migrants who are forced to rely on smuggling networks to navigate across securitised borders. People fleeing conditions of persecution—such as those faced by Rohingya in Myanmar—will take any opportunity for migration available, regular or irregular, to seek relative safety. This leads to a merging of migration flows so that, for instance, Rohingya refugees from the Myanmar-Bangladesh border join Bangladeshi workers in seeking employment in Malaysia.

In Southeast Asia, it is common for migrant workers to cross borders by informal and irregular means, because these are easier and more accessible than formal processes. For many border areas in the region, including the Thailand-Myanmar and Indonesia-Malaysia borderzones, communities living on both sides of the territorial border are more socially and geographically proximate to one another than they are to their respective national centres. Crossing the border informally, with the help of existing social networks, is easier, cheaper and more familiar to many migrants than the process of acquiring formal travel documents and visas, which would often require multiple trips to the capital city of their home country and considerable time and expense.

Conclusion

By far the largest source of refugees and asylum seekers in Southeast Asia and the Pacific is Myanmar, reflecting the long-standing and ongoing conflicts and persecution of ethnic and religious minorities in the country. Of the more than half a million refugees and asylum seekers from Myanmar in 2015, around half were living in Bangladesh, with most of the remainder in Malaysia and Thailand. These populations are an order of magnitude greater than the smaller numbers of refugees and asylum seekers from outside the region, some of whom attempt onward travel to Australia through Southeast Asia. The countries of origin and pre-departure circumstances of these refugees and asylum seekers also reflect situations of conflict and persecution, with research showing that the primary motivating factor for these movements is to seek safety and security.

The largest sources of labour migration in Southeast Asia and the Pacific are middle-income countries, where workers are more likely to have the capacity, opportunity, and aspiration to migrate. The scale of migration from the Philippines, and to a lesser extent from Indonesia, is also attributable to efforts by the respective governments to facilitate labour export and encourage migrants to send remittances home. This supports the findings of de Haas (2010) and Clemens (2014) that rates of labour migration have an inverse U-curve relationship to economic development. The outlier case in the region is Myanmar, where much higher numbers of workers have migrated to neighbouring Thailand than is the case for other states at a similar level of economic development, including Lao PDR and Cambodia. An examination of the motivations of migrant workers from Myanmar in the context of conditions in their home areas shows that in addition to the normal motivation of migrants to find economic opportunities, migrants from Myanmar are motivated by insecurity and conflict in their home areas. The logic of path dependence applies here as well, so that the informal logistics and social networks of migration established in the context of decades of political and economic instability in Myanmar will continue to enable labour migration as conditions at home improve.

Notes

1. For ease of comparison, migration data based on World Bank estimates is generally used in this chapter, including in Table 3.1.

2. The GMS comprises Cambodia, Lao PDR, Myanmar, Thailand, Vietnam, Yunnan Province and Guangxi Zhuang Autonomous Region of the PRC.
3. As the 2007 election of indigenous leader and independence campaigner Oscar Temaru in French Polynesia showed, there is continuing support for renegotiation of the terms of colonial relationships in the Pacific, including the possibility of future independence for these incorporated territories.
4. General Ne Win introduced the 'four cuts' policy in 1962 to deprive the rebel Karen National Union of food, funds, intelligence, and recruits (Grundy-Warr and Wong Siew Yin 2002, 101).
5. Many of these asylum seekers were unsuccessful in their initial claims, with only 123 refugees of Malaysian origin registered in Australia by UNHCR (2017) in 2015. Asylum seekers from Malaysia made 2006 of the 4622 applications for review to the Migration Review Tribunal in the 2015–16 financial year (Burton-Bradley 2016).
6. Arrivals in Lhokseumawe, Kuala Langsa, Bayeun, Lhokbani and Medan.

Bibliography

Ah Lek, Pook. 2016. The Dilemma of having Foreign Workers in Malaysia. *The Straits Times*, 17 September 2016. http://www.straitstimes.com/opinion/the-dilemma-of-having-foreign-workers-in-malaysia

Ambrosini, Maurizio. 2016. Why Irregular Migrants Arrive and Remain: The Role of Intermediaries. *Journal of Ethnic and Migration Studies*. http://www.tandfonline.com/doi/pdf/10.1080/1369183X.2016.1260442

Asis, Maruja M.B. 2006. *The Philippines' Culture of Migration*. Migration Policy Institute. http://www.migrationpolicy.org/article/philippines-culturemigration

The Border Consortium. 2016. Refugee and IDP Camp Populations. December 2016. http://www.theborderconsortium.org/media/76787/2016-12-dec-map-tbc-unhcr.pdf

The Borneo Post. 2014. New Policy to Limit Recruitment of Foreign Workers. *The Borneo Post*, 27 May 2014. http://www.theborneopost.com/2014/05/27/new-policy-to-limit-recruitment-of-foreign-workers/

Brees, Inge. 2008. Forced Displacement of Burmese People. *Forced Migration Review* 30: 4–5.

Brundige, Elizabeth, Winter King, Priyneha Vahali, Stephen Vladeck, and Xiang Yuan. 2004. Indonesian Human Rights Abuses in West Papua: Application of the Law of Genocide to the History of Indonesian Control. A paper prepared for the Indonesia Human Rights Network by the Allard K. Lowenstein International Human Rights Clinic Yale Law School. http://www.g-a-l.info/Yale%20Report%20on%20West%20Papuah%20rights.pdf

Burton-Bradley, Robert. 2016. 'We are Living Like a Dog': Explosion in Malaysians Seeking Asylum in Australia. *SBS World News*, 22 November 2016.

http://www.sbs.com.au/news/article/2016/11/21/we-are-living-dog-explosion-malaysians-seeking-asylum-australia
Castles, Stephen. 2013. The Forces Driving Global Migration. *Journal of Intercultural Studies 34* (2): 122–140.
Castles, Stephen, and S. Loughna. 2005. Trends in Asylum Migration to Industrialized Countries, 1990–2001. In *Poverty, International Migration and Asylum*, ed. G. Burjas and J. Crisp. New York: Palgrave Macmillan.
Clemens, Michael. 2014. Does Development Reduce Migration? *CGD Working Paper 359*. Washington, DC: Center for Global Development. http://www.cgdev.org/publication/does-development-reduce-migration-working-paper-359
Commission on Filipinos Overseas. 2014. *2014 CFO Compendium of Statistics.* http://cfo.gov.ph/images/pdf/pdf-migration/2014-CFO-Statistical-Compendium.pdf
DIBP—Department of Immigration and Border Protection. 2013. Asylum Trends—Australia 2012–13. https://www.immi.gov.au/media/publications/statistics/immigration-update/asylum-trends-aus-2012-13.pdf
DIBP. 2014. Asylum Statistics—Australia: Quarterly Tables—June Quarter 2014.
———. 2015a. *Strategy 2020.* https://www.border.gov.au/CorporateInformation/Documents/strategy-2020.pdf
———. 2015b. Border Technology Strategy. Presentation to DIBP Industry Summit. https://www.border.gov.au/Engagingwithindustry/Documents/industry-summit/border-technology-strategy.pdf
Firth, Stewart. 2007. Pacific Islands Trade, Labor, and Security in an Era of Globalization. *The Contemporary Pacific 19* (1): 111–134.
Grundy-Warr, Carl, and Elaine Wong Siew Yin. 2002. Geographies of Displacement: The Karenni and the Shan Across The Myanmar-Thailand Border. *Singapore Journal of Tropical Geography 23* (1): 93–122.
de Haas, Hein. 2010. Migration Transitions: A Theoretical and Empirical Inquiry into the Developmental Drivers of International Migration. *International Migration Institute Working Paper 24.* https://heindehaas.files.wordpress.com/2015/05/de-haas-2010-migration-transitions-imi-wp-24.pdf
Henry, Nicholas. 2015. Trade union internationalism and political change in Myanmar. *Global Change, Peace & Security 27* (1): 69–84.
Huguet, Jerrold. 2014. Introduction. In *Thailand Migration Report*, ed. Jerrold Huguet, xix–xxi. Bangkok: United Nations Thematic Working Group on Migration in Thailand.
ILO. 2015. Analytical Report on the International Labour Migration Statistics Database in ASEAN
IOM Country Mission in Thailand and the Asian Research Center for Migration, Chulalongkorn University. 2013. Assessing Potential Changes in the Migration Patterns of Myanmar Migrants and their Impacts on Thailand. http://th.iom.int/index.php/migration-resources/func-download/201/chk,61c1a7e0a53f61289109191a7914141a/no_html,1/

IRC (International Rescue Committee). 2012. Surviving or Thriving on the Thai-Burma Border: Vulnerability and Resilience in Mae Sot, Thailand. https://www.academia.edu/6434599/2012_Surviving_or_Thriving_on_the_ThaiBurma_Border_Vulnerability_and_Resilience_in_Mae_Sot_Thailand_International_Rescue_Committee

Lewis, Daniel Ray, Nuarpear Lekfuangfu, Irena Vojackova-Sollorano, Federico Soda, and Claudia Natali. 2010. *Forecasting Migration Flows: The Relationships among Economic Development, Demographic Change and Migration in the Greater Mekong Subregion*. Asia Development Bank and International Organisation for Migration. http://pioneer.netserv.chula.ac.th/~ldaniel/Socrates/Migration/ADBIOM%20Draft%20Forecasting%20Migration%20Flows%20in%20GMS%202010.pdf

McAdam, Jane. 2011. Swimming against the Tide: Why a Climate Change Displacement Treaty is Not the Answer. *International Journal of Refugee Law 23* (1): 2–27.

McAulife, Marie. 2013. Seeking the Views of Irregular Migrants: Decision Making, Drivers and Migration Journeys. *Irregular Migration Research Program Occasional Paper Series 05/2013*, Department of Immigration and Border Protection. https://www.border.gov.au/ReportsandPublications/Documents/research/views-irregular-migrant-decision-drivers-journey.pdf

McNamara, Karen Elizabeth, and Chris Gibson. 2009. 'We Do Not Want to Leave Our Land': Pacific Ambassadors at the United Nations Resist the Category of 'Climate Refugees'. *Geoforum 40* (3): 475–483.

Ministry of Foreign Affairs of the People's Republic of China. 2014. *China's Relationship with United Nations High Commissioner for Refugees (UNHCR)*. Statement by the Permanent Mission of the People's Republic of China to the United Nations Office at Geneva and Other International Organizations in Switzerland. Accessed 5 January 2016. http://www.fmprc.gov.cn/ce/cegv/eng/rqrd/jblc/t85094.htm

Ministry of Immigration of Malaysia, Information Technology and Records Section. 2015. Statistik pekerja asing aktif mengikut sektor dan warganegara dari 1 januari 2015 sehinga 31 Oktober 2015 [Statistics on Foreign Workers by Sector and Citizenship from January 1, 2015 until October 31, 2015]. Copy of Unpublished Statistics Provided to the Author by Malaysia Trade Union Congress.

Ministry of Manpower, Singapore. 2016a. Foreign Workforce Numbers. http://www.mom.gov.sg/documents-and-publications/foreign-workforce-numbers

———. 2016b. Work Passes and Permits. http://www.mom.gov.sg/passes-and-permits

———. 2016c. Sector-Specific Rules for Work Permit. http://www.mom.gov.sg/passes-and-permits/work-permit-for-foreign-worker/sector-specific-rules

National Economic and Social Development Board. 2011. *The Eleventh National Economic and Social Development Plan (2012–2016)*. Bangkok: Office of the Prime Minister.

Nagl, John A. 2005. *Learning to Eat Soup with a Knife: Counterinsurgency Lessons from Malaya and Vietnam*. Chicago University Press.

Neumayer, Eric. 2004. Asylum Destination Choice: What Makes Some West European Countries More Attractive than Others? *European Union Politics* 5 (2): 156–180.

Phillips, Lawrence. 2000. British Slavery after Abolition: The Pacific Trade. *Race and Class 41* (3): 13–27.

Radio New Zealand. 2017. Pacific Concern Relayed at UN over West Papua Abuses. *Radio New Zealand News*, 2 March 2017. http://www.radionz.co.nz/international/pacific-news/325717/pacific-concern-relayed-at-un-over-west-papua-abuses

Robinson, Vaughan, and Segrott, Jeremy. 2002. Understanding the Decision-Making of Asylum Seekers. Home Office Research Study 243. UK Home Office Research, Development and Statistics Directorate. https://www.researchgate.net/profile/Jeremy_Segrott/publication/248205716_Understanding_the_Decision-Making_of_Asylum-Seekers/links/00b49537f535421143000000.pdf

Sampson, Robyn C., Sandra M. Gifford, and Savitri Taylor. 2016. The Myth of Transit: The Making of a Life by Asylum Seekers and Refugees in Indonesia. *Journal of Ethnic and Migration Studies* 42 (7): 1135–1152.

Shwegu Thitsar. 2014. Cheated Seafarers Speak Out: 'It's Simply Human Trafficking. *Myanmar Times*, 27 October 2014. http://www.mmtimes.com/index.php/national-news/12077-cheated-seafarers-speak-out-it-s-simply-human-trafficking.html

Small, Cathy A., and David L. Dixon. 2004. *Tonga: Migration and the Homeland*. Migration Policy Institute. http://www.migrationpolicy.org/article/tonga-migration-and-homeland

TBBC (Thai Burma Border Consortium). 2011. Displacement and Poverty in Southeast Burma/Myanmar. http://www.theborderconsortium.org/media/10447/report-2011-idp-en-1-.zip

UNDESA (United Nations Department of Economic and Social Affairs) Population Division. 2013. Trends in International Migrant Stock: The 2013 Revision (United Nations Database, POP/DB/MIG/Stock/Rev. 2013). http://esa.un.org/unmigration/migrantstocks2013.htm?mtotals

UNDESA. 2016. International Migration Report 2015. ST/ESA/SER.A/375. http://www.un.org/en/development/desa/population/migration/publications/migrationreport/docs/MigrationReport2015_Highlights.pdf

UNHCR. 2007a. Vietnamese Refugees Well Settled in China, Await Citizenship. http://www.unhcr.org/464302994.html

———. 2007b. Advisory Opinion on the Extraterritorial Application of Non-Refoulement Obligations under the 1951 Convention Relating to the Status of Refugees and its 1967 Protocol. 26 January 2007. http://www.refworld.org/docid/45f17a1a4.html

———. 2015a. *2015 UNHCR Country Operations Profile—Myanmar.* http://www.unhcr.org/pages/49e4877d6.html#

———. 2015b. *Bay of Bengal and Andaman Sea Initiative.* http://www.unhcr.org/557040af9.html

———. 2017. Population Statistics—Persons of Concern. http://popstats.unhcr.org/en/persons_of_concern

UNSW Human Rights Clinic. 2015. *Temporary Migrant Workers in Australia.* University of New South Wales.

Williams, Angela. 2008. Turning the Tide: Recognizing Climate Change Refugees in International Law. *Law & Policy 30* (4): 502–529.

World Bank. 2016. *Migration and Remittances Factbook 2016.* http://www.worldbank.org/en/research/brief/migration-and-remittances

CHAPTER 4

Framing Threats

The institutional framing of irregular migration as smuggling and trafficking has significant material effects on governance policy and practice and, in turn, on the lives and journeys of migrants. International efforts to counter trafficking in persons and migrant smuggling frame the facilitation of irregular migration and the exploitation of labour as exceptional acts of criminal deviance that constitute security threats to states. In the process, migrants with irregular status are framed as both victims and threats (Aradau 2004). This dichotomised framing leaves little room for consideration of the complex choices that migrants are compelled to make by circumstances and structural conditions beyond their control.

This chapter examines the twin processes of criminalisation and securitisation that frame irregular migration as an issue of importance to states at the same time as depoliticising the issue in public debate. The securitisation of migration is depoliticising in the sense described by Waever (1995) of removing an issue from the contested complexities of normal political debate, including through construction of crisis, use of emergency powers, and secrecy. Similarly, criminalisation of a social phenomenon is depoliticising in that it can bypass engagement with complex questions of structural power and social agency in favour of simplified and fixed categories of innocent victims and threatening criminals. As Andreas and Nadelman (2008, 233–235) have shown, the depoliticising effects of securitisation and criminalisation in the framing of transnational crime

N. Henry, *Asylum, Work, and Precarity*, Critical Studies of the Asia-Pacific, DOI 10.1007/978-3-319-60567-8_4

have enabled police forces and other state agencies to increase their international operations and coordination with relatively little scrutiny.

I describe the process by which counter-trafficking and counter-smuggling operations have come to define dominant responses to irregular migration as one of institutional framing. Institutional framing is more than a rhetorical process and has real consequences for those subject to the resultant processes of governance, in this case, migrants. Institutional framing shares the general characteristics of framing defined by Entman (1993) of selectively identifying issues of salience in ways that lead actors to define problems, diagnose causes, make moral judgments, and suggest remedies in common ways. However, an institutional frame describes more than the communication processes emphasised by Entman, because institutional framing involves the selection and definition of policy problems and governance approaches by international organisations and actors that command major resources of personnel, funds, coercive power, and influence. In policy governance contexts, and especially in processes of international regime formation where institutions are not yet fully formed or areas of responsibility remain contested, institutional framing allows international actors to have consequential impacts on how and by whom governance and enforcement will be coordinated, social agency enabled and constrained, and resources distributed.

Framing Trafficking in Persons and Migrant Smuggling as Global Threats

In the process of establishing trafficking in persons and migrant smuggling as institutional frames in the negotiations for the UN Convention on Transnational Crime, international lobbyists and negotiators set out to link the issues with states' existing concerns for border security. Through this issue linkage (Haas 1980), forms of irregular migration associated with asylum and migrant labour were grouped together with state concerns for border control to form the issue areas of counter-trafficking and counter-smuggling. The emergence of trafficking/smuggling as an issue area laid the basis for the formation of an international regime to target irregular migration through techniques of international cooperation already associated with criminal and security regimes of border control. UN General Assembly resolutions on trafficking in persons framing the problem in criminal terms persuaded a greater number and diversity of states to condemn trafficking in stronger terms than resolutions framed around human rights language (Charnysh et al. 2014, 345).

The securitised framing of trafficking and smuggling as transnational crime has also been effective in crossing over into the rights-based discourse of liberal humanitarianism. For instance, the 2005 report of the Global Commission on International Migration (GCIM) used the language of rights to present irregular migration as a threat to state sovereignty and human security, using the frames of migrant smuggling and trafficking in persons. The preamble to the chapter of the report dealing with irregular migration advocates for the rights of migrants as potential caveats to the more general sovereign rights of states to control borders:

> States, exercising their sovereign right to determine who enters and remains on their territory, should fulfil their responsibility and obligation to protect the rights of migrants and to re-admit those citizens who wish or who are obliged to return to their country of origin. In stemming irregular migration, states should actively cooperate with one another, ensuring that their efforts do not jeopardize human rights, including the right of refugees to seek asylum. Governments should consult with employers, trade unions and civil society on this issue. (GCIM 2005, 32)

In this framing, states are identified as the primary actors and their motivation in exercising the 'sovereign right to determine' is assumed to be 'stemming irregular migration'. The GCIM framework legitimates the goal of migration border control with the limited caveat that in exercising their sovereign rights states should 'protect the rights of migrants'. While employing the rights-based language of liberal humanitarianism, the report frames states rather than migrants as the primary rights holders. Rather than framing freedom of movement as a human right that may be conditionally limited in the interests of state security and public order, the report frames sovereign control of borders as the primary right that is conditionally limited by the rights of migrants.

The GCIM report generally frames irregular migration in terms of trafficking and smuggling and focuses on negative consequences, emphasising the dangers to migrants as well as claiming negative impacts for state sovereignty and public attitudes towards migrants. State sovereignty is deemed threatened by loss of control over migration borders, as well as by growth in organised crime and corruption associated with smuggling and trafficking. The Commission further argues that widespread irregular migration contributes to undermining public confidence in migration policy and fuels 'xenophobic sentiments that are directed not only at migrants with irregular status, but also at established migrants, refugees and ethnic minorities' (GCIM 2005, 34). By suggesting that irregular migration is a danger to migrants and states, and is a cause of rising xenophobia, the Commission frames migrants with irregular status simultaneously as victims and as threats, portraying them as responsible for their own experiences of abuse as well as partially responsible for the abuse of others.

Defining migrant smuggling and trafficking in persons as international crimes has been a project driven by states, international organisations and non-government campaign networks. Both migrant smuggling and trafficking in persons are defined in protocols supplementing the 2000 UN Convention on Transnational Organised Crime. The Protocol against the Smuggling of Migrants by Land, Sea and Air (Smuggling Protocol) is explicit in framing irregular movement as the core problem. The protocol obliges states to take action to criminalise conduct that enables or profits from irregular migration, to monitor and inspect vessels at sea, and to share information on the identities, movements and methods of those suspected of smuggling. The Protocol to Prevent, Suppress and Punish Trafficking in Persons, Especially Women and Children (Trafficking Protocol) frames the core problems of trafficking as coercion and exploitation, but identifies the primary acts to be criminalised as including facilitation of movement. State parties are obliged to create specific criminal offences to target 'perpetrators' of trafficking, while migrants with irregular status subject to coercion and exploitation are defined as victims in need of protection. The decision to define and counter migrant smuggling and trafficking in persons through international instruments targeting organised crime is significant as it allows opponents of irregular migration to shift attention from more complex obligations of humanitarian protection and labour standards to a singular focus on criminalisation.

Framing Trafficking

The definition of trafficking in Article 3(a) of the Trafficking Protocol includes an *act* of facilitating the movement or transfer of persons, a *means* of coercion, and a *purpose* of exploitation:

> 'Trafficking in persons' shall mean the recruitment, transportation, transfer, harbouring or receipt of persons, by means of the threat or use of force or other forms of coercion, of abduction, of fraud, of deception, of the abuse of power or of a position of vulnerability or of the giving or receiving of payments or benefits to achieve the consent of a person having control over another person, for the purpose of exploitation. Exploitation shall include, at a minimum, the exploitation of the prostitution of others or other forms of sexual exploitation, forced labour or services, slavery or practices similar to slavery, servitude or the removal of organs (UN 2000)

By defining the arrangement of movement as the central criminal act of trafficking, the protocol sets up border control as a key means of state action to combat international trafficking. Some, including the US State Department, have pointed out that the definition of trafficking in persons is not limited to cases where the victim crosses an international border. However, the language of the protocol emphasises movement and its institutional framing in relation to international crime produces a focus on border enforcement that is reflected in the interpretation and responses of states. The choice to describe the criminal activity in terms of movement, where it is most easily captured by state control, seems to be a pragmatic move, rather than focusing on the more harmful acts of coercion and exploitation that are harder to define and capture. The definitions of coercive means and exploitative purpose then serve as filters for selecting whose movement should be prevented and intercepted. This is also significant, as it shifts the focus from combating exploitation through industry-wide enforcement of labour standards, to profiling potential victims of exploitation through border security and criminal law enforcement.

Profiling of potential victims of trafficking in persons at the point of entry inevitably draws on racialised and gendered frames of policing to assess risk. Here, the definition of sexual exploitation is especially significant in creating a large category of those defined as victims of trafficking who can be profiled and intercepted. While the Protocol specifies 'sexual exploitation', including 'exploitation of the prostitution of others', as forms of exploitation, neither term is defined. This was a deliberate decision by the drafters of the protocol so as to allow states to interpret sexual exploitation in relation to their own national laws on sex work (UNODC 2015, 27–28). It is clear, however, that the terms create a broader scope for including various forms of sex work within the rubric of exploitation than is the case for other forms of labour, where a more general label of 'labour exploitation' was considered and rejected by the drafters and only 'forced labour' is specified (UNODC 2015, 26).

The relationship between forced labour and trafficking is somewhat complex, however, with only subtle differences in definition but major divergence in the approaches implied by each term. Forced labour is in many ways a competing institutional frame to that of trafficking in persons. The ILO's efforts to eradicate forced labour date to the origin of the organisation in 1919 and have been strengthened over time, particularly associated with the dismantling of colonial administrations. The ILO definition of forced labour includes any situation in which compulsory labour is exacted 'by menace of any penalty' (ILO 2012). As an institutional frame for responding to the worst forms of labour exploitation, forced labour differs considerably from trafficking in persons, putting the focus on compulsion of work rather than mobility as the primary problem, and framing solutions in terms of structural changes in labour institutions to promote workers' rights rather the law enforcement mode of counter-trafficking.

The international discourse around the negotiation of the Trafficking Protocol and more generally the growing attention from the 1990s onwards to the issue area of trafficking in persons shared many features with the moral panic over 'white slavery' at the turn of the twentieth century, with a common focus on the supposedly widespread coercion of vulnerable women and children into sex work (Doezema 2010). In a commentary on the document that became the Trafficking Protocol, then referred to as the Draft Protocol To Combat International Trafficking In Women And Children, the Global Network of Sex Work Projects (NSWP) argued that the discourse around trafficking remained 'more concerned with protecting women's 'purity' than with ensuring the human rights of those in the sex industry' (NSWP 1999, 1). Arguing that the often precarious conditions of migrant sex workers are worsened by a lack of legal protection associated with widespread criminalisation of the sex industry, the NSWP opposed the draft protocol on the grounds that the criminalisation of trafficking in persons would lead to further discrimination and exclusion from protection for migrant sex workers (NSWP 1999, 2). Noting that '[s]ex workers share the concern about the abuses in labour migration' the NSWP problematised the use of the term 'trafficking' with its 'history of being used against migrant prostitutes/sex workers', in particular, through the conflation of trafficking with migration for sex work, or with sex work in general. These concerns are well supported by statements from organisations that campaigned in favour of the trafficking declaration, many of which saw the campaign for the criminalisation of trafficking in persons as one component of a broader effort to oppose sex work.

In the view of Dorchen Leidholdt (2003, 168), co-founder of the Coalition Against Trafficking in Women (CATW) that actively lobbied in favour of the Trafficking Protocol, trafficking for sex work is a 'uniquely horrific' element of transnational crime. Leidholdt argues that trafficking in women is inseparable from the globalisation of the sex industry, which she describes as the 'merchandising of women's bodies for the sexual gratification of men'. Leidholdt's conflation of trafficking with the sex industry is echoed in the same volume by editor Melissa Farley, who describes trafficking as 'simply the global form of prostitution', which she in turn describes as a 'toxic cultural product' that is invariably harmful and traumatic to sex workers, who Farley directly compares to survivors of mass rape as a weapon of war (Farley 2003, xi–xvii). In her article, Leidholdt (2003, 169) takes aim at a rival organisation, the Netherlands-based Foundation Against Trafficking in Women (FATW), which she accuses of serving the interests of the sex industry and the Dutch government by adopting an 'exceedingly narrow' definition of trafficking due to their position that 'trafficking is a human rights violation while prostitution is work'. This dispute reflects a foundational split in international feminist organisations between those campaigning to improve the status of sex workers as workers and those such as CATW seeking to abolish and criminalise the sex industry.

From its inception, CATW pushed for criminalisation of trafficking as part of a broader anti-prostitution agenda, forming alliances with fundamentalist Christian lobbies and finding a powerful international ally in the George W. Bush administration from 2000 (Buss and Herman 2003). To counter the criminalisation agenda, other feminist organisations, including FATW in the Netherlands, formed the Global Alliance Against Traffic in Women (GAATW) to combat exploitation of women migrant workers and support the decriminalisation of sex work as part of this effort. The GAATW originated in Southeast Asia, at a 1994 conference in Chiang Mai, Thailand responding to the emerging framing of trafficking as a category of criminal law. The founding organisations of the alliance were concerned that 'women were being treated as criminals for violating immigration laws and stigmatised by society for having worked in prostitution' (GAATW 2016a). Part of GAATW's early work was to develop and promote a set of Human Rights Standards for the Treatment of Trafficked Persons in an effort to influence legal framing of trafficking towards protection rather than criminalisation of migrant workers who had suffered coercion and exploitation. The standards seek to ensure that legal frameworks provide those identified as trafficked persons with 'effective legal remedy, legal protection, non-discriminatory treatment, and restitution, compensation and rehabilitation' (GAATW et al. 1999, 1). GAATW has continued in its concern that the rights and interests of migrant sex workers are infringed by counter-trafficking operations focused on criminalisation. The International Secretariat of GAATW (2016b) supported Amnesty International's 2016 call for the decriminalisation of sex work by declaring that: 'Sex workers' struggle for rights is the same struggle as that of women, migrants and workers around the world'. The organisation has also opposed the so-called 'Nordic model' of criminalising clients of sex workers, arguing that this approach contributes to marginalisation and stigmatisation that particularly hurts migrant sex workers (GAATW 2014; see also Amnesty International 2016a).

While the work of GAATW reflects a pragmatic approach to working within the emerging trafficking paradigm, many organisations of migrant workers, especially migrant sex workers, hold the view that counter-trafficking efforts are a threat to their livelihoods and security (Empower 2012). The two positions are not inconsistent, but rather, are a response to the institutional framing processes that sweep together diverse and disparate areas of policy and practice under the label of countering trafficking in persons. In the field of work defined by the intersection of migration and labour exploitation, organisations with longstanding commitments to the welfare and interests of migrant workers have found their access to funding and influence increasing framed in terms of counter-trafficking. This can be an uncomfortable position for organisations that have a practical need to continue engaging with governance processes as they are while remaining critical of the framing of those processes. This concern was expressed in interviews with staff from a range of organisations active on migrant labour issues in the Asia-Pacific, from NGOs and trade unions to UN agencies.

The contradictions of the trafficking frame are particularly pronounced in attitudes toward migrant sex workers, where organisations with diametrically opposed goals are swept together under the rubric of counter-trafficking. The involvement in counter-trafficking operations of Christian NGOs, which found their funding and profile dramatically boosted from 2000 onwards, has contributed to the growth of what Agustín (2007) terms the rescue industry and Bernstein (2012) has referred to as carceral politics. Agustín traces a continuous history of social reformers who have advocated for the abolition of prostitution since the nineteenth century and argues that this perspective has always involved the marginalisation of the voices of sex workers and working class women.

Quantifying Trafficking: The Politics of Large Numbers

Several international organisations, government agencies and NGOs have attempted to quantify the extent of trafficking in persons, with varying results. A claim by the US State Department that between 600,000 and 800,000 people were trafficked across borders each year has been widely cited, including in the Congressional Findings of the US Trafficking Victims Protection Reauthorization Act (TVPA) of 2005. However, the figure has been described as 'questionable' in a report by the US Government Accountability Office, which found that the estimate was developed by an intelligence analyst 'who did not document all of his work, so the estimate may not be replicable, casting doubt on its reliability' (USGAO 2005, 10). The figure was derived by statistical sampling of previously published regional and global estimates of trafficking by a range of agencies, including NGOs. However, such estimates also tend to be based on highly problematic methodology. For example, a widely cited Global Slavery Index produced by the Walk Free Foundation claimed to estimate country-specific numbers of trafficked persons, described as 'modern slaves'. However, academics and practitioners have criticised the index for making spurious extrapolations from limited and questionable data (Broome and Seabrooke 2015; Gallagher 2016).

As Lewis et al. (2010, 16) point out, many of the authors and organisations making exaggerated claims about the scale and nature of trafficking in persons stand to gain from overestimation of the problem. Funding, access and employment in the growing counter-trafficking sector all depend on continuing claims of a large and growing threat. In particular, claims about numbers of women and children trafficked into sex work frequently exceed the total size of the industry to the point that 'it simply would not be possible to absorb the number of migrants sometimes ascribed to persons so trafficked'.

International organisations have taken different approaches to the production of data on trafficking in persons. UNODC and IOM have each produced data based on their areas of work, without extrapolating to global estimates of trafficked persons. UNODC (2014, 17) collated data from member states on reported criminal prosecutions of trafficking offenses affecting 40,177 victims worldwide in the period 2010–12, while IOM (2016) provided assistance to 7000 people defined as victims of trafficking worldwide in 2015. The ILO took a different approach to estimate the global prevalence of forced labour at 20.9 million persons, extrapolating from published reports of specific incidents of involuntary labour.[1] The relationship between forced labour and trafficking is somewhat complex however, with only subtle differences in definition but major divergence in the approaches implied by each term. The forced labour frame also allows for more recognition of states as perpetrators of abuse, with the ILO estimating that 20% of forced labour globally is exacted by states, including from prison populations in Western states.

Framing Smuggling

Associating migrant smuggling with trafficking in persons as a pair of transnational crimes has been productive for opponents of irregular migration. International efforts to combat migrant smuggling emphasise the dangers to migrants of organised irregular migration, as well as the threat to state border control. However, as detailed in subsequent chapters, the criminal law-enforcement response to smuggling produces greater incarceration, danger, and precarity for migrants.

The framing of irregular migration as criminal smuggling is problematic in several respects. First, the framing of migrant smuggling as transnational organised crime assumes a level of coordinated organisation and profit motive that is not always evident in the activities of those who assist migrants to cross borders. Second, the claim that smuggling operations cause harm to migrants is not universally or uniformly true. Third, to the extent that smuggling is organised for profit and causes harm to migrants, it is not at all clear that criminalisation will improve conditions for migrants—rather, it is likely to worsen them.

The introduction of the definition of migrant smuggling as a transnational crime in the Migrant Smuggling Protocol introduces overlapping conflicts with international law on asylum and rescue at sea. By criminalising the act of assisting migrants to cross state borders without visas, rather than criminalising specific acts of abuse against migrants, the Migrant Smuggling Protocol also contributes to the criminalisation organisations or individuals who provide life-saving assistance to migrants involved in dangerous border crossings, including rescuing migrants in distress at sea in accordance with international maritime law (Landry 2016). By conflating all forms of assistance to irregular migrants with criminal smuggling, the protocol contributes to shifts in institutional framing whereby jurisdiction over border zones is increasingly dominated by military or militarised agencies. An example of this conflation of rescue and smuggling was shown in documents leaked from the European border agency FRONTEX in 2016 accusing charities running rescue operations in the Mediterranean of colluding with smugglers. The agencies, including Medicins Sans Frontiers (MSF), were accused of assisting smugglers by rescuing asylum seekers from boats in distress off the coasts of Libya and Turkey (Robinson 2016).

Framing Threats in Southeast Asia and the Pacific

The institutional framing of migration governance to give primacy to state powers of border control is also found in the Asia-Pacific region. In translating and adapting the international norms of migration governance identified in the conventions and other instruments discussed above, governments in the Asia-Pacific have tended to emphasise commitments to strengthening state capacity to control migration borders, while de-emphasising or diluting reference to the rights of migrants. This trend is matched in the implementation of regional agreements by states, where a further layer of filtering occurs in favour of emphasising state interests in border control.

The Bali Process on People Smuggling, Trafficking in Persons and Related Transnational Crime (Bali Process) was initiated by Australia and Indonesia in 2002, comprising a broad membership of states in the wider Asia Pacific area. In 2011, participating states along with UNHCR and IOM agreed to a Regional Cooperation Framework to address irregular movement of asylum seekers. The first core principle of the framework states that '[i]rregular movement facilitated by people smuggling syndicates should be eliminated and States should promote and support opportunities for orderly migration'. The remaining principles express support for 'consistent assessment processes', 'durable solution[s]', return of those 'found not to be in need of protection', and targeting people smuggling and human trafficking through border security and law enforcement cooperation (Bali Process 2016)

The non-binding nature of regional coordination of migration and asylum policies in Southeast Asia and the Pacific allows for selective adoption of multi-lateral agreements by states. Regional agreements tend to emphasise cooperation on capacity building for border management and control rather than strengthening mechanisms for humanitarian protection and regular migration. The issue of selective adoption has particularly affected the implementation of commitments made under the Bali Process since 2002. In formal terms, the Bali Process is considered to comprise four pillars of work on irregular migration: detection, prevention, protection, and migration management. However, in practice there has been relatively little progress on advancing regional mechanisms for humanitarian protection and regular migration management, compared to the intensive web of coordination and capacity-building activity that has developed around techniques of detection and prevention of irregular migration in the region.

International organisations, including IOM and UNHCR, organised a number of regional consultative processes that were forerunners to the Bali Process. In 1996, the IOM initiated a meeting of government representatives to exchange information on irregular migration and trafficking in the Asia-Pacific that became known as the Manila Process, —involving 17 countries by the last of the four annual meetings hosted by Indonesia in 2000. In the same period, UNHCR cooperated with IOM and the Australian government to host an annual Asia Pacific Consultation, initially focused on refugee issues before expanding to consider broader issues of migration management, with a focus on regional cooperation to address irregular migration. In the context of these two processes, Thailand hosted a ministerial meeting of 19 Asia-Pacific governments in cooperation with IOM in 1999, resulting in the Bangkok Declaration on Irregular Migration.

The Bangkok Declaration (see UN-ACT 2016a) adopts much of the language of the earlier GCIM report, while avoiding any mention of human rights and diluting references to state obligations towards migrants. Whereas the GCIM had spoken of state obligations to abide by international agreements on the rights of refugees and the human rights of all migrants, the Bangkok Declaration merely notes that 'there is a number of international conventions and instruments dealing with humanitarian issues relating to migration'. Following this cursory acknowledgment of the existence of unspecified international conventions and instruments, the Bangkok declaration gives a more fulsome endorsement of the sovereign powers of states to control borders:

> Respecting the sovereign rights and legitimate interests of each country to safeguard its borders and to develop and implement its own migration/ immigration laws, and also recognizing the obligations of the country of

> origin to accept its nationals back, and the obligation of the countries of transit and destination to provide protection and assistance where appropriate, in accordance with their national laws;

The following articles of the declaration set out a number of non-binding commitments by signatory states to 'reinforce their efforts to prevent and combat irregular migration', including through strengthening domestic laws, criminalising migrant smuggling and trafficking, sharing information and coordinating the '[t]imely return of those without right to enter and remain' as a 'strategy to reduce the attractiveness of trafficking'. In contrast, the interests of migrants are mentioned in only one commitment, Article 14, which makes no reference to the human rights and fundamental freedoms of migrants guaranteed in international law:

> Irregular migrants should be granted humanitarian treatment, including appropriate health and other services, while the cases of irregular migration are being handled according to law. Any unfair treatment towards them should be avoided.

In this, the Bangkok Declaration echoes the language of the GCIM in treating protection obligations towards migrants as a limited caveat to the more general rights of states to control borders, where protection of migrants is to be considered in the context of carrying out border protection activities. But the Bangkok declaration goes further down this path by replacing reference to human rights obligations with a more diffuse and unspecified commitment to humanitarian treatment. While reference to protection obligations grounded in binding international law could be read as introducing a conflict with the untrammelled sovereign rights of states, and could limit state action in some circumstances—such as preventing the return of migrants and asylum seekers to countries where they face persecution or torture—the vague reference to humanitarian treatment in the Bangkok Declaration is intended as guidance on how states should carry out border protection, rather than imposing any restriction. For instance, rather than preventing deportation in certain circumstances, the norms codified in a non-binding form by the declaration would merely require states to treat deportees fairly and humanely according to the domestic laws, with no obligation to consider the consequences for the deportee once they are outside the borders of the state.

Trafficking

The United Nations Action for Cooperation Against Trafficking in Persons (UN-ACT) is a project of the UN Development Program (UNDP) that seeks to coordinate counter-trafficking operations in the Greater Mekong Sub-region (comprising Myanmar, Cambodia, Vietnam, China [Yunnan state] and Lao PDR). The project continues the work of the United Nations Inter-Agency Project on Human Trafficking in the Greater Mekong Sub-Region (UNIAP) from 2000 to 2012. In addition to initiating independent campaigns, publications and events, UN-ACT is the secretariat for the Coordinated Mekong Ministerial Initiative against Trafficking (COMMIT). COMMIT formed in 2004 with a Memorandum of Understanding recognising 'the need for a strengthened criminal justice response to trafficking' (UN-ACT 2004). UN-ACT (2016b, 2) describes its governance roles as 'a facilitator and manager as well as expert and innovator'. In particular, the UN agency seeks to use its 'agenda-setting function as the COMMIT secretariat to introduce relevant research into policy and programming considerations'. One of the core roles of COMMIT under UN-ACT's leadership has been to coordinate and support the establishment of dedicated anti-trafficking taskforces in each of the member states to coordinate law enforcement responses and anti-trafficking campaigns, including through cooperation with non-government agencies.

The approaches taken by government and NGO counter-trafficking campaigns in Southeast Asia are criticised by some labour activists as presenting a rather extreme view of the dangers of trafficking that is unhelpful to people considering migrating for work:

> When I was in Myanmar I was very surprised to see some of the NGOs had put up banners with a picture of a child crying and a message about trafficking. Some of them still present like 'don't migrate, otherwise you will end up in a trafficking situation', but when you talk to the people on the ground, that is not helpful for them to make a better migration. Save the Children and World Vision do this type of campaign. (Interview, Migration Working Group Thailand)

While some public campaigns may be seen as unhelpful or difficult for workers to relate to, other practices by state and NGO agencies targeting trafficking can be more overtly harmful to migrant workers.

Counter-trafficking operations targeting sex workers in the Asia-pacific have been strongly criticised by workers' organisations for contributing to the incarceration, deportation, and abuse of workers. In the words of members of the Thai sex workers' organisation Empower (2012):

> We see that the anti-trafficking law cannot assist anyone in sex work to improve their quality of life. The more there are rescues the worse our lives become, by many times. After the rescue, the people affected are forced to do vocational training, are detained and forced to return home. This increases their debt and vulnerability to brokers who are actually authorities in disguise, both in their home country and in the country they are working in.

In 2012, Empower published an in-depth participatory study of women sex workers' experiences with anti-trafficking operations in Thailand, including migrant sex workers from the Greater Mekong Sub-region. Drawing on the organisation's networks across 13 provinces, including major urban centres and border areas, a team of 4 staff and 36 Empower members led the research, working with 170 other sex workers as research partners and interviewing business owners, police, officials, and NGO staff. Women interviewed for the report who had been apprehended in police raids of brothels and entertainment venues and identified as victims of trafficking 'overwhelmingly stated they came independently to Thailand and are working voluntarily in work they have chosen to do' (Empower 2012, xi). Empower described counter-trafficking operations in Thailand since 2008 as 'confused and frantic efforts' to comply with the requirements of the USTIP process that had resulted in a 'punitive, criminal justice response' that disproportionately targeted and disadvantaged sex workers (Empower 2012, 26).

NGOs are increasingly active in counter-trafficking activity in the Asia-Pacific in partnership with state agencies. The activities of the NGOs, many of which are Christian faith-based groups, range from vigilante-style investigations by ex-police officers to programs that aim to rescue and rehabilitate people defined as victims of trafficking.[2] In a study based on her participatory fieldwork as a volunteer with Christian faith-based anti-trafficking projects in Bangkok and Beijing, Thai Light and China Star, Shih (2014, 74–75) describes how the NGOs recruited sex workers by visiting entertainment bars and offering the women alternative jobs manufacturing jewellery for sale by the NGOs. As part of their work with the NGO, workers were required to abstain from sex work and attend daily

Christian prayers and bible study, even though most were Buddhist. In conversations with the women she was working with, Shih reports that they were shocked to learn they were being portrayed as victims of trafficking in promotional materials for US-based customers and supporters of the NGOs. The women insisted that they had voluntarily chosen to work in the sex industry, just as they had chosen to take up the NGOs' offers of alternative work, and they rejected the claim that they had been rescued.

According to interviews with staff at the ILO and Migrant Worker Resource Centres, workers seeking assistance from the centres were not interested in being involved in pursuing criminal charges of trafficking. As one ILO staff member put it, 'the approach to border control in that criminal justice system sense is not something we see resonate with migrant workers'. Instead, workers sought assistance to make compensation claims under labour protection laws against exploitative employers and migration agents.

People Smuggling

The release of the UN Office of Drugs and Crime (UNODC 2015) report *Migrant Smuggling in Asia: Current Trends and Related Challenges* was a deliberate move of institutional framing. The purpose of a document like this is not merely to inform, but to assert the 'cognitive authority' (Broome and Seabrooke 2015) of the institution to define and manage the field. The report opens by describing migrant smuggling as an international crime defined by the Smuggling of Migrants Protocol to the UN Convention on Transnational Organised Crime, with the UNODC describing itself as the 'guardian of the Convention' and its protocols (UNODC 2015, 1). The UNODC promotes its role in coordination and capacity building for Asia-Pacific states to combat migrant smuggling and identifies the report as a 'knowledge product' that will 'fill the information gaps' and 'raise awareness' among states in the region. As with the trafficking frame, migrant smuggling is framed as an objectively criminal activity. States that have not completely adopted the smuggling frame to crack down on irregular migration are judged to be insufficiently aware of the problem or insufficiently capable of responding.

The reporting of Australia's interception of maritime arrivals of asylum seekers is an example of how the UNODC report participates in the framing of irregular migration as migrant smuggling. Since the election of the Coalition government in 2013, the (newly renamed) Department of Immigration and Border Protection has been required to refer to asylum seekers arriving on Australia's shores as 'illegal maritime arrivals (IMAs)'. The DIBP's (2013) *Asylum Trends Report 2012–2013* declares that 'a total of 18,119 people who arrived by sea were screened into a refugee status determination process' and refers to this group collectively as IMAs. Clearly, these are asylum seekers, and are recognised as such by UNHCR and the Australian government. The decision to apply the pejorative label of 'illegal' was a part of an attempt by the new government to be seen to take a hard line on asylum seekers to meet their election promise to 'stop the boats,' but has no particular basis in Australian law. There is certainly no criminal offence that asylum seekers could be charged with for arriving by boat, although anyone actively assisting them could be charged with migrant smuggling. Nevertheless, in using the term IMA, the Australian government has sought to emphasise the mode of arrival, to associate asylum seekers with criminal smuggling and undermine their claims for asylum. The UNODC report takes this process of discursive delegitimation a step further with statements like, 'In 2012, Australian authorities apprehended 1,198 Pakistani migrants trying to enter the country illegally,' with no mention anywhere in the report that these were asylum seekers who were recognised as such by the Australian government and UNHCR. Data provided by the Australian government of 'smuggled migrants' intercepted in 2012 is cited as evidence of criminal smuggling operations. Although conflict and fear of persecution are briefly mentioned as 'push factors' for irregular migration, UNODC emphasises the economic impact of insecurity and suggests that migrants are motivated by economic factors. One of the few mentions of asylum in the report is the statement that irregular migration from South-West Asia to Western states including Australia 'is predominantly driven by the search for better economic and social conditions as well as the prospect of asylum for those who seek it' (UNODC 2015, 20).

A 2013 UNODC report on transnational organised crime identifies four main areas of transnational crime affecting East Asia (including Southeast Asia) and the Pacific: trade in illegal *drugs*; *environmental* crime including waste disposal and trafficking in wildlife; trade in counterfeit *goods* including fraudulent medicines; and facilitation of irregular migration and exploitation of *people*. The report attempts to quantify each area of transnational crime based on estimates of generated revenue. Migrant smuggling is identified with six main areas of threat: deadly risks and loss of human life; human rights abuses; economic impact; threat to state security; corruption; and cost of law enforcement. These categories establish a broad constellation of social, economic, and political threats with irregular migration at the centre. The threat of human rights abuse identified by UNODC relates to the irregular status of migrants increasing risk of exploitative and dangerous work, as well as exclusion from health, education, and social welfare services. Economic threats from irregular migration are framed in terms of unfair competition, undermining wages and social protection, and loss of tax revenue. Irregular migration is framed as a threat to state security in general through the profits it generates for organised crime, the undermining of migration border controls, contributions to corruption of officials bribed to facilitate irregular movement, and the cost of law enforcement operations associated with border security.

The Australian Crime Commission's (ACC 2015) *Organised Crime in Australia* report devotes a section to 'crimes against the person', which it identifies as human trafficking and slavery, maritime people smuggling and child sex offending. The Commission also claims that visa and migration fraud is an emerging area of organised crime, often facilitated by migration brokers. The commission includes both false documents and legitimate visas obtained through false claims in this category of fraud, which it claims 'has the potential to pose a significant threat to Australia's migration system' and is a 'possible threat to Australia's national security' because it undermines the ability of border agencies to accurately determine identity.

Since Prime Minister John Howard responded to the imminent arrival of asylum seekers rescued at sea by the Norwegian freighter Tampa with the statement 'we will decide who comes to Australia and the manner in which they come', Australian government policy on asylum across the political spectrum has been defined by the principle that the state must control migration and the perception that migrant smuggling constitutes a serious threat to this primary principle of state control. The opprobrium levelled at migrant smuggling operators—or people smugglers as they are referred to in Australian political discourse—is consistent across the political spectrum of parliamentary parties and has escalated over time, as political parties have competed to find the harshest policies to crack down on the 'people smugglers' business model'. The focus on people smugglers has also increased as an evolution from political discourse during and after the Tampa crisis that initially targeted asylum seekers directly as the primary threat to border security. Politicians such as Liberal Minister for Immigration Phillip Ruddock and Labour Minister for Foreign Affairs Bob Carr described asylum seekers as 'Queue jumpers' and 'economic migrants' in attempts to delegitimise their claims for protection. But while this message resonated with some voters, others remained sympathetic to the humanitarian impulse to offer assistance and protection to asylum seekers. Labour leader Kevin Rudd was able to appeal to this constituency in the 2007 general election, promising a more compassionate response to asylum seekers. Politicians seeking to sell a border security message portraying the arrival of boats carrying asylum seekers as a threat found a new and more popular target by focusing their attacks on people smugglers rather than asylum seekers. Liberal leader Tony Abbott adopted this strategy in opposition with his promise to 'stop the boats' and Kevin Rudd adopted the same message of targeting people smugglers to justify the 2012 policy pivot to a deterrence framework, including mandatory detention and offshore processing for asylum seekers arriving by boat.

Australia has responded to people smuggling as a non-traditional security threat (Maley 2001, 351). In the security paradigm epitomised by Australia's counter-smuggling security response, the state remains the central referent object of security, even as its security and sovereignty is seen as besieged by non-state threats. The framing of Australia's security has become so tightly linked to border control that Devetak (2004) has suggested asylum seekers are perceived as an existential threat to Australia in a similar way to how communists were seen in the Cold War. As Maley argues, the securitisation of asylum in Australia takes no account of the human security of the refugees and other migrants categorised as smuggled. However, the security narrative of Australia's response to asylum seekers is also not based on any empirical or objective threat to state security. Maley identifies a range of factors contributing to the political construction of asylum seekers as a threat to Australia, all of which originate in Australia's political culture. From the early 2000s, asylum seekers became a target for a backlash against policies of liberal multiculturalism led by federal government politicians. The rhetoric and policies of John Howard's government rivalled those of Pauline Hanson's One Nation party in stoking and appealing to xenophobic sentiment among white Australians. Fifteen years after Maley's analysis, Hanson's re-election to the Australian Senate in 2016, with One Nation's attacks on multiculturalism revised to explicitly target Australian Muslims, served as a reminder of the continued relevance of xenophobic anxiety to the white Australian electorate.

Another factor identified by Maley that remains relevant to explaining Australia's extreme political opposition to asylum seekers is the 'culture of control' in Australia's immigration agencies and public discourse (Maley 2001, 352–353). The culture of control, exemplified by Howard's 'we will decide' rhetoric, also has its roots in the racially based immigration system of the 'White Australia' policy, which established the power of the state to decide who enters and settles in the country as a central element of nation-building and national identity for white Australians. The political construction of asylum seekers as a threat builds on Australia's history of race-based migration policy and associated narratives of racial threat to the white settler majority (Devetak 2004, 104). Understanding this history of explicitly racist immigration policy is vital to understanding how asylum seeker arrivals, which are relatively small in international terms (Koser 2010, 5), have remained such a prominent issue in Australian politics. In particular, political attachment to state control over borders helps to explain why arrivals of asylum seekers are treated with such public and official hostility while larger populations of refugees are routinely resettled in Australia through the UNHCR quota system with relatively little fuss.

The perception that asylum seeker arrivals represent a loss of control over migration borders reflects the particular anxieties of Australian nationalism. In part, it is the ability of the general public to perceive the border as a stable and fixed natural entity that is threatened. When state agencies intercept boats carrying asylum seekers, they are described as 'defending' or 'protecting' a border that is assumed to have some separate existence and to be under threat. In this sense, border politics in settler societies like Australia and New Zealand display the ambivalent character of colonial discourse described by Bhabha (2004, 95) 'that vacillates between what is always "in place", already known, and something that must be anxiously repeated.' If asylum seekers pose a threat to borders, it is only by compelling the state to make visible the relations of force on which the border depends.

Mechanisms of Persuasion

The criminalisation and securitisation of trafficking in persons and migrant smuggling has been strongly promoted at the regional level in Southeast Asia and the Pacific. Policy convergence is promoted at the regional level in three main ways, through policy templates, inter-agency cooperation and data sharing, and training and capacity building. In addition, the adoption of technologies of border control associated with counter-trafficking and counter-smuggling operations is facilitated through financial incentives and sanctions for non-compliance.

Implementation of the Regional Cooperation Framework is tasked to the Regional Support Office (RSO) to the Bali Process, established in 2012. The priorities and work plan of the office were updated following a 2014 review, focusing on four 'pillars' of the response to irregular migration:

early detection, prevention, protection and migration management. Across these four pillars, the mechanisms of action coordinated by the office are to encourage the sharing of information, best practice and technical resources, and to coordinate capacity building activities and joint projects (RSO 2014c, 4). The continuity of cooperation on these activities through the Regional Support Office is significant given that diplomatic dialogue on irregular migration in the region has frequently broken down. Although the foreign ministries of Indonesia and Australia appoint the RSO co-convenors, the co-convenors see their function as facilitating politically neutral cooperation and collaboration.

Policy Templates

The Bali Process RSO has produced policy guides on criminalisation of Migrant Smuggling and Trafficking in Persons. The guides were developed by a committee of experts nominated by Australia, Thailand, New Zealand, Sri Lanka and UNODC, with support from the RSO and IOM. While emphasising the differences between migrant smuggling and trafficking in persons as distinct criminal offences, the two guides promote a shared formula of policy responses. Both policy guides focus on encouraging state policymakers to develop new specific criminal offences for migrant smuggling and trafficking in persons. States are encouraged to establish extraterritorial jurisdiction to cover these crimes, due to the perceived risk that 'organized criminal groups can exploit gaps in laws between different States to escape prosecution' (RSO 2014a, 9). There is also a strong focus on international cooperation, with states encouraged to develop effective laws and agreements for extradition and mutual legal cooperation. Continuing the focus on combating international organised crime, each policy guide exhorts states to 'follow the money' to 'target the profits and finance of organised criminal groups' (RSO 2014a, 12; RSO 2014b, 13).

According to Australian Co-Chair of the RSO Lisa Crawford, the impact of the policy guides can be partly attributed to the state-driven consultative process through which they were developed. The RSO focused on creating the space for state representatives to engage in 'robust conversations' in a private forum, and with the delegated authority from their governments, to 'work together to find solutions'. Governments felt confident to engage in the dialogue because it was a non-binding and voluntary process, with no obligation to endorse the final document. The consultation phase, centred on a two-day workshop where the working group presented and revised the documents with representatives of the 45 Bali Process member states, was described by Crawford as an important part of persuading states to be 'enthusiastic stakeholders' in the project goal of furthering the criminalisation of migrant smuggling and trafficking in persons. For example, Sri Lanka has used the policy guide process to help develop standard operating procedures for identifying and prosecuting cases of migrant smuggling and trafficking in persons.

Inter-agency Cooperation and Data Sharing

A significant aspect of the RSO structure is that the office primarily coordinates between state officials and personnel, rather than members of government or heads of state. This reflects a division of labour in the Bali Process, where political decisions and agreements are made through semi-regular meetings of heads of state or their representatives, while the RSO coordinates between officials in responsible ministries and agencies. This has allowed the RSO to remain insulated from political disputes and to carry on their work even while the governments of Australia and Indonesia have clashed publicly over Australia's policy of turning back boats to Indonesia.

By promoting data sharing and cooperation between agencies in different countries, regional organisations are encouraging new ways of seeing the problem of irregular migration as well as new ways of responding. A deliberate effect of the regional coordination meetings arranged by the Bali Process RSO is to create demand for data from responsible officials who want to appear well informed with up-to-date situation reports to present at meetings. This creates incentives for officials to implement formal and informal monitoring and reporting mechanisms to collect information on trafficking and smuggling cases from colleagues and subordinates. A similar effect was noted by a UNODC consultant responsible for collecting data on cases of migrant smuggling and trafficking in persons from member states. Since few states in Southeast Asia have central databases or formal processes for tracking these cases, data was collected and shared through personal connections and informal networks among border officials. For instance, in Thailand where many border posts dealing with irregular migration lack internet facilities, border officials shared information on personal mobile phones, using messaging apps such as Line. Promoting the development of these informal information networks by providing opportunities for personal trust building was identified as a goal of the face-to-face meetings between mid-level border officials organised by UNODC, including the border liaison office program. UNODC was able to access information gained from informal networks of border officials for use in formal contexts and reports, as well as encouraging the regionalisation of informal information sharing between officials in different states.

Data on 'people smuggling and related conduct' collected by UNODC in the Asia Pacific through a voluntary reporting project is shared with member states via a closed network, with access only granted to states that provide data. The data-sharing network targets the 48 members of the Bali Process, with 22 states having joined so far. A UNODC consultant working on the project said that data collection had been a challenge in the region but was 'absolutely vital' to UNODC's work in countering trafficking in persons and migrant smuggling. UNODC's (2015) report *Migrant Smuggling in Asia* recommended further efforts to collect and analyse data to shape policies. By facilitating informal and voluntary information sharing networks, UNODC is able to benefit from access to data that would otherwise be time-consuming and difficult to collect.

In addition to contributing to reports that promote the role of the international organisation and have a policy impact, the process of data collection in itself is seen as a technique of policy change. By encouraging states to collect data on trafficking and smuggling, organisations like UNODC contribute to the visibility and framing of the problem.

Training and Capacity Building

One of the key processes involved in the institutional framing of irregular migration as the smuggling and trafficking of migrants is the coordination of training and capacity building for mid-level government officials, including border and immigration staff and law enforcement. This is because, as Broome and Seabrooke (2015) argue, transnational training programs of this type can play a central role in socialising officials across different states into common ways of diagnosing and solving problems.

Training and capacity building is a major part of the work coordinated by the Bali Process RSO. Working with the IOM, the RSO developed a curriculum on standardised induction training for frontline border officials. The Curriculum document sets out the structure of a full training program, including learning objectives divided by knowledge, skills and attitude. In addition to practical skills of document inspection and traveller assessment, the curriculum includes a section of modules on migration and border management covering irregular migration, transnational organised crime, migrant smuggling, trafficking in persons, refugees and detention. Skills to be developed include identifying smuggled migrants and victims of trafficking. RSO Co-Chair Lisa Crawford described the purpose of the curriculum development project as giving state policy makers the practical tools to implement change, filling the gap between political will and practice on the ground. For instance, Lao PDR was in the process of investigating using the RSO Curriculum as their primary training framework for border staff.

The development of standardised curriculum frameworks by the RSO had the deliberate aim of creating further demand from member states for assistance with developing training content. National training programs, supported by further development of content and train-the-trainer programs by the RSO, would then be supplemented by coordinated regional training (RSO 2014c, 7). In 2015, the RSO announced plans to develop a regional training curriculum on comprehensive approaches for addressing irregular movements of people by the sea. The standardised curriculum will be developed and delivered by UNHCR and IOM through the International Law Enforcement Academy in Bangkok and the Jakarta Centre for Law Enforcement Cooperation (JCLEC). In addition, RSO and JCLEC initiated a regional training coordination mechanism to promote coordination between law enforcement training centres, develop a catalogue of existing courses, and liaise with states to promote existing courses and assess demand for further programs. The RSO has continued to develop and add to its own programs, including training on Regional Intelligence Analysis planned for development in 2015–17 to assist border officials to 'collect, analyse and share information using a regional perspective' (RSO 2014c, 5), as well as training on 'risk profiling' and 'visa integrity' for staff of foreign missions as part of a broader project developing tools for 'risk-based approaches on border management', including further training programs for Immigration Liaison Officers (RSO 2016, 5). The RSO also promotes the involvement of civil society organisations in counter-trafficking operations through a training partnership with IOM and the Kuala Lumpur CIFAL centre for local government and NGO staff on 'identification, assistance and support of victims of human trafficking' (RSO 2014c, 8).

The Australian government has also given significant bilateral support to governments in the ASEAN region for training and capacity building for criminal justice responses to trafficking. The Australia-Asia Program to Combat Trafficking in Persons (AAPTIP) provides AU$50 m across five years for a 2013–18 work program of collaboration and expert advice to law enforcement, prosecutors and judges across the region. Management of the project is contracted to Cardno, an Australian engineering firm that describes itself as 'a world leader in the provision of professional services to improve the physical and social environment'. Cardno also held contracts to manage the previous Australian funded initiatives, the Asia Regional Cooperation to Prevent People Trafficking (2003–06) and the Asia Regional Trafficking in Persons Project (2006–13). The same company runs the Australian government's Labour Mobility Assistance Program (LMAP), which brings seasonal workers from Pacific states to work in Australian agriculture (Cardno 2016a, b).

By providing significant funding to developing countries in the region conditional on cooperation in counter-trafficking programs, Australia contributes material incentives to the development of a regional migration border regime, as well as facilitating the learning processes of the emerging regime through provision of training and capacity building. By contracting these programs to transnational corporations, the state also provides the means and incentive for the creation of powerful private actors to carry the counter-trafficking norms and practices of the migration border regime across the region.

Incentives and Sanctions

Since it was first launched in 2001, the annual US Trafficking in Persons (USTiP) report has become a central tool in a global incentive structure for the emergence of counter-trafficking regimes. The power of the USTiP report rests as much on an instrumental logic of consequences as a normative logic of appropriateness (March and Olsen 1998), with the ratings allocated by the report integrated into the assessment of eligibility for US government aid, together with the use of trade and other sanctions against states deemed not to be in compliance with US expectations of counter-trafficking programs. Countries included in the USTiP report are ranked into three tiers based on their level of compliance with minimum standards outlined in US legislation, the Trafficking Victims Protection Act (TVPA) of 2000 and successive acts of Congress that have reauthorised its provisions. As Gallagher (2006, 139) argues, the ranking process of the USTiP report is not based on international agreements and conventions, but rather, on an extrapolation of US law, norms and policies. The TVPA requires states to prohibit, punish, and make 'serious and sustained efforts to eliminate' severe forms of trafficking in persons, but the definition of severe forms of trafficking is one of US rather than international law. The TVPA defines severe trafficking as inducing a commercial sex act by a person under 18 years of age, or by means of force, fraud, or coercion; or 'the recruitment, harboring, transportation, provision, or obtaining of a person for labor or services, through the use of force, fraud, or coercion for the purpose of subjection to involuntary servitude, peonage, debt bondage, or slavery'. This means that the US definition sets a higher bar for 'severe' forms of trafficking in the case of forced labour than the UN trafficking protocol does, but a significantly lower bar in the case of commercial sex. This dual standard reflects both the legal situation of criminalised sex work in the US, as well as the politics of anti-prostitution described above, which the US government seeks to export and enforce using the USTiP instrument.

In requiring states to demonstrate progress in eliminating severe forms of trafficking compared to previous years, the USTIP report assumes that reliable data on prevalence of trafficking can be found and that a reduction in numbers signifies progress. However, as with any project of criminalisation, data on prevalence are dependant on rates of reporting and categorisation of criminal cases as trafficking. A state attempting to comply with US standards for counter-trafficking could reasonably expect to see an increase in reported cases of trafficking, at least in the short-term, due to new requirements for reporting and categorising cases (Gallagher and Rebecca 2012, 25).

The USTiP report has become an influential instrument of international governance since the ranking of states' counter-trafficking actions are linked to US trade and funding. Receiving a poor ranking on the USTiP report has both reputational and material consequences for states, which are taken seriously by policy makers. Therefore the standards and criteria used to judge a country's actions in the USTiP report are of international significance, since the report functions as intended to promote the diffusion of US norms of counter-trafficking.

Governments listed as tier one are judged to be fully compliant with TVPA standards, those on tier two are judged as non-compliant but making significant efforts to become compliant, while those on tier three are judged to be non-compliant and not making significant efforts to improve. States on tier two that are judged to not be making fast enough progress may be placed on a watch-list for future downgrade to tier three and, from 2013, states that have been at tier two for more than two years will be automatically downgraded to tier three unless granted special dispensation. Tier three states are subject to restrictions on assistance and funding from the US government, including restrictions on US government support for multilateral assistance such as IMF and World Bank loans (US State Department 2005, 39–40). A consultant to UNODC working with states in Southeast Asia and the Pacific, interviewed in 2015, identified the USTiP report as a significant driver of interest from states in policy change and regional cooperation in order to maintain or upgrade status on the report.

Conclusion

Institutional framing of irregular migration in terms of trafficking and smuggling, including through the adoption of the Trafficking in Persons and Migrant Smuggling Protocols to the UN Convention on Transnational Crime, has contributed to the criminalisation and securitisation of the movement of migrants across international borders. In the Asia-Pacific, regional organisations including UN agencies have played a significant role in promoting institutional frames that criminalise and securitise irregular migration at national levels. Regional organisations have developed and disseminated policy templates on criminalisation that align with existing state interests as well as international pressure. Cooperation between government agencies has been promoted through data sharing initiatives that shape the problem-solving approaches of state agencies in line with the counter-trafficking and counter-smuggling agenda. Training and capacity-building for personnel at all levels of border, immigration and law enforcement agencies across the region have provided further opportunities to embed institutional frames in the daily practice of government. Incentives for states to participate in these processes of institutional change are created through the provision of significant funding for the activities, as well as the threat of sanctions for non-compliance.

Notes

1. Reported cases were collected by two independent research teams and combined as a capture-recapture sample. A key variable in the study is the estimated ratio of reported to unreported cases, which is calculated based on ILO migrant worker survey data to be 1:27 or 3.6%.
2. For an example of a faith-based anti-trafficking organisation using undercover investigation techniques by ex-police officers, see www.Nvader.org. Nvader promote their role in 'investigation and prosecution', 'survivor care', and 'capacity building' to combat trafficking in Southeast Asia, with a strong focus on the sex industry.

Bibliography

ACC (Australian Crime Commission). 2015. Organised Crime in Australia. https://www.acic.gov.au/sites/g/files/net1491/f/2016/06/oca2015.pdf

Agustín, Laura. 2007. *Sex at the Margins: Migration, Labour Markets and the Rescue Industry*. London: Zed Books.

Amnesty International. 2016a. Norway: The Human Cost of 'Crushing' the Market: Criminalization of Sex Work in Norway. https://www.amnesty.org/en/documents/eur36/4034/2016/en/

Andreas, Peter, and Ethan Nadelmann. 2008. *Policing the Globe: Criminalization and Crime Control in International Relations*. Oxford University Press.

Aradau, Claudia. 2004. The Perverse Politics of Four-Letter Words: Risk and Pity in the Securitisation of Human Trafficking. *Millennium—Journal of International Studies* 33 (2): 251–277.

Bali Process—Regional Support Office. 2016. Regional Cooperation Framework. www.baliprocess.net/regional-cooperation-framework

Bernstein, Elizabeth. 2012. Carceral Politics as Gender Justice? The "Traffic in Women" and Neoliberal Circuits of Crime, Sex, and Rights. *Theory and Society 41* (3): 233–259.

Bhabha, Homi K. 2004. *The Location of Culture*. Abingdon: Routledge.

Broome, André, and Leonard Seabrooke. 2015. Shaping Policy Curves: Cognitive Authority in Transnational Capacity Building. *Public Administration 93* (4): 956–972.

Buss, Doris, and Didi Herman. 2003. *Globalizing Family Values: The Christian Right in International Politics*. Minneapolis: University of Minnesota Press.

Cardno. 2016a. http://www.cardno.com/en-au/AboutUs/Pages/Home.aspx

———. 2016b. http://www.cardno.com/en-au/Projects/Pages/Labour-Mobility-Assistance-Program-(LMAP).aspx

Charnysh, Volha, Paulette Lloyd, and Beth A. Simmons. 2014. Frames and Consensus Formation in International Relations: The Case of Trafficking in Persons. *European Journal of International Relations* 21 (2): 323–351.

DIBP—Department of Immigration and Border Protection. 2013. Asylum Trends—Australia 2012–13. https://www.immi.gov.au/media/publications/statistics/immigration-update/asylum-trends-aus-2012-13.pdf

Devetak, Richard. 2004. In Fear of Refugees: The Politics of Border Protection in Australia. *The International Journal of Human Rights* 8 (1): 101–109.

Doezema, Jo. 2010. *Sex Slaves and Discourse Masters: The Construction of Trafficking*. London; New York: Zed Books.

Empower. 2012. Recommendations Regarding Trafficking from Sex Workers of Empower. http://www.empowerfoundation.org/sexy_en.php?id=6

Entman, Robert M. 1993. Framing: Toward Clarification of a Fractured Paradigm. *Journal of Communication* 43 (4): 51–58.

Farley, Melissa. 2003. Preface—Prostitution, Trafficking, and Traumatic Stress. In *Prostitution, Trafficking, and Traumatic Stress*, ed. Melissa Farley. New York: Routledge.

GAATW—Global Alliance Against Traffic in Women, Foundation Against Trafficking in Women, and International Human Rights Law Group. 1999. Human Rights Standards for the Treatment of Trafficked Persons. http://www.hrlawgroup.org/resources/content/IHRLGTraffickin_tsStandards.pdf

GAATW. 2014. Criminalising Clients Endangers Sex Workers and Creates Barriers to Exiting Sex Work: Lessons Learned from the Anti-Trafficking Industry. Brief to the Senate Legal and Constitutional Affairs Committee on Bill C-36: Protection of Communities and Exploited Persons Act Submitted 8 September 2014 by the Global Alliance against Traffic in Women, International Secretariat (GAATW-IS) and Global Alliance Against Traffic in Women—Canada (GAATW-Canada). http://www.gaatw.org/advocacy/Bill_C-36-GAATW_brief.pdf

———. 2016a. The Early Years. http://gaatw.org/about-us/history/156-about-us/history/440-the-early-years

———. 2016b. GAATW-IS Statement on Amnesty International's Policy on Sex Work. http://gaatw.org/events-and-news/68-gaatw-news/847-gaatw-is-statement-on-amnesty-international-s-policy-on-sex-work

Gallagher, Anne. 2006. Human Rights and Human Trafficking in Thailand: A Shadow TIP Report. In *Trafficking and the Global Sex Industry*, ed. Karen Beeks and Delila Amir, 139–163. Lanham, MD: Lexington Books.

———. 2016. Unravelling the 2016 Global Slavery Index. *Open Democracy*, 28 June 2016. https://www.opendemocracy.net/anne-gallagher/unravelling-2016-global-slavery-index

Gallagher, Anne, and Rebecca Surtees. 2012. Measuring the Success of Counter Trafficking Interventions in the Criminal Justice Sector: Who Decides—and How? *Anti-Trafficking Review 1*: 10–30.

Global Commission on International Migration. 2005. *Migration in an Interconnected World: New Directions for Action*. http://www.iom.int/jahia/webdav/site/myjahiasite/shared/shared/mainsite/policy_and_research/gcim/GCIM_Report_Complete.pdf

Haas, Ernst B. 1980. Why Collaborate? Issue-Linkage and International Regimes. *World Politics 32* (3): 357–405.

ILO—International Labour Organisation. 2012. ILO Global Estimate of Forced Labour: Results and Methodology. http://www.ilo.org/wcmsp5/groups/public/@ed_norm/@declaration/documents/publication/wcms_182004.pdf

IOM. 2016. https://www.iom.int/news/iom-assists-7000-victims-human-trafficking-globally-2015

Koser, Khalid. 2010. Responding to Boat Arrivals in Australia: Time for a Reality Check. *Lowy Institute for International Policy*. http://m.lowyinstitute.org/files/pubfiles/Koser,_Responding_web.pdf

Landry, Rachel. 2016. The 'Humanitarian Smuggling' of Refugees: Criminal Offence or Moral Obligation? *Oxford University Refugee Studies Centre Working Paper Series No. 119.*

Leidholdt, Dorchen A. 2003. Prostitution and Trafficking in Women: An Intimate Relationship. In *Prostitution, Trafficking and Traumatic Stress*, ed. Melissa Farley. Hoboken: Routledge.

Lewis, Daniel Ray, Nuarpear Lekfuangfu, Irena Vojackova-Sollorano, Federico Soda, and Claudia Natali. 2010. *Forecasting Migration Flows: The Relationships among Economic Development, Demographic Change and Migration in the Greater Mekong Subregion.* IOM.

Maley, William. 2001. Security, People-Smuggling, and Australia's New Afghan Refugees. *Australian Journal of International Affairs* 55 (3): 351–370. doi:10.1080/10357710120095216.

March, James G., and Johan P. Olsen. 1998. The Institutional Dynamics of International Political Orders. *International Organization 52*: 943–969.

NSWP (Global Network of Sex Work Projects). 1999. Commentary on the Draft Protocol to Combat International Trafficking in Women and Children Supplementary to the Draft Convention on Transnational Organized Crime. http://www.nswp.org/resource/commentary-the-draft-protocol-combatinternational-trafficking-women-and-children-supplemen

Robinson, Duncan. 2016. EU Border Force Accuses Charities of Collusion with Migrant Smugglers. *Financial Times*, 15 December 2016. https://www.ft.com/content/3e6b6450-c1f7-11e6-9bca-2b93a6856354

RSO. 2014a. Policy Guide on Criminalizing Trafficking in Persons.

———. 2014b. Policy Guide on Criminalizing Migrant Smuggling.

———. 2014c. RSO Forward Work Plan 2015–17. http://www.baliprocess.net/files/Forward%20Work%20Plan%202015-2017.pdf

———. 2016. Bali Process Strategy for Cooperation: Update. http://www.baliprocess.net/UserFiles/baliprocess/File/BP%20Strategy%20-%20Presented%20to%20SOM%20March%202016.pdf

Shih, Elena. 2014. Globalising Rehabilitative Regimes: Framing the Moral Economy of Vocational Training in After-Trafficking Work. In *Human Trafficking in Asia: Forcing Issues*, ed. Sallie Yea, 64–77. Oxon: Routledge.

UN. 2000. Protocol to Prevent, Suppress and Punish Trafficking in Persons, Especially Women and Children, Supplementing the United Nations Convention Against Transnational Organized Crime. United Nations.

UN-ACT. 2004. Memorandum of Understanding on Cooperation Against Trafficking in Persons in the Greater Mekong Sub-Region. http://un-act.org/publication/view/2004-commit-mou/

———. 2016a. The Bangkok Declaration on Irregular Migration. http://un-act.org/publication/view/the-bangkok-declaration-on-irregular-migration-1999/

———. 2016b. Coordinating and Innovating Counter-Trafficking. http://un-act.org/wp-content/uploads/2016/04/UN-ACT-Brochure.pdf

UNODC. 2014. Global Report on Trafficking in Persons. https://www.unodc.org/documents/data-and-analysis/glotip/GLOTIP_2014_full_report.pdf

———. 2015. Issue Paper on 'The Concept of "Exploitation" in the Trafficking in Persons Protocol'. http://un-act.org/wp-content/uploads/2015/06/The-Concept-of-Exploitation-in-the-Trafficking-in-Persons-Protocol.pdf

USGAO (United States Government Accountability Office). 2005. Human Trafficking: Better Data, Strategy, and Reporting Needed to Enhance U.S. Antitrafficking Efforts Abroad. http://www.gao.gov/products/GAO-06-825

US State Department. 2005. Trafficking Victims Protection Reauthorization Act of 2005. http://www.state.gov/j/tip/laws/61106.htm

Waever, Ole. 1995. Securitisation and De-securitisation. In *On Security*, ed. Ronnie D. Lipschultz, 46–86. New York: Columbia University Press.

CHAPTER 5

Screening Migrants

Institutional framing processes centred on international efforts to criminalise and securitise trafficking in persons and migrant smuggling have produced a proliferation of common techniques in state practices towards mobile populations. Even as states fail to reach substantive agreement on common normative frameworks for dealing with irregular migration, there has been a convergence in practice around techniques of surveillance and control.

The central argument of this chapter is that the evolving mechanisms of migration screening are increasingly coordinated between states in Southeast Asia and the Pacific through a web of bilateral and soft multilateral mechanisms that create a regional border regime, even as these mechanisms work against core principles and norms of humanitarian protection ascribed to the international 'refugee regime' (Betts 2009) and the international labour standards regime (Hughes 2002). Screening of migrants therefore takes place at the conjunction of multiple overlapping and contradictory international regimes.

States are selective in their adoption of international norms, and the patterns of change are enabled and influenced by regional cooperation. In the process of norm localisation (Acharya 2004), regional regimes play an intervening role in translating international norms into regional contexts and setting agendas and timetables for change. This chapter shows that even the informal regional regime of coordinated border management that operates in Southeast Asia and the Pacific has a significant impact in setting the priorities for change in state policy and practice. The powerful

N. Henry, *Asylum, Work, and Precarity*, Critical Studies of the Asia-Pacific, DOI 10.1007/978-3-319-60567-8_5

institutional resources for change provided by international organisations are channelled by regional priorities. In the process, sets of norms that are packaged together in international policy discourse can be separated and subject to two-speed implementation at regional and local levels.

In response to the perceived threats of trafficking in persons and migrant smuggling, international organisations, NGOs and Western states have promoted a package of policy responses centred around criminalisation and securitisation of irregular migration, described in the previous chapter. Many liberal humanitarians have been persuaded to support this package of counter-trafficking and counter-smuggling policies, not only because they share with conservatives a commitment to preserving state control over migration borders, but also because the criminalisation and securitisation agenda has been packaged together with commitments to enhancing protection for asylum seekers and migrant workers. However, at the point of implementation at regional and state levels, this packaging tends to come apart and, while international resources for securing borders and criminalising smugglers have been eagerly taken up by states, efforts to promote safe travel, access to asylum, legal status and improved working conditions for migrants have been relegated to the slow lane of international cooperation.

As the previous chapter showed, movements of migrants with irregular status have been securitised to an unprecedented degree. To a great extent this securitisation has been pursued by framing irregular migration in terms of transnational organised crimes, migrant smuggling and trafficking in persons, which pose threats to state sovereignty and national security. The criminalisation and securitisation of irregular migration, pursued through efforts to counter migrant smuggling and trafficking in persons, has had a significantly detrimental impact on the freedom of movement of migrant workers and asylum seekers, exposing these migrants to greater risk and precarity in their lives during and after migration. This chapter reviews the mechanisms and processes by which the securitisation and criminalisation of irregular migration has been put into practice in Southeast Asia and the Pacific. I focus on the techniques through which the agents and agencies of state borders encounter migrants and seek to intervene in migrant journeys, including through regulating permission to enter or remain in the territory of the state. These encounters and interventions are increasingly dispersed from the physical boundaries of state territories and involve coordination between multiple state agencies and private actors.

Migration border controls have externalised beyond the territory of states in an effort to detect and prevent unwanted or irregular migration before migrants are able make claims for asylum. Border controls have also been internalised within the territories of states by the growth of dedicated police units and police-like immigration enforcement agencies. These twin processes of externalisation and internalisation combine to form a mobile regime of surveillance and control of migrant populations, producing the continuum of interventions that Australian authorities refer to as the 'layered border'.

Modes of Migration Control

Across the region of Southeast Asia and the Pacific, migration governance displays varying combinations of three typical modes: *formal management* according to legally established rules, including capacity-building for border and immigration agencies, and efforts to regularise existing migrant populations through amnesties and registration schemes; *informal tolerance* of irregular migration, often in response to demand from employers, including through systematically lax or corrupt enforcement of immigration rules; and *arbitrary enforcement* through police-style actions, often framed in security terms as a crackdown on irregular migration, whether under emergency regulations or existing laws.

Each country in the region exhibits some combination of the three modes in different proportions, according to varying capacities and political will for formal migration border management, and typically with some degree of cyclical alternation between informal tolerance and arbitrary enforcement in response to irregular labour migration. As Battistella (2007, 209–211) argues, informal tolerance of irregular migration is widely prevalent throughout the broader Asia-Pacific region, enabled by long and porous borders, close historical and cultural ties between neighbouring countries, social networks, and the involvement of private recruitment agencies. The extent of opportunities for irregular migration, combined with growing demand for migrant labour in multiple states in the region, means that the degree of irregular migration is largely shaped by limitations on opportunities for regular migration imposed by state policies. The informal tolerance for irregular migration shown in states such as Thailand and Malaysia reflects the structural conditions of economic reliance on migrant labour combined with political reluctance to extend formal status for migrants.

The preference for formal management of migration on the part of international organisations, including IOM, UNHCR and UNODC, is commonly imagined by participants in these organisations as a process of embedding liberalism (Ruggie 1982). By extending the rule of law and institutional capacity of states to more fully and formally manage migration flows, it is assumed that a concomitant expansion of formal rights and protections for asylum seekers and migrant workers will be facilitated. However, as I show in this and subsequent chapters, the international resources that have been contributed to the promotion of formal migration governance in Southeast Asia and the Pacific, have so far produced hybrid modes of formalised and arbitrary border enforcement, with little progress towards openness and protection for migrants.

In practice, regional coordination of border management in Southeast Asia and the Pacific amounts to a distribution of common techniques and capacities in addition to largely ad hoc processes for sharing information. The absence of formal or binding mechanisms for cooperation becomes especially problematic when states take unilateral actions designed to externalise perceived security risks associated with irregular migration. In addition to unilateral actions by which states seek to displace risk onto neighbours by turning away migrants, states in Southeast Asia and the Pacific have demonstrated a commonly held reticence to take responsibility for protecting migrants and have cooperated to resist international pressure to adopt protection norms. Reticence towards migrant protection has been expressed through the two-speed adoption of international norms and resources noted above, whereby migrant protection is deprioritised and delayed compared to swift action on border security, as well as through coordinated inaction among states in the region in the provision of minimal and delayed protection responses.

The events of May 2015 provided a stark example of coordinated inaction on migrant protection by states in Southeast Asia and the broader region, including Australia. In the midst of a crackdown by Thai authorities on migrant smuggling operations, more than 5000 migrants were abandoned by boat crews and left drifting in the Andaman Sea, off the coasts of Thailand and Myanmar. The boats carrying a mix of Bangladeshi migrant workers and Rohingya asylum-seekers from Myanmar were refused disembarkation and pushed back to sea by authorities in Thailand, Malaysia and Indonesia. Australia made no official offer of assistance and when asked if Australia would offer help with resettlement of refugees, Prime Minister Tony Abbott responded in typically blunt fashion: 'nope, nope,

nope' (Medhora 2015). Interviews conducted by UNHCR indicated at least 70 people died at sea during May 2015, with the causes of death including thirst, hunger and violence (UNHCR 2015, 1).

As UNHCR officials have noted, including in an interview for this book, the situation in the Andaman Sea in 2015 was not a crisis of migration numbers. The crisis and the deaths were caused by states combining a crackdown on migrant smuggling with inaction on migrant protection. The more than 5000 migrants who were abandoned at sea were those who were already embarked when Thai authorities launched the crackdown, leaving the boat crews with nowhere to land. In normal circumstances, the migrants would have come ashore in Southern Thailand and continued by land to Malaysia, assisted by a network of military and immigration officers paid by the smugglers. According to regular monitoring by UNHCR and the Arakan project, the numbers of irregular migrants travelling by sea in April–May 2015 were not unusual for the season. The numbers were also small compared to irregular migration in other regions, a point that a UNHCR official emphasised in refusing the label of 'migration crisis' to describe the situation, pointing out that the total number stranded at sea in May 2015 was fewer than the numbers being disembarked to European state territories from the Mediterranean every day in the same period.

At the end of May 2015, state leaders from the region met in Jakarta to discuss resolutions to the crisis. By this point, most of the stranded migrants had already been brought ashore in Indonesia and Malaysia. In the case of Indonesia, around 1200 migrants were rescued by local fishing communities in Aceh province and looked after by local associations, including the Geutanyoe Foundation. The governments of Indonesia and Malaysia agreed to provide temporary protection for Rohingya asylum seekers, although they announced that they expected Western states to provide resettlement within a year for those found to be refugees. This condition was criticised by an official at UNHCR (interview 2015) as an unrealistic expectation that was announced without consultation with UNHCR. The official suggested that Southeast Asian leaders needed to recognise changes since Western states provided resettlement under the 1989 Comprehensive Plan of Action for Indochinese refugees. In this official's view, significant economic growth in Southeast Asia in recent decades meant that states in the region should be taking more responsibility for providing protection and work opportunities for asylum seekers within their own countries.

During the crisis, existing regional plans and international rules for cooperation on maritime search and rescue were disregarded, with states primarily using information sharing mechanisms to locate and turn back boats. This was despite an ongoing process led by the Regional Support Office (RSO) to the Bali Process to promote coordinated approaches to search and rescue for migrant vessels in distress at sea. A regional meeting in January 2014, convened by UNHCR, IOM and the New Zealand government under the Bali Process, had discussed contingency plans for cooperation in responding to large-scale movements by sea, including search and rescue operations. The concept note for the meeting on 'Mapping Disembarkation Options: Towards Strengthening Cooperation in Managing Irregular Movements by Sea' referenced the 2013 Regional Roundtable on Irregular Movements by Sea, convened by UNHCR and the governments of Indonesia and Australia, that had identified the need to identify 'places of safety for disembarkation', harmonisation of guidelines for protection and processing, and regional support for states hosting rescued migrants. The January 2014 meeting aimed to 'discuss and agree upon the parameters, structure, content and modalities of a mapping exercise of disembarkation options' (RSO 2013).

By late 2015, the RSO remained in the early stages of work on the disembarkation mapping exercise. According to a senior official at the RSO, interviewed in December 2015, the office was waiting for a new staff member to be seconded to investigate what was achievable and planning to proceed cautiously:

> We're not going to change things in a day. We're not going to shift decades of thinking, but what we can do is help states when they want to respond to something be capable of doing that.

Whereas state responses and coordination during the events of May had been handled 'at the political level', the RSO saw its role as making such a situation 'a less likely occurrence in the future' by developing the capacity of personnel across state agencies to be able to offer concrete policy alternatives to state leaders.

> We want something that's realistic and that encourages further conversation rather than frightens states from wanting to contribute and participate for fear that they're going to be bound by something or overcommitted.

In many ways, the work of the RSO represents current best practice for coordination of protection of refugees and other migrants in the region. UNHCR, as a founding partner of the office, has frequently called for states to fully engage with the protection mechanisms and commitments contained in the Bali declaration. However, states have been relatively slow to respond to the protection 'pillar' of the RSO's work, compared with the enthusiasm for preventing and deterring irregular migration. The non-binding form of the Bali Process, and in particular the unspecified timelines of the commitments made by states, opens the process to a problematic two-speed implementation, where cooperation on tougher border enforcement has been implemented speedily and out of step with increased protection mechanisms for vulnerable migrants, which remain largely at the stage of abstract in-principle agreements.

This problem is reflected throughout the work of international organisations on migration management in the Asia-Pacific, where support for criminalisation and securitisation of irregular migration is justified in terms of broader programmes of liberalised formal migration management and protection of vulnerable migrants that frequently fail to receive equivalent commitment or priority from states. A similar framing is commonly found in academic arguments from scholars who approach irregular migration as a problem of international law and institutions. For instance, Schloenhardt (2008, 36–37) makes an explicit argument in favour of the securitisation and criminalisation of irregular migration, stating that the two 'must go hand in hand' to 'prevent and suppress illegal migration and migrant smuggling in the Asia-Pacific'. Schloenhardt's approach to criminalisation of irregular migration follows the agenda of his former employer UNODC with proposals to make 'illegal migration and the smuggling of migrants less attractive by increasing the costs for perpetrators and minimising the profit their activities generate'. In common with other present and former staff of international organisations like UNODC, Schloenhardt (37–39) justifies criminalisation as an approach to harm-reduction for migrants, who he describes as the 'victims of migrant smuggling', as part of a package of policy proposals. For Schloenhardt, these proposals include decriminalising irregular migration for refugees—including for smugglers and others who assist them to cross borders—and reforms to increase legal channels for the movement of both migrant workers and asylum seekers. As such, Schloenhardt's argument provides a concise and coherent articulation of a complete package of formal migration management that forms the broad consensus among international organisations and their regional representatives in the Asia-Pacific.

Within this broad consensus, the prioritisation of border security reflects the interests of states and is reflected in the institutional capture of migration issues by forums primarily concerned with security and crime. Within ASEAN for instance, state responses to irregular migration are coordinated by the Senior Officials Meeting on Transnational Crime (SOMTC). A UNHCR staff member with responsibility for responding to maritime movements of asylum seekers, interviewed in 2015, described why this is seen as problematic:

> The transnational crime body is the one that's been dealing with this issue, even though we're not always happy with that, because we don't want to see it just as a law enforcement or crime issue.

The activities coordinated by SOMTC focus on information sharing and capacity building, including joint training programs (Emmers et al. 2008, 68). These activities facilitate the development of a regime of common techniques and cooperative action of migration border control among states in the region, while the non-binding nature of ASEAN activities maintains the sovereign independence of states, rather than seeking to construct a supranational normative or institutional structure.

Regionalisation of Australia's Border Security Regime

Pickering and Weber's (2013) observation that Australian immigration authorities were becoming more police-like in their operations, as well as increasingly working with police and other agencies on migration border enforcement, identified the trend that led to the formation of the Australian Border Force in 2015. A product of the merger of the Australian Customs and Border Protection Service into the recently renamed Department of Immigration and Border Protection, the Australian Border Force combined the enforcement divisions of the two agencies and was intended to have a higher profile, with clearly identifiable police-style uniforms and an active media presence. The DIBP (2015a, 13) defines itself as a part of Australia's 'law enforcement and national security community' The redefinition of the department around border protection as part of the law enforcement and national security establishment has been advanced by the structure of the Border Force within the DIBP, with a uniformed Commissioner reporting directly to the Minister of Immigration and Border Protection. In turn, the

Minister of Immigration and Border Protection sits on the permanent National Security committee of Cabinet.

DIBP's law enforcement and national security focus is expressed through three interrelated goals, identified as priorities by the department (DIBP 2015a, 13). The first, 'effectively securing our borders through a programme of prevention, deterrence and enforcement' summarises the department's responses to perceived threats to Australia, including from irregular migration. Because each element of these responses extend beyond and within the boundaries of Australian territory, this goal identifies the temporal and geographical layering of the border as a continuum of interventions to be made in the process of journeys deemed to be security risks.

DIBP's second strategic goal of 'safeguarding and streamlining lawful trade and travel' reinforces the dual nature of the border as a screening process that seeks to enable and facilitate trade and travel deemed desirable, as well as filtering out unwanted arrivals. As a DIBP (2015b, 5) Industry Summit presentation described the role of the department, it seeks to be 'Australia's trusted global gateway':

> This means we will be the conduit through which legitimate travellers, migrants and potential citizens, as well as legitimate goods, can freely pass, and we must be able to firmly and quickly shut that gate against those who would do Australia harm.

This strategic goal emphasises that the screening processes of the border, both for trade in goods and movement of people, operate as a channelling of flows where the gating process involves directing movements into more or less smooth paths through the border depending on risk assessment and profiling.

The extent to which Australia's border security strategy overlaps with criminal and national security functions is emphasised in DIBP's third strategic goal of 'contributing to efforts to disrupt and dismantle transnational criminal and terrorist organisations'. In combination with the institutional framing of irregular migration as a transnational crime of people smuggling, detailed in the previous chapter, this goal serves to further the securitisation and criminalisation of Australia's migration border. By addressing transnational crime, including the facilitation of irregular migration as a serious threat to Australia comparable with terrorism, the department seeks to legitimate the extended range of 'layered' techniques used to screen out migrants with potentially irregular documentation.

DIBP works with other Australian government agencies and international partners to profile travellers and migrants deemed to be security risks, and prevent these people from reaching Australia. To this end, DIBP maintains a Movement Alert List (MAL) comprising a Person Alert List (PAL) of over 700,000 individuals flagged as a risk for a range of reasons, and a Document Alert List (DAL) of more than two million travel documents, primarily documents reported as lost, stolen, or cancelled (DIBP 2016a, b, c). Figures for December 2013 released by DIBP (2014a, b) show 44% of individuals on the list were flagged on 'national security' grounds based on secret assessments by ASIO. Other significant categories included criminal convictions (18%), health concerns (11%), debt to the Commonwealth of Australia (10%), and a range of immigration issues including previously overstaying a visa (5%), breaching visa conditions (2%), and 'organised immigration malpractice' (2%). The number of people on the PAL has continued to grow rapidly, which DIBP has attributed to 'heightened concerns about national security, fraud and irregular people movements' (ANAO 2009, 19).

As a screening tool, the MAL comes into use well before passengers reach the Australian border. Airlines and sea carriers are required to apply for clearance to board passengers at the point of check-in through the Advance Passenger Processing (APP) system operated by DIBP. APP is an automated document screening process based on the DAL database and generates one of two responses: 'OK to board' or 'Do not board'. Passengers denied document clearance may be directed to DIBP Airport Liaison Officers, located at each airport with direct flights or last ports of embarkation to Australia. Strict penalties, known as carrier sanctions, apply to any transport operator that fails to assure screening of travel documents and DIBP approval for all passengers arriving in Australia. For passengers cleared for boarding, an expected movement record is sent to DIBP's Travel and Immigration Processing Systems (TRIPS) for automated checking of the passenger record against the PAL database and additional risk profiling by automated systems and DIBP analysts. If a passenger is denied clearance by the TRIPS process, including as a result of a PAL listing, they may be denied boarding by the transport carrier or, if already en route to Australia, will be flagged for interception at the border. Data on expected passenger movements and immigration directives are passed from TRIPS to the Passenger Analysis Clearance and Evaluation (PACE) system used by DIBP's Customs and Border Protection staff. Passengers who are denied entry or flagged for further investigation in PACE are referred to DIBP staff at the airport. For passengers approved for entry at the border, PACE generates an entry record.

In 2014, I was at check-in for an Air New Zealand flight from Wellington to Melbourne when the APP system stopped functioning. To board the flight, airline staff separated passengers into two queues, one for those with Australian and New Zealand passports who did not require visas to enter Australia, and another queue for those with other passports who were individually screened by telephone with a DIBP official in Canberra. All passengers were issued with handwritten boarding passes, since the airline system would not issue boarding passes without APP authorisation. This experience underscored how central the APP system has become to the smooth functioning of travel to and through Australia and other Western countries, even if most passengers would be unaware of the existence of the system or their processing through it. The temporary replacement of the automated system by a manual screening process also highlighted the differential levels of security screening applied to holders of different categories of passports and the role of DIBP officers and systems in Canberra in security screening and clearance for boarding at foreign ports.

The requirement for transport carriers to screen the travel documents of passengers prior to boarding is enforced by sanctions, introduced by a 1979 amendment to Australia's Migration Act (section 229). In 2017, the fine for allowing the travel to Australia of a passenger without a valid visa was 18,000 Australian dollars. Given the role of carrier sanctions in preventing the travel to Australia of a wide class of migrants who cannot obtain visas, including the majority of asylum seekers, some authors have drawn comparisons to preceding carrier sanctions which were first used in Australia in the 1855 *Act to Make Provision for Certain Immigrants* to oblige shipping companies to limit the numbers of Chinese migrants they carried and to require Chinese migrants to pay an arrival tax, also designed as a deterrent (Cronin 1999). As several authors have noted, the effect of carrier sanctions is to privatise a key aspect of migration border enforcement, with the particular effect of preventing the arrival of asylum seekers, thus preventing the engagement of Australia's obligations to offer humanitarian protection (Taylor 2008, 100–101; Hyndman and Mountz 2008; Rodenhäuser 2014).

Whereas the implementation of carrier sanctions required legislative change, the growth of the Advance Passenger Processing system, along with the Movement Alert List and associated tools, and their increasing importance as a tool for information sharing and coordination, are examples of change in border management driven by an enhanced technical capacity to fulfil an existing mandate. As noted by the ANAO (2009, 25–26), the MAL is an 'administrative tool' with 'no specific basis in law'. Where there have been changes to legislation governing Australia's migration border management these have often been specific and instrumental responses to short-term operation needs and perceived threats. Between 2010 and 2016, 41 separate amendments were passed to the Migration Act 1958, in addition to 74 amendments in the decade 2000–09, compared to 42 in the 1990s, 22 in the 1980s and seven between 1958 and 1979. The escalating pace of legislative change in migration governance, especially since the Howard Liberal government of 2000 reflects the turbulence of a policy environment in which such fundamental issues as the location of the migration border and the approach to detention of irregular migrants have been in constant flux.

Going into the 2013 election, joint Coalition policy on border security from the Liberal and National parties focused on accusations of a lack of coherence and resolve in the Labour government's approach. The Coalition policy proposed to achieve coherence in border management through operational restructuring, with legislative changes to be introduced where necessary to serve operational requirements. This approach reflects an ongoing approach of continuous ad hoc changes to Australia's migration legislation.

Introduced by the Abbott Liberal-Coalition Government, the Joint Agency Task Force (JATF) Operation Sovereign Borders (OSB) was established by Prime Ministerial directive under DIBP. Although the operation is structured as a whole-of-government task force responsible to the Minister for Immigration and Border Protection, the public framing of the operation emphasises that it is 'military-led', referring to the appointment of a senior general of the Australian Defence Force (ADF) as head of the task force. OSB is composed of three operational task groups bringing together the border-related enforcement activity of a range of federal government agencies: Disruption and Deterrence, led by the Australian Federal Police (AFP); Detection, Interception and Transfer, led by the Australian Border Force (ABF); and Offshore Detention and Returns, led by DIBP. These three task groups each extend in different ways beyond Australia's territory, making up the multi-layered border response to irregular maritime arrivals of asylum seekers,

The Disruption and Deterrence Task Group led by AFP makes use of resources from the Australian Security Intelligence Service (ASIS) and the Australian Security Intelligence Organisation (ASIO) (Attorney

General 2015). ASIO's involvement was enabled by the Anti-People Smuggling and Other Measures Act 2010, which amended the definition of 'security' in the ASIO Act to define people smuggling operations as a threat to Australia's border security.

The Detection, Interception and Transfer Task Group is led by the Maritime Border Command (MBC) of the Australian Border Force. Like the OSB which it contributes to, the MBC is a military-led civil agency combining personnel and resources from the ABF and the ADF. The MBC is led by a Rear Admiral of the Australian Navy appointed from the Department of Defence, who is also sworn in as an ABF officer to give authority over MBC personnel from both agencies. ADF contributions to OSB through the MBC are made through Operation Resolute, which aims to 'protect Australia's maritime domain from security threats' including 'illegal maritime arrivals' (Australian Department of Defence 2016).

The Offshore Detention and Returns Task Group, managed by DIBP, runs the detention camps known as Regional Processing Centres (RPCs) in Nauru and Papua New Guinea, using a combination of department staff and contractors. In 2016, the primary contractor for the operation of the RPCs was Broadspectrum (previously known as Transfield), with Wilson Security as a subcontractor providing guards for the detention centres. Health services in the RPCs were contracted to International Health and Medical Services (IHMS), while other welfare services were contracted to the Salvation Army and Save the Children, before being taken over by Broadspectrum in late 2016.

Each of the Australian agencies tasked with aspects of Operation Sovereign Borders maintain their own regional networks with similar agencies in other states of Southeast Asia and the Pacific. These networks have contributed to the diffusion of techniques and tactics of migration border policing and have been used by Australia to promote criminalisation of migrant smuggling to coordinate counter-smuggling operations. In a study of cooperation between Australia and Indonesia to prevent and deter movement of asylum seekers to Australia, Nethery and Gordyn (2014) describe the bilateral relationships Australia has fostered with neighbouring states as processes of 'incentivised policy transfer' of techniques of migration border security.

The Australian Federal Police (AFP) takes part in a regional law enforcement network known as the Joint Management Group on People Smuggling (JMG) with counterparts from Malaysian, Pakistani, Sri Lankan, Thai and Vietnamese agencies. Annual meetings rotate between the member countries and are a further chance for senior law enforcement officers to network and build personal relationships that contribute to the implementation of bilateral and multilateral agreements. The AFP also runs an international Law Enforcement Cooperation Programme (LECP), with a focus on countering transnational organised crime in the Asia Pacific. The LECP was established as part of efforts to counter trafficking in illicit drugs, but expanded from 2008 with funding from the Australian government's New Policy Initiatives to counter people smuggling.

Australian agencies the AFP and ASIS have engaged in activities aimed at directly disrupting migrant smuggling operations in neighbouring countries since 2000, which are now grouped under the Disruption and Deterrence task group of OSB. Disruption and Deterrence operations take a variety of forms, and many of the details remain obscure since these extra-territorial activities have generally been conducted without substantial public or parliamentary disclosure. The AFP operates a Joint Services People Smuggling Strike Team with DIBP that coordinates disruption activities, primarily focused on investigating the organisational and financial networks of smugglers. The AFP also seeks to disrupt the recruitment of crew members for people smuggling operations. AFP officers were involved in running public meetings in fishing areas of Indonesia designed to deter fishers from acting as crew for boats attempting to reach Australia. The AFP also maintains a network of informants among smuggling organisations in the region. Information from this network has been used to arrest smugglers for prosecution in Australia, or used in efforts in transit countries such as Indonesia to directly prevent boats from departing or reaching Australia. In 2001, the AFP and ASIS were accused of paying local agents to sabotage boats, although the government has denied that either agency was directly involved. Giving evidence to a Select Committee Inquiry, AFP Commissioner Keelty stated that '[t]he AFP, in tasking the INP to do anything that would disrupt the movement of people smugglers, has never asked—nor would it ask—them to do anything illegal… The difficulty is that once we ask them to do it, we have to largely leave it in their hands as to how best they do it' (Stewart 2004). In 2015, according to witnesses and Indonesian authorities, ASIS officers paid a crew to return to Indonesia after their boat carrying asylum seekers was intercepted by Australian Customs in international waters (Roberts 2015).

High level meetings between immigration officials in Australia and Malaysia are convened through the Joint Working Group on Transnational Crime, originally established in 2009 as the Malaysia-Australia Working

Group on People Smuggling and Trafficking in Persons (Xinhua 2009). Speaking at a ceremony for the transfer of the first of two Bay Class patrol vessel to Malaysia in 2015, Australia's Minister for Immigration and Border Protection Peter Dutton (2015) praised the bilateral cooperation between the two countries for contributing to his government's effort to 'stop the boats'. Dutton emphasised the significance of joint maritime border security operations in the Malacca Strait, code-named Operation Redback, which he described as 'a targeted maritime operation aimed at deterring and disrupting people smuggling operations'. Between 2011 and 2016, the Australian Border Force and Malaysian Maritime Enforcement Agency (MMEA) have conducted seven rounds of joint operations under the Redback programme. In 2016, the joint operation was preceded by a training program on vessel search techniques conducted by the ABF for MMEA staff. Operation Redback focuses on maritime law enforcement in response to threats to border security, which DIBP (2016b) identified as including 'people smuggling, human trafficking and piracy and robbery at sea'.

As migration borders are securitised, the surveillance and screening of migrants converges with the existing military and para-military activity of counter-terrorism operations. In comments to the Malaysian press, MMEA Director-General Ahmad Puzi emphasised the role of the operations in preventing the movement of international terrorists into Malaysia, a threat that he linked to irregular migration. According to Puzi, Operation Redback had begun with a joint interest in preventing 'human smuggling and the entry of immigrants from West Asia' and was important because of 'new threats posed by international terrorists' (The Sun Daily 2016a). Speaking on an earlier occasion, Puzi also emphasised the role of MMEA in protecting Malaysia from international terrorist threats, which he linked to undocumented migrants from Afghanistan, Sri Lanka and Somalia: 'We must be careful, investigate and pay attention on how they try to enter our country illegally and should not overlook them. We must not compromise on the safety of Malaysia' (The Sun Daily 2016b). Puzi said in November 2015 that there had been no indication of irregular migration routes restarting, but that the agency was sharing information with neighbouring countries and actively patrolling Malaysian waters bordering the territories of Indonesia and Thailand. Puzi declared that if there were reports of boats carrying migrants with irregular status from Myanmar and Bangladesh via Thailand, the agency would 'swing into action' to 'not only deploy ships and boats but aircraft as well, to thwart the influx of the illegals' (The Sun Daily 2015).

States in Southeast Asia have existing interests in expanding their capacity to patrol and control maritime borders and to manage migration. These interests overlap with the interest of the Australian state in extending its securitised migration border regime beyond Australian territory, primarily to prevent and deter the movement of asylum seekers to Australia.

Screening Asylum Seekers

The issue of managing the movements and status of asylum seekers does not have the same level of political priority and public resonance in any other state of the Asia-Pacific as it does in Australia. States in Southeast Asia have been persuaded to participate in joint operations to target irregular movements of asylum seekers and other migrants where these coincide with existing security concerns of these states to control borders and migration in general. Similarly, in the Pacific, Nauru and Papua New Guinea have been persuaded to host detention and processing centres under the effective control of Australian authorities and contractors in return for substantial aid packages and direct income from the centres. However, where Australia's approach to deterring movements of asylum seekers conflicts has come into conflict with the general border security and sovereignty of other states, as it has with the repeated incursions of Australian Navy vessels into Indonesian territory, the instrumental basis of cooperation has quickly broken down.

UNHCR and NGOs advocating for refugees and asylum seekers have advocated the development of regionally integrated refugee status assessment and protection mechanisms, but there has been little progress in this direction. Australia, committed to policies of extra-territorial border enforcement and deterrence, has refused to support any policies that might be perceived to create incentives for asylum seekers to travel to Southeast Asia in the hope of onward travel to Australia. States in Southeast Asia have also been reluctant to adopt any system of refugee status assessment that might be interpreted as imposing protection obligations or costs on the state, and have instead largely maintained policies of informal tolerance for undocumented asylum seekers, combined inconsistently with arbitrary enforcement of migration regulations.

Like other Western countries, Australia has increased security and screening requirements for regular passenger services to the point where it is very difficult for migrants, including asylum seekers and refugees, to reach Australian ports of entry without approved travel documents and visas.

As asylum seekers have resorted to paying smugglers to travel by boat to Australia, successive governments have introduced extra-territorial screening mechanisms as part of increasingly militarised border security operation within and beyond Australia's territorial waters.

In October 2012, the Gillard Labor government of Australia introduced 'enhanced screening' processes for asylum seekers on boats intercepted travelling from Sri Lanka. Under the new protocols, asylum seekers would be screened at sea by teleconference with Immigration officers to decide whether they had a valid basis for an asylum claim. The officers' decisions were made on the basis of the response to the questions: 'What are your reasons for coming to Australia? Do you have any other reasons for coming to Australia? Would you like to add anything else?' If the immigration officer did not believe the migrant had clearly and credibly stated a well-founded fear of persecution, they would be 'screened out' and returned to Sri Lanka without further opportunity to lodge a claim for asylum. Under Coalition governments from 2013, Australia's screening out procedures have been combined into the range of techniques used by Operation Sovereign Borders to prevent and deter the arrival of irregular migrants at Australia's territorial borders, including for the purposes of claiming asylum. As of early 2016, the enhanced screening process had only been applied to migrants intercepted on routes from South Asia, primarily carrying asylum-seekers from Sri Lanka.

The majority of irregular migrants on sea routes between Sri Lanka and Australia are Tamils displaced or fleeing persecution in the aftermath of the defeat of the Liberation Tigers of Tamil Eelam by Sri Lankan government forces in the North of the country. The Australian government has demonstrated an unwillingness to recognise refugee claims by Sri Lankan Tamils since the end of the conflict and has taken steps to increase cooperation with the Sri Lankan government, including on border protection and efforts to counter irregular migration. The program of cooperation to return intercepted asylum seekers to Sri Lanka was introduced by Australia, despite evidence that returned asylum seekers were frequently detained and tortured by the Sri Lankan Police, Criminal Investigation Department and military (Immigration and Refugee Board of Canada 2013; Doherty 2012). Cooperation continued even after reports that people screened out and returned by Australian forces continued to be detained on arrival by Sri Lankan authorities and faced prosecution for leaving the country without permission (Doherty 2016).

The Australian enhanced screening process is similar in function to the so-called 'Shout Test' applied by the US coastguard to routinely return irregular migrants intercepted in Caribbean waters unless the migrants manage to shout out a claim for asylum as they are being detained and returned. Both are techniques designed to maintain a superficial claim of adherence to international norms of non-refoulement, while in practice making it difficult or impossible for asylum seekers to lodge their claims.

Under Operation Sovereign Borders since 2013, asylum seekers arriving by sea from Indonesia have been intercepted and turned back, without claims for asylum being screened or assessed. Australian agencies have used a variety of methods to turn back asylum seekers, including towing boats back to Indonesian waters and leaving them with limited fuel, paying boat crews to return to Indonesia, and forcibly embarking asylum seekers in life-rafts off the coast of Indonesia. By facilitating the return of undocumented migrants to Indonesian territory without permission from Indonesian authorities these actions by Australia fit the definition of 'Smuggling in Migrants' under the UN Smuggling Protocol, with the aggravating factor that the migrants being smuggled are being transported against their will (See Amnesty International 2016; ABC News 2016). The Indonesian government has strongly protested the violations of their territorial sovereignty by Australian Navy vessels entering Indonesian waters in the process of turning back boats. Despite international condemnation, the 'policy of turnbacks' has bipartisan support from both the Liberal/National Coalition and Labour parties in Australia.

The policy of turnbacks has also received qualified support from some members of the humanitarian NGO community in Australia. Father Frank Brennan (2016), despite previously using his high public profile and position in the Catholic Church to support acceptance of asylum seekers, argued that refugee supporters and advocates should accept turnbacks of boats to discourage asylum seekers from taking dangerous journeys. The leader of Welcome to Australia, an NGO providing settlement services to refugees, also publicly supported a bipartisan policy of boat turnbacks to 'neutralise' a divisive debate by 'closing the ocean route to Australia' (Chilcott 2015). Writing in The Australian, Save the Children Australia CEO Paul Ronalds (2015) made a more reluctant argument for the same conclusion, that organisations supporting refugees should embrace the opportunity for consensus by abandoning active support for the principle of non-refoulement:

> Although we may not like turnbacks, it is clear the policy is here to stay. Now we and other advocates for the rights of asylum-seekers must look beyond this aspect of the policy and concentrate our efforts on implementing a genuine regional framework, which we have long called for.

Ronalds urged those supporting asylum seekers to seek pragmatic opportunities in the emerging consensus between the major parties, including through lobbying for increased resettlement quotas. These NGOs, with moral and financial investment in formally managed approaches to refugee resettlement, have been persuaded to support arbitrary enforcement against irregular movement of asylum seekers out of a combination of political pragmatism and carceral humanitarian arguments that border enforcement is required to 'save lives at sea'.

The policies of 'screening out' migrants for return, turning back boats and imposing carrier sanctions, along with other tactics and techniques of disruption, deterrence and prevention, are part of what Hyndman and Mountz (2008) have called neo-refoulement. Neo-refoulement leaves the legal rights of asylum intact in states that have ratified the Refugee Convention and Protocol, but works to prevent asylum-seekers from being able to claim their rights to protection by preventing them from reaching the territory of the state. As techniques of migration border management, these tactics of extra-territorial screening and externalisation of border controls have diffused beyond the agencies of the rich states to which the label of neo-refoulement directly applies. In the regional context of Southeast Asia and the Pacific, developing states that form the geographical and economic periphery to Australia's border protection efforts have been drawn into an extended regime of migration border controls in pursuit of their own interests. For these states, the motivations for limiting freedom of movement for asylum seekers have little in common with the particularly politicised status of the issue in Australia, but rather, are subsumed within concern for the wider issue of irregular migration, primarily focused on the issue of how best to socially control and economically exploit populations of migrant workers.

Of the states in Southeast Asia, only the Philippines has a functioning system for registration of asylum seekers and refugee status determination. Other states effectively delegate responsibility by allowing UNHCR to conduct refugee status determination in their territories. This includes Cambodia, which is the only state in Southeast Asia other than the Philippines to be a signatory to the Refugee Convention and Protocol.

In addition to advocating for other states in Southeast Asia to sign and ratify the Refugee Convention and Protocol, UNHCR has made significant efforts to lobby states to establish independent refugee screening and status determination procedures. This lobbying has a basis in international law in that the requirement of non-refoulement is now considered a peremptory norm even for states not signatory to the Refugee Convention and Protocol. Therefore, even states not offering permanent sanctuary to refugees under the terms of the Convention and Protocol are required to develop processes to avoid returning refugees to states where they face persecution. All states are also required under the UN Convention against Torture not to return migrants to states where they face torture, regardless of refugee status.

There is also a pragmatic side to UNHCR's lobbying for Southeast Asian states to establish independent refugee screening processes, in that UNHCR seeks to persuade states that the presence in their territory of asylum seekers with irregular migration status is an unavoidable fact, and that establishing refugee screening processes will enable states to better monitor and govern this population. In 2015, UNHCR Thailand organised a study tour for Thai immigration officers to Hong Kong to understand how the territory had implemented refugee status determination and protection systems despite not being a signatory to the Refugee Convention and Protocol.[1] In an interview, a staff member with Asylum Access Thailand described the country's approach to refugees and asylum seekers as 'very much below minimum standards', with considerable room for improvement under existing Thai laws even without ratification of the Refugee Convention. The Asylum Access staff member had recently attended a roundtable on refugee screening processes organised by UNHCR. Examples of positive practices that could be applied in Thailand had included presentations on refugee processing and protection in Zambia and Indonesia's process for alternatives to detention for children of migrants and unaccompanied minors, who are transferred to shelters operated by Church World Service.

In 2017, Indonesia introduced a Presidential Decree that provides a clear legal basis, for the first time, to clarify the responsibilities of government departments for asylum seekers, including search and rescue operations. The decree had been lobbied for by Indonesian human rights organisations over a period of several years and had existed in draft form since 2010. As signed by President Joko Widodo on 31 December 2016, the decree provided for government agencies to develop further policy and take responsibility for the detection, shelter, security, and supervision of asylum seekers and refugees arriving into Indonesia. This work was to be coordinated by the Ministry of Foreign Affairs and in particular required agencies dealing with maritime search and rescue to actively respond to reports of boats carrying refugees and to disembark passengers from boats in distress. The regulations provide a translation into Indonesian of the internationally recognised definition of refugees from the 1951 Convention and required that refugees be treated in accordance with 'generally accepted international regulations' in cooperation with UNHCR. However, the decree still carries the presumption of detention for most refugees and asylum seekers, with release into community shelters only mandated for minors and those who are sick, pregnant or elderly (Sekretariat Kabinet Republik Indonesia 2017).

The decree was welcomed by representatives of SUAKA, Indonesia's human rights advocacy organisation for refugees and asylum seekers, as a positive step away from treating refugees as illegal immigrants. By incorporating the internationally accepted definition of refugees, the regulation was seen as a hopeful step forward in recognising the basic rights of asylum seekers and refugees. SUAKA also welcomed the clarification of official roles and responsibilities, especially regarding search and rescue, since in the absence of a clear mandate local authorities had tended to act conservatively and to prioritise existing mandates on border control and security, which had contributed to boats carrying asylum seekers being pushed back to sea (SUAKA 2017).

Screening Workers

The accessibility and criteria of screening processes for migrant workers are uneven across the region of Southeast Asia and the Pacific. In each of the destination countries surveyed below, restrictive conditions and cumbersome or expensive processes for applying for work permits were drivers of irregularity. Where concerted efforts have been made by government agencies to improve accessibility and efficiency of registration processes for workers, there has been progress in improving the prevalence of regular status among migrants.

Australia

Unlike other countries in the region, Australia has no visa category designed for the admission of low skilled migrant workers. Instead, labour migration to Australia has developed in an ad hoc manner through the expansion of the size and purpose of multiple visa categories to accommodate migrant workers, including: international students with limited work rights and temporary graduate workers; those on skilled temporary work visas (subclass 457), working holiday visas (subclass 417) and the seasonal workers program; in addition to those without regular work or migration status. As described in Chap. 3, the majority of the 736,124 temporary migrant workers in Australia with regular work and migration status in 2014 were international students or working holidaymakers.

The Australian government has used the conditions of temporary labour migration visas to channel migrants towards industries and locations in rural Australia with labour shortages. The Seasonal Workers Program for specified Pacific Islands aims to bring migrant workers to work in seasonal agricultural jobs. Additional agricultural labour is provided by working holiday visa-holders under a provision where, in order to qualify for an extension of one-year visas for an additional year, working holiday migrants are required to show that they have worked for at least three months in specified industries, primarily agricultural, in rural Australia. A similar condition was imposed in a new class of visa offered to asylum seekers as an alternative to Temporary Protection Visas from 2015. Asylum seekers in Australia who were classed as 'illegal maritime arrivals' were able to apply for Safe Haven Enterprise Visas, with temporary rights to remain and work in Australia on the condition that they found employment in specified rural industries. Conditional temporary visas for working holidaymakers and asylum seekers have been used in part to make up a shortfall in the numbers of migrants taking up places in the Seasonal Workers Programme, which were lower than expected.

Thailand

Thailand has consistently relied on ad hoc temporary systems of migrant worker registration since the 1990s. Over that period, the population of migrant workers has steadily grown to over 3 million, while the number who hold regular immigration status and work permits has fluctuated depending on the registration scheme in force at the time. As Martin (2007, 5) suggested in a report for the ILO, 'Thai migrant worker policy is best described as a series of employer-initiated registrations of foreign workers that defer their removal'.

Thailand's migration regime remains governed by 1979 legislation that makes no allowance for labour migration except in a limited number of skilled professions. Exceptions to the general legislative ban on labour migration may be extended by cabinet regulations under Article 17 of the Immigration Act, and this is the mechanism that has been used since the 1990s to respond to the economic reality of Thailand's dependence on migrant labour. The ad hoc system of labour registration introduced since 1992 overlaps with Thailand's approach to registering and issuing identity cards for non-Thai residents. The system of identity cards is an extension of that introduced in 1936 for non-Thai residents, primarily urban Chinese workers, and for Thai citizens since 1962. The cards are colour coded according to a classification system defined by cabinet resolutions to grant either limited rights of residence or temporary deferral of deportation to particular groups of migrants with irregular status present in Thailand.

Attempts to introduce formal management of labour migration in Thailand have generally been temporary and short term and have had to take account of the large population of irregular migrant workers already in the country. In 1992, a limited scheme was introduced for migrants from Myanmar working in ten of Thailand's border provinces. Only 706 work permit registrations were completed, but over 100,000 identity cards were issued by immigration authorities. These purple colour-coded cards conveyed no official legal status, identifying the holder as *Lop-Nee-Khao-Kuang* or 'illegal immigrant', but gave temporary protection from deportation. Workers were forbidden from travelling outside the province in which their identity card was issued and were required to live in accommodation provided by their employers. A broader scheme introduced in 1996 allowed employers to register workers in 43 provinces across 11 industries and resulted in 303,988 two-year work permits issued to migrants, 88% from Myanmar, who had often already been working in Thailand for several years (Martin 2007, 2; Pongsawat 2007, 176–177).

The economic downturn following the Asian Financial Crisis saw registrations and renewals of work permits suspended in 1997 and 1998, with the Ministry of Labour announcing plans to reduce the number of migrant workers by 300,000 per year. This was a period of heightened vulnerability for migrants as the suspension of the formal management system of registration was accompanied by an intensification of arbitrary enforcement with workplace raids and street operations targeting unregistered workers. However, as economic conditions returned to normal so did the policy balance, with registration and renewal of work permits reopened in 1999 and 2000.

With the election victory of businessman Thaksin Shinawatra's populist Thai Rak Thai party in 2001, the policy balance shifted further towards informal tolerance and formal management, with expanded opportunities for employers to register migrant workers. The shift reflected the close connections of the new government with Thailand's business community, particularly in the expanding export industries and construction, which heavily depended on migrant labour. The policy approach from 2001 to 2003 followed the same basic system of temporary work permits that had been followed since 1996. This remained a system for migrants with irregular status already in the country to register with the government and gain temporary permission to work, albeit with heavy restrictions on their effective legal rights. Workers remained confined to their province of registration and bound to specific employers. The registration process was open to employers rather than workers, and employers often retained workers' identity cards, leaving workers vulnerable to arrest and deportation outside their worksites. Registration was expanded to 37 provinces, with 568,245 migrant workers registered in 2001 for temporary 6-month permits, renewable for a further 6 months. However, registration was far from universal and, of the 409,339 permits issued in 2002, only around 350,000 were extensions of previous permits, implying that many workers lapsed back into irregular status (Martin 2007, 3). In 2004, the Thai government shifted its approach, launching a nationwide process for workers to register individually rather than relying on employers to initiate registration. The scheme proved popular, with 1,284,920 migrants and 103,100 dependents registering for the new pink-coded Tor Ror 38/1 identity cards. Approximately 70% of those registering were from Myanmar, with 15% from Cambodia, and 15% from Lao PDR. Of those migrant workers who registered for identity cards, 849,552 were granted work permits. Their status was still only semi-regular though, with their categorisation in Thai law translating to 'illegal entry and work while awaiting for deportation' (MMN 2014, 10).

In the same period, Thailand negotiated Memoranda of Understanding with neighbouring countries to facilitate the establishment of regular channels for labour migration. The first memorandum with Lao PDR in October 2002 was soon followed by similar agreements with Cambodia and Myanmar in May and June 2003. These MOUs remain in force, with the addition of an agreement with Vietnam signed in 2015. In addition to initiating government-to-government channels for facilitating regular labour migration, the MOU set out processes for regularising migrant workers already working in Thailand who were nationals of the neighbouring countries. Registration of migrant workers already in the country was conducted in two stages. In the first stage, workers registered for a non-Thai identity card, the Tor Ror 38/1, and an associated temporary work permit. To receive this document, a worker needed to show employment in Thailand and have the support of their employer to register, but did not need any additional documentation to prove identity or nationality. This process allowed a path to regularisation for undocumented workers and was taken up by more than 2 million workers by the end of 2015. The second stage of Nationality Verification was conducted in partnership with the governments of the neighbouring states that are the largest origin countries for migrant workers in Thailand: Myanmar, Cambodia and Laos. At the conclusion of this process, workers would receive a temporary passport issued by their country of origin permitting them to reside and work in Thailand.

The implementation of the regularisation agenda detailed in the MOUs was briefly interrupted in 2014 by the 22 May military coup leading to the formation of the National Council for Peace and Order (NCPO) military government in Thailand. As described in the following chapter on carceral responses, the military government made public statements threatening a crackdown on migrant workers with irregular status. Following a mass exodus of Cambodian migrant workers and a backlash from employers, the government reconsidered its approach. Instead of embarking on mass arrests and deportations on the scale that had been threatened, the government moved quickly to open One Stop Service Centres in provinces with large populations of migrant workers to facilitate issuing identity cards, work permits, health checks and insurance registration in a single appointment. In 2014, around 1.6 million migrant workers registered through the centres. The events of 2014 demonstrated the structural significance of migrant labour for Thailand's economy. In this context, policies based on a securitising rhetoric of repudiating migrant workers could not survive long in the face of economic dependence on migrant labour.

A Thailand country-specialist on labour migration at the IOM praised the One Stop Service Centre initiative as being beneficial to migrants by speeding up the process of registration and making it more accessible. However, the IOM staffer described the subsequent process of Nationality Verification carried out in partnership with neighbouring governments as failing on multiple counts:

> It takes a long number of months, years in fact; it costs a lot of money; it's been hijacked by brokers to a large extent. At the end of the day, the migrants may not even receive or be able to access the benefits that should come with the regular status. So often what happens is they drop out at various stages of the process and slip back into irregular status.

The early period of NCPO rule also saw a crackdown on smuggling of migrants through Thailand, including the arrest of military personnel and police accused of involvement in smuggling. The crackdown was prompted by the discovery of mass graves near migrant camps in the South of Thailand amid public revelations of abuses suffered by Rohingya asylum-seekers and Bangladeshi migrants in the course of their journeys through Thailand.

Malaysia

Malaysia's policies towards irregular migrant workers have followed the cycle between informal tolerance and arbitrary enforcement to an even greater extent than Thailand, with fewer opportunities created for formal labour migration or regularisation. As described in Chap. 3, Malaysia's economy is structurally dependent on migrant labour, with as many as 7 million migrant workers in the country, of whom 2.1 million hold work permits. Devadason and Meng (2013, 20) note that Malaysia's ad hoc approach to migration policy follows an oscillation between crackdowns and laxity in which 'retrenchments, deportations and migration bans are quickly followed with return migration and lifting of those bans within short periods of time'.

As in Thailand, Malaysia's legislative framework makes little allowance for unskilled labour migration. The sector remains governed by the 1955 Employment Act and 1959 Immigration Act, inherited from the British administration and the newly independent state of Malaya respectively, which were aimed at limiting and restricting foreign labour. Following the formation of Malaysia, further measures in the 1968 Employment Restriction Act limited the mobility of migrant workers and restricting the sectors and occupations in which they are permitted to work. Kaur (2014, 348) argues that migration policies in this period 'were not aimed at addressing labour shortages, but rather focused on expelling Indian and Chinese non-citizens'.

During the New Economic Policy period 1971–90, government policy aimed to reduce the number of non-citizens working in Malaysia, with many Indian and Chinese workers deported. Labour policy has continued to be based on the assumption that Malaysia should reduce dependence on foreign labour in order to promote local employment, and that employment of migrant workers is at best a temporary measure (Kaur 2014, 348–349). However, these policy assumptions are out of step with the economic realities of demand for labour in a situation of near full employment for Malaysian citizens, who are generally unwilling to do the kinds of jobs that employ migrant workers. In 2001, a strike by Indonesian factory workers who had been employed without work permits led Prime Minister Mahathir Mohammed to describe migrant workers as a security threat and introduce new laws allowing for caning and deportation of male migrant workers. A diplomatic confrontation with Indonesia and the return of large numbers of Indonesian workers led the Malaysian government to solicit migrant workers from other countries including from South and Central Asia. The laws allowing for harsh punishment of undocumented migrant workers remain in effect, including fines, deportation and caning for men (Devadason and Meng 2013, 23).

Attempts to respond to labour shortages by facilitating and regulating labour migration have been promoted at times by government policies. The Committee for the Recruitment of Foreign Workers introduced the first formal scheme in 1982 for employers to recruit migrant workers, primarily to meet demand for plantation labour. However, the scheme was unable to meet the scale of demand, and irregular migration continued to grow in response to labour shortages. The main features of the current system of labour migration were introduced by the 1991 Comprehensive Policy on the Recruitment of Foreign Workers, with an annual government levy for each migrant worker and permits that restricted workers to particular employers, regions and occupations (Kaur 2014, 349). The system of government levies remains in place as an attempt to use a market mechanisms to limit reliance on migrant labour, but Devadason and Meng (2013, 20) argue the policy has failed in this regard, as even after amended laws in 2009 required employers rather than workers to pay the levy, employers have continued to pass the costs on to workers.

An amnesty on harsh punishments for undocumented workers as part of a general registration scheme for migrant workers in July–August 2011 saw 1.3 million migrant workers with irregular status come forward, despite uncertainty about whether they would be allowed to stay in the country. Eventually the government announced that they would be given permits to work in high demand sectors of manufacturing, plantations, agriculture, construction and services (Devadason and Meng 2013, 20).

Applying for official permission to employ migrant workers in Malaysia via regular channels can be time consuming and expensive, so many employers take shortcuts which result in workers having irregular status. Employers wishing to hire migrant workers must apply to the Ministry of Home Affairs and show that they have advertised and made efforts to hire workers locally. The Ministry will then approve a number of workers to be recruited, specifying the source country and recruitment agency to be used. The need to apply for formal approval before initiating recruitment and migration means that the process takes many months, and is impractical for employers who often need to increase staff at short notice. To fill the gap, employers prefer to hire migrants with irregular status who are already in Malaysia and available to start work immediately. Recruitment of migrant workers in Malaysia is primarily organised by private labour supply companies, of which there are more than 2000 operating with little regulation.

Singapore

Allocation of permits to employ foreign workers in different economic sectors is used as an instrument of developmental planning by the state in Singapore. Singapore's developmental state has shown a strong concern for maintaining social stability based on a multi-racial society in which the Chinese majority coexists with significant minorities of Malay and Indian ethnicity (Ooi 2005). As part of maintaining the racialised economic segmentation and hierarchy that is integral to Singapore's social structure, the state allocates work permits from different source countries to specific sectors and occupations.

Labour migration to Singapore is permitted under three main visa classes, stratified by salary level. Professional employees earning over 3600 Singapore Dollars per month are covered by the Employment Pass. Mid-level skilled staff earning between 2200 and 3600 Singapore Dollars are covered by the S-Pass. Lower-skilled workers are covered by the general Work Permit, applying to any worker earning less than 2200 Singapore Dollars per month.

Eligibility for Work Permit visas is restricted by source country and economic sector. Employers in the manufacturing and services[2] sectors who wish to recruit migrant workers are restricted to hiring from Malaysia, China and 'North Asian Sources' including Hong Kong, Macau, Taiwan and South Korea. While workers from Malaysia and North Asian Sources are eligible to extend their visas indefinitely, migrants from China are restricted to a maximum of ten years residency. For the construction, marine (ship-building and repair) and process[3] sectors, the list of permitted source countries is expanded to included so-called 'Non-Traditional Sources': India, Sri Lanka, Thailand, Bangladesh, Myanmar and Philippines. Like workers from China, migrants from this category of Non-Traditional Sources are restricted to ten years in Singapore (Ministry of Manpower 2016).

Work permits are also limited to a specific employer, so that workers who change employers become irregular in their status, in addition to those who work in a different economic sector or industry to that specified on their permit. According to a staff member at the advocacy group Transient Workers Count Too, interviewed in 2015, both situations are reasonably common, since migrant workers report they can earn more money and have better control over the terms and conditions of their work by working informally than they have access to in their government-approved jobs. Some workers continued to work for their mandated employer while taking on additional work informally for other employers. Others were willing to take the risk of working entirely outside the conditions of their permits in order to escape adverse treatment or conditions in their original employment.

Conclusion

This chapter analysed approaches to migration across Southeast Asia and the Pacific in terms of three modes of governance: informal tolerance, formal management and arbitrary enforcement. Each country in the region has displayed elements of each mode of migration governance in varying proportions at different times. Policy changes advocated by international organisations and Western states, including Australia, have generally emphasised a transition from informal tolerance of irregular migration to formal management. However, while formal management of migration tends to be imagined and justified in liberal humanitarian terms as a package including liberalised channels for regular labour migration and humanitarian protection measures for asylum seekers, the implementation of formalisation has tended to prioritise securitisation and criminalisation of irregular migration.

This two-speed process of formalisation, neglecting progress on access to regular and safe channels for migration and protection, has resulted in migration governance across the region being pushed toward arbitrary enforcement.

Notes

1. Although China signed and ratified the Refugee Convention and Protocol, the former British colony of Hong Kong did not. Under the One Country Two Systems approach, Hong Kong has retained many aspects of its separate economic, political, and legal systems, including not applying China's ratification of the Convention and Protocol to the territory of Hong Kong.
2. Broadly defined to include Financial, insurance, real estate and business services; Transport, storage and communications services; Commerce (retail and wholesale trade); Community, social and personal services (excluding domestic workers); Hotels; Restaurants, coffee shops, food courts and other approved food establishments.
3. Includes manufacturing of petroleum, petrochemicals, specialty chemicals and pharmaceutical products.

Bibliography

ABC News. 2016. Fact Check: Would Paying People Smugglers to Turn Back Boats be Illegal? http://www.abc.net.au/news/2015-07-07/fact-check-paying-people-smugglers-to-turn-back-boats-illegal/6566184

Acharya, Amitav. 2004. How Ideas Spread: Whose Norms Matter? Norm Localization and Institutional Change in Asian Regionalism. *International Organization* 58 (2): 239–275.

Amnesty International. 2016. *By Hook or By Crook: Australia's Abuse of Asylum-Seekers at Sea.* https://www.amnesty.org.nz/sites/default/files/By_Hook_or_by_Crook_Australias_abuse_of_asylum_seekers_at_sea.pdf

ANAO (Australian National Audit Office). 2009. Management of the Movement Alert List. https://www.anao.gov.au/work/performanceaudit/management-movement-alert-list

Attorney General of Australia. 2015. Portfolio Budget Statement: Australian Security Intelligence Organisation. https://www.ag.gov.au/Publications/Budgets/Budget2015-16/Documents/Portfolio-budget-statements/PBS-ASIO-2015-16.pdf

Australian Department of Defence. 2016. Operation Resolute. http://www.defence.gov.au/operations/BorderProtection/

Battistella, Graziano. 2007. Migration without Borders: A Long Way to Go in the Asian Region. In *Migration Without Borders: Essays on the Free Movement of People*, ed. Antoine Pécoud and Paul de Guchteneire. New York: Berghahn.

Betts, Alexander. 2009. *Protection by Persuasion: International Cooperation in the Refugee Regime*. Cornell University Press.

Brennan, Frank. 2016. The Cruelty of Offshore Detention is Compounded by Its Pointlessness. *ABC*. http://www.abc.net.au/religion/articles/2016/02/04/4400032.htm

Chilcott, Brad. 2015. End Uncertainty on Refugees. *Brisbane Times*, 3 March 2015. https://www.brisbanetimes.com.au/national/queensland/enduncertainty-on-refugees-20150303-13tn8a.html

Cronin, Kathryn. 1999. Controlling Immigration: Australian Legislation and Practice. *Reform 19* (75): 6–9.

Devadason, Evelyn Shyamala, and Chan Wai Meng. 2013. Policies and Laws Regulating Migrant Workers in Malaysia: A Critical Appraisal. *Journal of Contemporary Asia* 44 (1): 19–35.

DIBP. 2014a. FOI Release to Sean Parnell on Movement Alert List. https://www.border.gov.au/AccessandAccountability/Documents/FOI/FA140100764.pdf

———. 2014b. Asylum Statistics—Australia: Quarterly Tables—June Quarter 2014.

———. 2015a. *Strategy 2020*. https://www.border.gov.au/CorporateInformation/Documents/strategy-2020.pdf

———. 2015b. Border Technology Strategy. Presentation to DIBP Industry Summit. https://www.border.gov.au/Engagingwithindustry/Documents/industry-summit/border-technology-strategy.pdf

———. 2016a. Movement Alert List Factsheet. https://www.border.gov.au/about/corporate/information/fact-sheets/77mal

———. 2016b. ABF Assists Malaysian Maritime Enforcement Agency in Maritime Security Operation. Australian Border Force Press Release. 29 June 2016. http://newsroom.border.gov.au/releases/b504bc51-9d8e-47bb-a7c1-d62caf14a85a

———. 2016c. Subclass 457 Quarterly Report: Quarter Ending at 30 June 2016. https://www.border.gov.au/ReportsandPublications/Documents/statistics/457-quarterly-report-30-06-2016.pdf

Doherty, Ben. 2012. We Live in Fear Every Day. *The Age*, 24 July 2012. http://www.theage.com.au/world/we-live-in-fear-every-day-20120723-22koc.html

———. 2016. Asylum Seeker Forcibly Returned by Australia says his Refugee Claim was Ignored. *The Guardian*, 17 May 2016. https://www.theguardian.com/australia-news/2016/may/18/asylum-seeker-forcibly-returned-by-australia-says-his-refugee-claim-was-ignored

Dutton, Peter. 2015. Stronger Regional Maritime Security. Minister for Immigration and Border Protection Press Release. 27 February 2015. http://www.minister.border.gov.au/peterdutton/2015/Pages/stronger-regional-maritime-security.aspx

Emmers, Ralf, Beth K. Greener, and Nicholas Thomas. 2008. Securitising Human Trafficking in the Asia-Pacific: Regional Organisations and Response Strategies. In *Security and Migration in Asia: The Dynamics of Securitisation*, ed. Melissa G. Curley and Wong Siu-lun. Oxon: Routledge.

Hughes, Steve. 2002. Coming in from the Cold: Labour, the ILO, and the International Labour Standards Regime. In *Global Governance: Critical Perspectives*, ed. Rorden Wilkinson and Steve Hughes, 155–171. London: Routledge.

Hyndman, Jennifer, and Alison Mountz. 2008. Another Brick in the Wall? Neo-Refoulement and the Externalization of Asylum by Australia and Europe. *Government and Opposition* 43 (2): 249–269.

Immigration and Refugee Board of Canada. 2013. Responses to Information Requests (August 2011–January 2013). Ottawa: Research Directorate, Immigration and Refugee Board of Canada. https://www.justice.gov/sites/default/files/eoir/legacy/2014/03/06/LKA104245.E.pdf

Kaur, Amarjit. 2014. Managing Labour Migration in Malaysia: Guest Worker Programs and the Regularisation of Irregular Labour Migrants as a Policy Instrument. *Asian Studies Review 38* (3): 345–366.

Martin, Phillip. 2007. The Economic Contribution of Migrant Workers to Thailand: Towards Policy Development. *ILO Sub-regional Office for East Asia.* http://natlex.ilo.ch/wcmsp5/groups/public/---asia/---ro-bangkok/documents/publication/wcms_098230.pdf

Medhora, Shalailah. 2015. 'Nope, Nope, Nope': Tony Abbott says Australia will Take no Rohingya Refugees. *The Guardian*, 21 May 2015. https://www.theguardian.com/world/2015/may/21/nope-nope-nope-tony-abbott-says-australia-will-take-no-rohingya-refugees

Ministry of Manpower, Singapore. 2016. Sector-Specific Rules for Work Permit. http://www.mom.gov.sg/passes-and-permits/work-permit-for-foreign-worker/sector-specific-rules

MMN—Mekong Migration Network. 2014. The Precarious Status of Migrants in Thailand: Reflections on the Exodus of Cambodian Migrants and Lessons Learnt. http://www.mekongmigration.org/wp-content/uploads/2014/12/FINAL-REPORT-The-precarious-status-of-migrants-in-Thailand.pdf

Nethery, Amy, and Carly Gordyn. 2014. Australia-Indonesia Cooperation on Asylum-Seekers: A Case of 'Incentivised Policy Transfer'. *Australian Journal of International Affairs* 68 (2): 177–193.

Ooi, Giok Ling. 2005. The Role of the Developmental State and Interethnic Relations in Singapore. *Asian Ethnicity 6* (2): 109–120.

Pickering, Sharon, and Leanne Weber. 2013. Policing Transversal Borders. In *The Borders of Punishment. Migration, Citizenship, and Social Exclusion*, ed. Katja Franko Aas and Mary Bosworth, 93–110. Oxford: Oxford University Press.

Pongsawat, Pitch. 2007. Border Partial Citizenship, Border Towns, and Thai-Myanmar Cross-Border Development: Case Studies at the Thai Border Towns. Doctoral dissertation in City and Regional Planning, University of California, Berkeley.

Roberts, George. 2015. Indonesian Police Documents detail Boat Turn-back and Alleged Payments to People Smuggling Crew. *ABC News*, 17 June

2015. http://www.abc.net.au/news/2015-06-17/indonesian-documents-detail-boat-turnback-and-alleged-payments/6551472

Rodenhäuser, Tilman. 2014. Another Brick in the Wall: Carrier Sanctions and the Privatization of Immigration Control. *International Journal of Refugee Law 26* (2): 223–247.

Ronalds, Paul. 2015. Abbott Must Back a Genuine Regional Approach to Asylum-Seekers. *The Australian*, 29 July 2015. http://www.theaustralian.com.au/opinion/abbott-must-back-a-genuine-regional-approach-to-asylumseekers/newsstory/1ce7754264a5295a48abd9a34e06fff8

RSO—Regional Support Office to the Bali Process. 2013. Concept Note: Meeting under RSO Auspices on "Mapping Disembarkation Options: Towards Strengthening Cooperation in Managing Irregular Movements by Sea". http://www.baliprocess.net/regional-support-office/movements-by-sea/

Ruggie, John G. 1982. International Regimes, Transactions, and Change: Embedded Liberalism in the Postwar Economic Order. *International Organization 36* (2): 379–415.

Schloenhardt, Andreas. 2008. Illegal Migration and Migrant Smuggling in the Asia-Pacific: Balancing Regional Security and Human Rights. In *Security and Migration in Asia: The Dynamics of Securitisation*, ed. Melissa G. Curley and Wong Siu-lun. Oxon: Routledge.

Sekretariat Kabinet Republik Indonesia. 2017. President Jokowi Signs Presidential Regulation on Handling of Refugees from Abroad. 16 January 2017. http://setkab.go.id/en/president-jokowi-signs-presidential-regulation-on-handling-of-refugees-from-abroad/

Stewart, Cameron. 2004. Put Out of Business. *Weekend Australian*, 21 August 2004.

SUAKA. 2017. Refugee Protection Must Answer Key Issues Regarding Asylum Seekers and Refugees in Indonesia. *SUAKA Press Release*. https://suaka.or.id/2017/01/18/press-release-suaka-perpres-ri-no-1252016-tentang-penanganan-pengungsi-dari-luar-negeri/

The Sun Daily. 2015. No Indication of Second Wave of 'Boat People' at the Moment, says MMEA. 13 November 2015. http://www.thesundaily.my/news/1610306

———. 2016a. MMEA Probes Possibility of Terrorists Entering M'sia through National Waters. 16 January 2016. http://www.thesundaily.my/news/1667889

———. 2016b. Curbing Movement of Terrorists New Focus of Ops Redback. 25 October 2016. http://www.thesundaily.my/news/2015537

Taylor, Savitri. 2008. Offshore Barriers to Asylum Seeker Movement: The Exercise of Power without Responsibility? In *Forced Migration, Human Rights and Security*, ed. Jane McAdam. Portland, OR: Hart Publishing.

UNHCR. 2015. South-East Asia: Mixed Maritime Movements, April–June 2015.

Xinhua. 2009. Malaysia, Australia to Jointly Curb Human Trafficking. 26 August 2009. http://news.xinhuanet.com/english/2009-08/26/content_11949076.htm

CHAPTER 6

Carceral Responses

The previous chapter introduced the argument that variation in migration governance in Southeast Asia and the Pacific could be described with the combination of three broad tendencies: formal management, informal tolerance and arbitrary enforcement. In focusing on the screening processes applied to migrants, the previous chapter dealt with the techniques of surveillance and control by which states encounter and categorise migrant bodies, lives and journeys, and the consequences for the status of migrants. This chapter deals with the mechanisms that states use to enforce the categories of migration status. Congruent with the criminalisation and securitisation of irregular migration discussed in Chap. 4, these enforcement mechanisms can be broadly described as carceral; including arrest, detention, and deportation. In discussing the different ways these carceral responses have been applied in the region, this chapter argues that aspects of arbitrary enforcement can be found across the region, but that the significance and consequences of carceral techniques differ greatly between systems that are broadly characterised by informal tolerance of irregularity and those based on formal migration management.

Systems of informal tolerance found in most parts of Southeast Asia, with the combination of irregular status and the constant threat of arbitrary enforcement, produce the situations of structural precarity described in the next chapter. However, when systems largely based on formal management of migration employ arbitrary enforcement as a mechanism of politicised deterrence in response to perceived threats of irregular

N. Henry, *Asylum, Work, and Precarity*, Critical Studies of the Asia-Pacific, DOI 10.1007/978-3-319-60567-8_6

migration, as has been the case in Australia's detention of asylum seekers, the outcomes for migrants have been found to be among the most extremely harmful of any incarcerated population. In short, the combination of informal migration management with arbitrary enforcement produces generalised precarity, while the combination of formal migration management with arbitrary enforcement has the potential to produce a more absolute carceral regime.

Migration border enforcement tends to be arbitrary in two senses, both related to its status as carceral techniques governed by administrative law in the context of securitisation. First, enforcement is arbitrary when it is applied unevenly and inconsistently. Second, enforcement is arbitrary when it is exercised without due process, judicial limit, or independent oversight, including rights of appeal. The unevenness and inconsistency of immigration enforcement is most obvious at the point of arrest, where immigration raids or crackdowns on asylum seekers and migrant workers are often launched for political reasons and as public spectacle, targeting particular populations seen as other to the dominant national group and visibly defined by some combination of characteristics—such as race, gender, occupation, and location of work or residence—that makes them identifiable as a target. The arbitrariness of the profiling of migrants for arrest is exacerbated by uneven and inconsistent treatment in the processes of detention and deportation. In many cases, decisions on whether to hold migrants in detention or release them back into the community is made by individual staff without clear criteria. Outcomes for migrants facing detention or deportation depend on access to advocacy and support from NGOs and International Organisations, as well as financial resources for bail payments or bribes. Arbitrary and inconsistent decisions on detention and deportation are also made for political reasons and in attempts to deter other potential migrants. For instance, some of the asylum-seekers detained in indefinite offshore detention by the Australian government arrived on the same boats as others who have since been released on temporary or permanent protection visas in Australia.

Immigration enforcement is also arbitrary in that the powers of arrest, detention and deportation can often be exercised without public transparency, or independent limit and oversight. As carceral powers, the techniques of migration border enforcement have the function of punishment, if not the official designation. When carceral functions are used to detain migrants indefinitely or to deport them to places where they face danger, and especially when this is done as a deterrent to other potential migrants, it becomes clear that migration borders function as an arbitrary form of extra-judicial punishment.

Prohibition of arbitrary detention is codified in the International Convention on Civil and Political Rights (ICCPR), which states in Article Nine:

> 1. Everyone has the right to liberty and security of person. No one shall be subjected to arbitrary arrest or detention. No one shall be deprived of his liberty except on such grounds and in accordance with such procedure as are established by law.
>
> ...
>
> 4. Anyone who is deprived of his liberty by arrest or detention shall be entitled to take proceedings before a court, in order that that court may decide without delay on the lawfulness of his detention and order his release if the detention is not lawful. (UNOHCHR 2017)

In a decision in support of a complaint by an asylum seeker detained in Australia for four years, the UN Human Rights Committee (UNHRC 1997) declared that in interpreting Article Nine of the ICCPR, arbitrariness 'must not be equated with "against the law" but be interpreted more broadly to include such elements as inappropriateness and injustice'. Although asylum seekers are detained in accordance with the law in Australia and other states in Southeast Asia and the Pacific, the detention may still be defined as arbitrary in legal terms if it is not necessary and proportionate in the particular circumstances of the case, and if it is not subject to review by a court with the power to order the release of those detained.

Arbitrary enforcement, including prolonged detention, is often linked to dysfunctional bureaucratic processes, whether due to a lack of capacity or as part of a deliberate strategy of deterrence. Therefore, in contexts where migrants are detained, efforts to improve procedural fairness can be one strategy to limit the scope and duration of detention. Together with efforts to abolish detention of migrants, improvements to the procedural fairness of migration governance also help to reduce the precarity of migrant lives, including by ensuring clear and reliable pathways to regular legal status. Minimum standards recommended by the International Detention Coalition (IDC 2016, vi) include access to legal status and documentation, independent legal advice for migrants during any assessment of their status including refugee status determination, fair and timely resolution of cases, and regular review of any detention or other restrictions on migrants. Fundamentally though, the IDC advocates for alternatives to detention and a presumption of liberty for migrants, including asylum seekers.

In his final report to the UN Human Rights Council in 2011, the Special Rapporteur on the Human Rights of Migrants Jorge Bustamente drew attention to the increasing criminalisation of irregular migration and consequent abuses of migrants. The Special Rapporteur suggested that criminalisation was a part of broader policies and institutional frameworks aiming to restrict migration and was linked to 'anti-migrant sentiments'. The report raised a concern that increased violation of migrants' rights associated with criminalisation was driven by 'externalization of migration control policies' associated with intensifying international collaboration between police and other agencies. In concluding the section of his report dealing with criminalisation of migration, the Special Rapporteur noted the evidence that:

> many enforcement mechanisms designed to prevent irregular or unauthorized migration, including harsh policies of interception, carrier sanctions and immigration control, were responsible for violence and abuse and might have the side effect of encouraging the expansion of smuggling and trafficking networks.

This effect of carceral networks in increasing dependence on smuggling networks and associated exploitation of migrants has been widely noted. In particular, the imposition of carrier sanctions, combined with the expansion of extraterritorial border regimes described in the previous chapter are the key factors forcing asylum seekers and other migrants without visas to take dangerous journeys, due to their enforced lack of access to regular safe means of transport.

As Doty (2011) has shown in her work on the US-Mexico border, the effect of intensified border controls has been to displace migrant journeys onto more dangerous and hostile terrain. In fact, as Doty shows, this effect is well known by border agencies who have shown a tendency to prioritise their enforcement resources on preventing migrants from crossing safely in populated areas, in the knowledge that migrants will use smugglers to attempt more remote and dangerous desert crossings. Doty argues that the migrant deaths that inevitably result from such dangerous journeys are the result of deliberate decisions by the state, outlined in strategy documents such as those governing the US Border Patrol's 1994 Operation Gatekeeper, to channel migrant crossings towards more dangerous areas as part of a deterrent to irregular migration.

A similar effect of displacement of migrant journeys onto more dangerous routes has been seen at Europe's borders in the Mediterranean. The European Union combined border agency FRONTEX has responded to the situation of irregular migration by coordinating military operations in the Mediterranean to turn back boats and arrest smugglers, including through support for military and coastguard operations by Libyan and Turkish agencies. Military actions in the name of border control have included attempts to disrupt efforts by NGOs to conduct search and rescue operations. In 2016, Libyan Navy personnel trained and supported by FRONTEX fired shots and boarded an MSF ship in the Mediterranean (Kingsley and Stephen 2016). The militarised response to irregular migration to Europe has resulted in migrants becoming more dependent on smuggling networks and making more dangerous journeys in an attempt to evade the coordinated border policing operations. In 2016, even as fewer migrants attempted the journey to Europe, reported casualties increased as a result of tactics to avoid detection, including more dangerous migration routes (UNHCR 2016c).

Both state and non-state agencies have sought to frame their responses to the dangers faced by irregular migrants in terms of liberal humanitarianism. As a result, appeals to humanitarian norms have become ambiguous in their significance and impact. States in Europe and North America, as well as Southeast Asia and the Pacific, have used the language of humanitarianism to justify border enforcement by claiming to be preventing harmful smuggling and rescuing vulnerable migrants (Squire 2015; Vaughan-Williams 2015). Structuring humanitarian concern as an appeal for state intervention therefore has the potential to reinforce the securitisation of borders that forces migrants into unsafe journeys.

In Australia, there is an established consensus across both major parties of government that strongly carceral responses to irregular migration are necessary to 'save lives at sea' by deterring dangerous journeys. This variant of securitisation discourse, which could be described as carceral humanitarianism, has emerged as a post hoc justification for policies originally framed as a defence of national security against migrants defined as a threat. Well established in Australian politics, carceral humanitarianism is also emerging as a dominant discourse in state responses to irregular migration to the European Union (Vaughan-Williams and Little 2016). In order to appeal to a broader audience across electorates which have shown the potential at times to sympathise with refugees and asylum-seekers, politicians have shifted their discourse to focus on 'people-smugglers' as the primary threat, with asylum seekers presented as their victims. As Aradau

(2004) argues in relation to carceral responses to movements defined as human trafficking, there is a slippage in such discourses between dichotomised categories of migrants defined as worthy of 'pity' as victims and those seen to embody 'risk' as threats to border security. As an instrument of governmentality, carceral humanism has a greater potential than more overtly xenophobic nationalism to persuade liberal sections of civil society to support carceral border policies.

Flynn (2016) argues that adherence to certain liberal norms has lead governments and regional organisations to contribute to the spread of immigration detention by formalising and externalising the carceral network. With reference to North American detention facilities, Flynn shows that concerns expressed by liberal advocates, of poor conditions in migration detention and the housing of immigration detainees with the general prison population, had contributed to the expansion of dedicated immigration detention facilities. While conditions for those detained in the new facilities were improved, so was the capacity of the state to arrest, detain and deport a larger number of migrants. In addition, concerns about the legality of detaining migrants, especially asylum seekers, for extended periods of time, led liberal states to externalise the carceral network by co-opting neighbouring states where detainees could be held with less transparency and with plausible denial of responsibility on the part of the liberal state.

As the following analysis of the expansion of immigration detention in Southeast Asia and the Pacific shows, both of these concerns are borne out by the contribution of Australia to the formalisation and externalisation of a carceral network devoted to the prevention and deterrence of asylum seekers from reaching Australia. The expansion and formalisation of a regional carceral network centred on Australia has met and overlapped with an existing carceral network targeting migrant workers with irregular status in Southeast Asia. Resources provided by Australia and by International and Regional organisations have contributed to the development of an increasingly integrated carceral network for the interception and arrest, detention, and deportation of both asylum seekers and migrant workers.

Australia and the Pacific Carceral Network

In the evidence-based judgment of Australian and international human rights and medical organisations, the Australian government has subjected thousands of refugees to torture in the forms of mental and physical harm, arbitrary imprisonment and child abuse, as a deterrent to others seeking asylum at Australia's maritime borders.

Australia's carceral approach to immigration detention reflects the continued influence of two interconnected strands of white supremacist nationalism in Australian politics: the bias towards white immigration established in the colonial period and continued as formal policy after Federation from 1901 to 1966; and the preoccupation of the white Australian population with retaining control over those seen as racial, cultural and religious minorities. As Nethery (2010, 3) notes, Australia shares with other settler-colonial states a history of using administrative detention as a response to groups defined as a threat to the settler population: 'Aboriginal reserves, quarantine stations, and enemy alien internment camps are institutional predecessors to immigration detention' (see also Mitropoulos 2016). By describing these forms of carceral domination in Australia's history of settlement as elements of white supremacist nationalism, I mean to draw attention to the role of carceral techniques as generalised forms of physical and symbolic violence in the subjugation of groups defined as other to the white settler majority. As Ghassan Hage (2000, 34–35) writes, the core social problem of white supremacy in Australia is not the mere existence of racism and other prejudiced attitudes among the white population, but rather the institutionalised power of white Australian nationalists to exercise and enforce their fantasies of white supremacy through the subjugation of others. As Hage (2014, 236) argues, the structural and symbolic violence of carceral policies towards asylum seekers and other migrants in Australia function as a deliberate part of a policy of subjugation. It is not enough that the borders of the territory and population be policed, but the population excluded as undesirable must be made to publicly and abjectly suffer, as a marker of the power of white Australian nationalists holding state power to 'decide who comes to this country and the circumstances in which they come' and, equivalently, as a deterrent to others seeking to challenge that determining power.

Australia's immigration law requires mandatory detention for any person in the country without a visa. A consequence of this policy is that migrants with irregular status, including asylum seekers, cannot be released from immigration detention in Australia unless they are granted a visa. The policy of mandatory detention was introduced by the Keating Labour government in 1992, with legislation that also removed any limit to detention periods, allowing for indefinite detention. The bridging visas, which grant temporary status and allow detainees to be released from detention while their claims are assessed, are issued at the sole discretion of the Minister of Immigration, with no process for appeal or right to judicial review.

Australian border agencies are required to take on conflicting roles in both protection of life at sea and deterrence of irregular migration (Pickering and Weber 2011; Pickering 2014). The increasing priority placed on deterrence has come at the expense of compromising the responsibilities of border agencies under the international convention on Safety of Life at Sea (SOLAS). Operational resources are devoted to interdiction of vessels likely to reach Australian territory, rather than to search and rescue of vessels likely or known to be in distress at sea. The widely publicised shift to a policy of deterrence from 2001 onwards, under which Australian military and border agencies would attempt to intercept and return rather than rescue vessels carrying asylum seekers, also had the effect of encouraging smugglers to attempt to evade interception by using more dangerous open sea routes and avoiding calling for assistance.

In 2001, the Coalition government under Prime Minister John Howard had manufactured a sense of crisis around maritime arrivals of asylum seekers. Growing official hostility towards asylum seekers arriving by sea culminated in a military standoff with the Norwegian freighter MV Tampa, whose captain had responded to a distress call by a boat carrying asylum seekers and was attempting to bring the survivors to the nearest Australian port in accordance with maritime law and standard practice. After winning an election dominated by his party's promise to crack down on asylum seekers arriving on Australia's shores, Howard announced the 'Pacific solution' plan to transfer maritime asylum seeker arrivals to detention centres in Nauru and on Manus Island in Papua New Guinea. The xenophobic discourse used to justify the plan and associated restrictions on migration have become associated in retrospect with the war on terrorism, but the main features of the plan were already in place before the events of 11 September 2001. The deal with Nauru was announced in an administrative agreement signed on 10 September that year. A total of 1322 asylum seekers were transferred by Australia to detention on Nauru between 2001 and 2008, with the detained population peaking at 1155 in early 2002. The centre was closed by the Rudd Labor government in 2008, but reopened in 2012 as the government came under political pressure over increased arrivals (Senate Select Committee on the Recent Allegations relating to Conditions and Circumstances at the Regional Processing Centre in Nauru 2015).

The policy shift back to offshore detention in 2012 was framed as the Gillard Labor government's response to an advisory panel established after the government's 'Malaysia Solution' was struck down by the High Court. The 'Malaysia Solution' was an agreement with Malaysia that would have authorised the Australian government to send 800 detained asylum seekers to Malaysia in return for accepting 4000 UNHCR-recognised refugees from Malaysia. The agreement relied on a declaration by the Minister of Immigration that Malaysia met the requirements then in place in the Migration Act that asylum seekers could only be removed to another country if it provided procedures for assessing refugee status, effective refugee protection and other human rights standards. Lawyers representing two asylum seekers facing removal successfully challenged this declaration in the High Court on the grounds the Minister had not properly applied the test. Although the 'Malaysia Solution' was never implemented, amendments to the Migration Act were passed in 2012 that removed restrictions on removal of asylum seekers to any country that is a member of the Bali Process if the Minister considers it in the national interest. A state's membership in the Bali Process is not an appropriate measure of safety for refugees and asylum seekers since, as argued in the previous chapter, despite the commitments to refugee protection made in the Bali declaration, implementation of the process is non-binding and uneven, with a 'two-speed' prioritisation of border security over refugee protection. The 2012 amendments allowed the re-establishment of indefinite detention of asylum seekers, described as 'offshore processing', at the reopened Nauru and Manus centres. The Rudd Labor Government made offshore detention mandatory for all asylum seekers arriving by boat from 19 July 2013.

While UNHCR and other UN agencies have consistently condemned the Australian government's use of offshore detention of refugees and asylum seekers, the IOM has at times cooperated with the government in managing the detention centres on Nauru and Manus. The IOM was responsible for managing the Nauru and Manus detention centres from 2001 to 2008. The IOM has also acted as a conduit for Australian funding to expand the carceral capacity of neighbouring states in Southeast Asia to detain irregular migrants including asylum seekers. Australia has provided funding through the IOM, as well as bilaterally, to both Indonesia and Malaysia to increase immigration detention capacities in an effort to prevent asylum seekers from reaching Australia.

UNHCR has consistently argued that the transfer of asylum-seekers to Nauru and Papua New Guinea 'does not extinguish the legal responsibility of Australia for the protection of the transferred asylum-seekers and refugees' (UNHCR 2016a). The distinctions introduced in Australian law between asylum seekers arriving by sea and air are not relevant to Australia's international obligations as a signatory to the 1951 Convention on the Status of Refugees and its 1967 Protocol. In fact, the mode of arrival of asylum seekers and their documentation status are specifically ruled out as an acceptable basis for discrimination, prosecution or punishment in Article 33 of the 1951 Convention. In a general advisory note, UNHCR (2007) has also clarified that the legal obligations of protection and non-refoulement of asylum seekers and refugees are not limited or extinguished by extra-territoriality in the way that Australian government representatives have attempted to claim in relation to those transferred to Manus and Nauru.

Australian government agencies have used offshore detention to remove asylum seekers from the jurisdiction of Australia's courts, and at times to claim that these people are no longer Australia's responsibility. In submissions and testimony to a Senate inquiry into the detention centre on Nauru in 2015, DIBP argued that the centre was entirely under the jurisdiction of the government of Nauru which 'owns and administers' the centre, with Australia providing 'capacity building and funding'. However, as was argued in other submissions including those by the Australian Human Rights Commission and UNHCR, the detention centres on both Nauru and Manus are under the 'effective control' of the Australian government, including through contracts with private companies responsible for the day to day running of the centres, as well as through the regular presence and daily involvement of Australian officials in the running of the centres (Australia Senate 2015, 11–14).

The effective control that Australian authorities exercise over detention arrangements on Nauru and Manus has also been demonstrated by modifications in the detention regime in response to legal action in Australia, Nauru and Papua New Guinea. In 2015, the Human Rights Law Centre (HRLC) took legal action challenging the Australian government's authority to fund detention centres outside Australian territory. In response, the government passed legislation in parliament under urgency to retrospectively authorise the expenditure.[1] At the same time, the government of Nauru announced that the detention centre on the island would be converted to an 'open centre', with detainees free to come and go (HRLC 2015). Amnesty International (2016) has criticised this characterisation of the facility as an open centre by Nauruan and Australian authorities, arguing that with travel restrictions remaining in place, the entire island of Nauru is 'to all intents and purposes an open-air prison' being used by Australia to detain refugees and asylum seekers. A similar announcement of conversion to an open centre was made for the Manus detention camp in response to a ruling by the PNG Supreme Court in 2015 that the facility was unconstitutional and must close. However, the location of the Manus camp inside the Lombrum Naval base meant that, in practice, the men at the centre were only allowed to leave the camp on day trips under a curfew. In 2016, legal action by lawyer Ben Lomai on behalf of the refugees and asylum seekers on Manus was continuing, seeking a PNG Supreme Court order for the men to be compensated and returned to Australia. However, even if the court were to grant such a ruling, the Australian government has indicated that it does not consider itself bound by decisions of the PNG courts.

In practice, the detention centres on Nauru and Manus function as an extension of Australia's carceral network of immigration detention. The centres share the punitive aspects of the harsh physical environment and isolation of detention centres in Australia's own territory, including the desert camps at Woomera and Baxter and on Christmas Island. In addition, the location of the centres on Nauru and Manus allows the Australian government to maintain the legal and political construction of non-responsibility while retaining physical control over the detainees to prevent them from reaching Australia and pursuing their claims for protection. The offshore detention system also serves a propaganda purpose in signalling to asylum seekers and smugglers that the Australian government will not allow them to reach or remain on Australian territory. In summary, the system of mandatory offshore detention for asylum seekers arriving in Australia by boat has allowed the Australian government to create a punitive system of deterrence based on isolated and harsh conditions beyond those that would be possible on Australian territory.

By early 2017, the refugees and asylum seekers held on Manus and Nauru had not been presented with any viable options to end their detention other than returning to danger in their countries of origin. The Australian government paid for flights and handed out cash incentives, in cooperation with the IOM, for refugees and asylum seekers who abandoned their claims and agreed to return home. It is a mark of the desperate and hopeless conditions created by the regime of offshore detention that some refugees and asylum seekers had taken up these offers despite fearing for their safety on their return. In 2014, Australia persuaded the Cambodian government to accept refugees from Nauru in return for 55 million Australian dollars in aid. By 2017, only four refugees had been resettled under the deal, with two of these later opting to return to Iran rather than remain in Cambodia.

The obscurity of the location and administrative processes of offshore detention, described in Chap. 2 as a series of folds in political space, have been deliberately designed to frustrate attempts by detainees to obtain their freedom. In one incident in 2017, a young refugee managed to escape from Papua New Guinea by boarding a plane to Fiji under a false name. A lawyer in Fiji arranged for the young man to meet with the head of the Immigration Department to make a claim for asylum, but on their way to the meeting the car they were travelling in was stopped by police and the refugee was dragged from the car and deported back to PNG.

Detentions, deportations and transfers have a similar arbitrary character within the carceral network of border agencies in Australia. Migrants, including asylum seekers and refugees, who are targeted for detention, deportation or transfer are commonly not informed in advance and have little opportunity to contact supporters, advocates or legal representatives. Asylum seekers holding bridging visas are commonly detained without notice after being required to attend an interview with DIBP, while those in detention have been transferred across the country or into offshore detention without notice in the middle of the night or early hours of the morning.

The 'fold' of legality introduced by the overlapping jurisdiction and lines of responsibility between the governments of Australia, Nauru and Papua New Guinea has also frustrated and delayed attempts by those detained, and their advocates, to challenge their detention. The 2016 ruling of the PNG high court that the Lombrum detention camp was illegal and must close was ignored by the Australian government and the camp remained open into 2017. However, the ruling and subsequent statements by the Prime Minister created the sense that the days of offshore detention in PNG were numbered.

Similarly, pressure placed on core contractors to Australia's Pacific carceral network has caused some companies to announce they would no longer bid for renewal of their contracts. In particular, controversy over the role of Australian engineering and logistics firm Transfield Services as the primary contractor running detention centres in both Nauru and

Manus contributed to ongoing turmoil in the company's structure through 2015 and 2016, including the sale of the company to Spanish firm Ferrovial and a re-branding of the company to Broadspectrum Services. As Broadspectrum's parent company, Ferrovial then announced it would withdraw from involvement in offshore detention at the conclusion of its existing contract in 2018.

The folds of location, legality and logistics introduced into the political space of Australia's Pacific carceral network have given the offshore detention regime the mobility and flexibility to frustrate the legitimate claims of refugees and asylum seekers to access protection in Australia. At the same time, this folded space is subject to instability and a degree of fragility that requires it to be constantly remade and restructured. For Mitropoulos (2015), the evolution of Australia's Immigration Detention Network has produced an architecture of contingency in the physical and financial infrastructure of the system. The physical structure of the detention camps is modular, built from containerised units in a similar way to other temporary or remote facilities such as mining camps, and able to expanded or reconfigured according to changed circumstances. Mitropoulos argues that a similarly modular and contingent structure is created in the financial structure of the detention network through the use of an assemblage of contracting and subcontracting arrangements. Contingency accounting is concerned with the estimation of financial losses or gains resulting from possible events as a method for converting uncertainty to an estimate of measurable risk. Mitropoulos' analysis of the key contracts underpinning Australia's detention network emphasises the role of contracts as measures for the resolution of uncertainty (unpredictable and uninsurable forms of risk) into quantified risk and contingency. Contractors to the detention network, and the profits they expect to derive from the contracts, are protected from uncertainty by clauses guaranteeing payments even if services are no longer required as a result of changes in policy. Uncertainties associated with the delivery of services in challenging environments, deliberately chosen to be harsh, isolated and lacking in infrastructure, are quantified as manageable risk through clauses that outline variable payments and abatements related to performance, while contractors are insulated from cost fluctuations by DIBP's contractual commitment to pay all 'pass-through' costs, apparently without scrutiny or requirement to show value (ANAO 2017). Contracts with major suppliers of services to the detention network also contain substantial contingency funds for responses to unforeseen events.

Contractors to the offshore components of Australia's detention network have also been protected, at least in the short term, from individual or corporate liability for physical abuses of detained migrants and the deprivation of rights under local (PNG, Nauru, Australian) and international law. The Australian government's denial of responsibility and refusal to consider itself bound by the rule of law in the territories where it operates offshore detention centres has contributed to a culture of impunity that has extended to the evasion of accountability for criminal behaviour by contracted Australian staff. Australian staff working at the Manus detention centre have repeatedly evaded investigation by the PNG police by returning to Australia. Australian staff who were employed by security firm G4S are wanted for questioning by Manus police over their role in the murder of Reza Barati in 2014. Two local staff who were employed by the Salvation Army and G4S, contracted by the Australian government, were charged with the murder, but other Australian staff who were allegedly present during the fatal assault on Barati were flown back to Australia by their employers before they could be interviewed by police. In a later incident, staff working for Wilson security were hurriedly returned to Australia before they could be questioned by police over a sexual assault reported by a local female co-worker (Tlozek 2015; ABC News 2015). By setting up detention centres in foreign territory while using Australian contractors and staff on a 'fly in—fly out' system, the Australian government created the conditions that allow staff with power over asylum seekers and refugees to evade responsibility for abuses and criminal actions.

Conditions in the Australian-run detention centres in Nauru and PNG have been subject to international scrutiny and condemnation. The offshore detention camps have become the central symbol of Australia's harsh policies towards asylum seekers who arrive by boat. The policy of offshore detention was described in an editorial by the New York Times (2015) as 'inhumane, of dubious legality and strikingly at odds with the country's tradition of welcoming people fleeing persecution and war'. In a submission to an Australian Senate inquiry into serious allegations of abuse in the Nauru and Manus detention centres,[2] based on multiple site visits to the centres including in April 2016, UNHCR (2016a, b, c, d) reported its finding that the detention of asylum seekers and refugees in both locations, together with the lack of any viable solution for their protection needs had caused widespread harm to mental health, self-harm and abuse. In relation to the Manus centre, UNHCR reported 'excessive levels of security' creating an 'institutionalised and punitive environment', together with overcrowding at twice the limit set by international standards for prisons. During UNHCR's April 2016 visits, surveys by medical experts of a sample of 181 asylum-seekers and refugees on Manus and 53 on Nauru found extremely high levels of mental health disorders, with 88% of those detained on Manus and 83% of those on Nauru suffering from a depressive, anxiety, or post-traumatic stress disorder. The authors of the medical study attached to UNHCR's submission concluded that the rates of mental health disorder among the refugees and asylum seekers on Manus and Nauru were directly attributable to the conditions of their detention and were the 'highest of any surveyed population'.

In 2015, the Australian Human Rights Commission (AHRC) proposed specific alternatives to the continued detention of asylum seekers on Manus and Nauru. Addressing government claims that the detention regime has successfully prevented dangerous sea journeys, the AHRC suggests that this aim could better be achieved by increasing opportunities for safe entry to Australia. In particular, Australia should increase resettlement quotas and introduce a visa category for the purpose of seeking asylum as ways of guaranteeing safe travel. In addition, the commission advocated a shift to 'protection sensitive migration' in other categories of migration that would remove barriers for refugees to apply for work, family and study visas.

Writing from Manus Island in Papua New Guinea, where he was sent by Australian authorities in 2013, Kurdish journalist Behrouz Boochani, a refugee from Iran, has documented the effects of indefinite detention, drawing on his own experiences along with those of his fellow refugees. As well as being intensely personal, Boochani's pieces in Australian and international media follow a tradition of political prison writing by theorising the conditions of his detention in a broader context. Boochani (2016a) references Agamben's theory of sovereignty as the power of deciding on the state of exception to understand the use of administrative detention in Australian law and the 19 July 2013 decision to indefinitely detain maritime asylum seekers on Nauru and Manus island. He frequently returns to the theme of the body in writing of the daily humiliations of detention, arguing that the Australian government has 'used my body for propaganda to send a message to the world' by using detention as a strategy of deterrence (Boochani 2016b). Expanding on this theme of the reduction to the body experienced by those in detention, Boochani (2016c) describes the systematic denial of the political agency of asylum seekers by the Australian government, and the associated everyday practices of detention which materially enact and enforce the denial of individuality and humanity to the detainees.

Thailand

There are no official statistics or available estimates for the number of migrants detained in Thailand's 12 immigration detention centres. However, according to a Human Rights Watch (2014, 21) report on children in detention, approximately 4000 children are detained for short periods during a typical year, with 100 detained for longer than a month.[3] A separate publication by UNHCR (2016d, 72) on detention of asylum seekers and refugees does not disclose the size of this subset of the detained migrant population, but identified that around 15% were children. Assuming a similar proportion of children to adults in the general population of migrants in detention would place the total number detained for some period during each year at around 26,000. There is no data available on the duration of migrant detention although, as described below, detention can be prolonged indefinitely for some categories of migrants who cannot easily be deported, including refugees, asylum seekers, and migrants from countries not bordering Thailand who cannot afford to pay their own deportation expenses.

The only way for detained migrants, including asylum seekers, to access alternatives to indefinite detention is for an approved organisation to act as a guarantor and pay a 50,000-baht bail bond, equivalent to more than 1400 US Dollars, to the immigration department. Even this provision is periodically suspended in periods of heightened security concern and during immigration crackdowns. From August to December 2015, all releases on bail were suspended after the Ratchaprasong bombing. At other times, release has been arbitrarily denied to certain groups of asylum seekers, even if NGOs are willing to pay bonds. A spokesperson for Asylum Access (interview 2015) reported that Immigration officials had been refusing for some time to release any Pakistani male asylum seekers. Although there was no official explanation for this, Pakistani men were frequently targeted by the police and experienced discrimination (see also Rogers 2016). Somali asylum seekers had also been refused release due to the Immigration department's view that the situation in Somalia had improved and they should return home. Asylum Access had joined other groups in petitioning the immigration department to change this approach and recognise asylum claims from Somalia. Another group that had been consistently refused release was Falun Gong members from China, apparently due to diplomatic pressure over the group's regular protests outside the Chinese embassy in Bangkok.

People held in Thailand's immigration detention centres are not allowed phone calls and, if visits are allowed, they are strictly limited and brief, so it is very difficult for NGOs to advocate on behalf of detainees or to attempt to secure their release. NGOs like Asylum Access rely on community reports of arrests and communicate with detainees through contacts with UNHCR, who have access to the detention centres. NGOs also pass details of particularly vulnerable people to UNHCR to request their cases be given priority for assessment of refugee status, but with the backlog of cases growing in 2016 it could still take several months to arrange an interview.

Migrants without legal status who are arrested and charged with immigration offences in Thailand pass through both the criminal system and the immigration system. Any foreigner in Thailand without a valid visa is liable on summary conviction to be fined or imprisoned. Migrants are often held in overcrowded police cells until they are able to pay court-imposed fines, at which point they are transferred to immigration detention for removal.

In practice, migrants who encounter police without being able to show valid documentation can sometimes pay bribes to avoid being passed on to the immigration authorities and criminal justice system. Migrants may be able to pay a bribe on the spot, or may be held at police stations until they or an associate are able to negotiate a payment for their release.

Thai law also requires detainees to pay their own expenses while in immigration detention. This is a feature of a system that was designed for short periods of detention prior to departure or deportation from Thailand, as well as to function as a form of punishment for violating the country's immigration rules. For migrants who are unable to return home, the prospect of indefinite detention in the immigration system is a frightening one. Advocacy by NGOs and UNHCR has resulted in the Thai government providing meals and basic medical care, but both are described as of a very low standard. Since the immigration department has no legal obligation to provide anything for detainees, they are able to claim that even substandard care is more than they are required to provide. A US State Department (2015) report on human rights in Thailand cites persistent complaints from NGOs of forced labour, extortion by guards, poor ventilation, and inadequate and culturally inappropriate food in immigration detention centres.

Immigration detention in Thailand also applies to migrant children. NGOs like Asylum Access have had some success in having children under 14 years of age transferred to shelters under Department of Social Welfare jurisdiction, or released into care of other agencies. However, children aged 14–18 are treated as adults for detention purposes, according to administrative rules derived from Thailand's age of criminal responsibility. A report by Human Rights Watch (2014) documented appalling conditions in Thailand's Immigration Detention Centres, including for families with young children, many of whom were detained indefinitely. Families were separated in gender-segregated units with no visitation rights and unaccompanied minors were detained along with unrelated adults. Conditions were overcrowded, unsanitary, and often violent.

Camps for refugees from Myanmar on the Thai side of the border also serve a carceral function in limiting the freedom of movement of refugees. Although officially known as temporary shelters, the camps have existed since 1988 and are home to a generation of refugees who have never known life elsewhere. As described in Chap. 7, the official policy of treating camps as temporary shelters functions to enforce precarious conditions for inhabitants who are not allowed to construct permanent dwellings and face restrictions on their lives and movements. Under the NCPO military regime from 2014, restrictions on movement have been more strictly enforced, with refugees confined within the camps by military guards.

On 3 June 2014, a crackdown on migrant workers with irregular status began with the arrest of 163 Myanmar migrants and 80 Cambodians, and the closure of informal border crossings on the Thai-Myanmar border near Mae Sot. Arrests and deportations of migrants continued over the following week, with 2160 deported on 9 June with, and a further 2993 deported on 10 June. On 11 June, the first public statement on the crackdown was made by Thai army spokesperson Sirichan Ngathong, who stated that migrant workers with irregular status in Thailand 'will be arrested and deported'. The spokesperson added that the presence of large numbers of migrant workers in Thailand, with no clear plans to manage them, 'could lead to social problems'. Television channels under the control by the NCPO then broadcast messages declaring the crackdown on migrant workers to be part of an 'environmental cleansing' operation to build a 'pleasant' society (MMN 2014, 11).

As mass arrests and deportations targeting migrant workers continued to escalate, rumours of impending raids circulated among Cambodian migrant workers and tens of thousands fled the country in a mass exodus rather than wait to be deported. The IOM estimated that 120,000 Cambodian workers fled or were deported from Thailand in the two weeks following the initial crackdown. Pressure from employers who found themselves abandoned by their migrant workforce led the NCPO to quickly reassess their strategy, with Prime Minister General Prayut Chan-Ocha initially denying on 13 June that a crackdown was occurring and then calling on 17 June for all workers who had fled the country or been deported to 'return with legal paperwork'. The NCPO then ordered relevant government departments to facilitate the return, registration and regularisation of migrant workers. As a staff member at IOM's Thailand country office described the situation, the 'huge influence of employers in Thailand' prevented the kind of permanent crackdown on migrant labour that had been threatened by the military government, based on the 'implicit recognition that Thailand depends on these migrant workers for sustaining large components of their economy'. An organiser with the Migrant Worker Resource Centre in Bangkok agreed:

> Mostly this is a capitalist country, so the money speaks. So if there will be a benefit to the national economy, any government will do that way. Even though at the start we thought that this military government would make a crackdown, instead what they did was to legalise everyone. So a lot of people became semi-documented. Frankly, people cannot live without the migrant workers.

An NGO researcher familiar with migration policy attributed the turnaround in NCPO policy to inexperience with civil administration, adding that in consultation meetings NCPO officials responsible for migration policy demonstrated a 'lack of institutional knowledge'. This example demonstrates that systems based on informal tolerance of irregular migration status for workers in Southeast Asia are based on structural economic conditions and deliberate policy decisions, rather than a lack of capacity. When the Thai government under military control attempted a dramatic shift to arbitrary enforcement on the basis of securitisation of irregular migration, the reaction from employers who depend on informal tolerance of migrants with irregular status forced a rapid reversal of the policy.

Malaysia

The large number of migrants with irregular status in Malaysia combined with strict immigration law, means that large numbers of people are held in the twelve immigration detention centres spread throughout the country. According to figures cited by the Global Detention Project (2015), at least 68,000 people including more than 1400 children were held in immigration detention in 2013, with the largest groups being citizens of Myanmar, Indonesia and Bangladesh.

In addition to facing arrest by police and immigration agents, migrants with irregular status in Malaysia are targeted by RELA, a paramilitary volunteer force who use their quasi-police powers to demand papers from people they suspect to be undocumented migrants. Migrants who are unable to produce documents confirming their immigration status may be arrested by RELA members and passed over to police or immigration agents. In practice, migrants are often subject to violence and extortion by RELA members.

As in Thailand, irregular migration in Malaysia is treated as both a criminal and administrative matter. Migrants with irregular status are subject to arrest and criminal charges with harsh penalties, before being handed over to immigration authorities for detention and deportation. The Malaysian criminal justice system retains caning as a punishment introduced under British colonial administration and the practice was extended to punishment of undocumented migrants in 2002. The punishment, defined as a form of torture by Amnesty International, can be applied to men aged 18–50. The majority of victims of caning in Malaysia are now migrant workers. Of the 8481 prisoners caned in 2013, 5986 were non-citizens of Malaysia (Global Detention Project 2015).

In 2016, two Cambodian domestic workers who had been detained in Juru, Penang State, reported witnessing multiple deaths of migrant workers after beatings by guards at the detention centre. Their story led the Cambodian government to instruct its embassy in Malaysia to search for Cambodian workers in Malaysian detention centres and arrange for their repatriation (Peter and Naren 2016). The Human Rights Commission of Malaysia called for inquests to be made mandatory for all deaths in custody at immigration detention centres (Divakaran 2016).

UNHCR (2015a) noted that an administrative instruction had been issued in 2015 to avoid the detention of asylum seekers. Police and immigration officers were instructed to check the UNHCR status of people arrested for irregular migration status and to release persons of concern to UNHCR. However, this instruction relies on the knowledge and discretion of frontline officers and does not create any formal legal status for asylum seekers, who are still subject to arrest. In practice, refugees and asylum-seekers are likely to face continued arrest and detention, although the instruction will provide an avenue for UNHCR and NGO advocates to secure the release of persons of concern. Although UNHCR has access to the immigration detention centres, there is no process for access to prisons where migrants serve sentences under the Immigration Act before being transferred to Immigration Detention. In the absence of formal legal status, the instruction not to arrest asylum seekers remains ambiguous at best.

Singapore

In stark contrast to neighbouring Malaysia, Singapore has a strictly enforced formal migration regime, including criminal punishment for migrants with irregular status. Entering Singapore without a visa, or overstaying a visa, is a criminal offence punished by up to six months in prison and at least three strokes of the cane. There are also harsh punishments for employing or 'harbouring', which includes renting accommodation, to irregular migrants. Singapore has three immigration detention centres for male migrants, while female migrants are detained at Changi women's prison. There were 1408 new convictions resulting in imprisonment on immigration charges in 2015, down from 2023 the previous year and 2704 in 2013 (SPS 2016, 109).

Singapore's Immigration and Checkpoints Authority (ICA 2017) uses the language of security to warn citizens about the dangers of 'harbouring' migrants with irregular status:

> Overstayers and illegal immigrants may pose security problems to your family and neighbourhood. You can help keep your home and neighbourhood safe and secure by denying them a place to stay through ensuring that your prospective foreign tenants have valid travel documents and immigration/work passes before renting a room/flat/house to them.

Landlords are required to check immigration passes and passports of prospective tenants and confirm the validity of the tenant's immigration pass before renting accommodation to them. Failure to do so can result in fines and prison terms from six months to two years.

Indonesia

Over the course of 2014, a total of 5782 refugees and asylum seekers were held across Indonesia's network of 14 immigration detention centres and 20 temporary detention centres, with a total of 4273 detained in February 2016 (UNHCR 2015b, 2016d, 47). Those detained made up nearly a third of the refugees and asylum seekers registered as persons of concern to UNHCR in the country, with a total of 13,829—comprising 6269 refugees and 7560 asylum seekers. Changes to Indonesia's immigration law in 2011 introduced mandatory detention for up to ten years for all foreigners without a valid visa, including refugees and asylum seekers, with limited exceptions for children, those in need of medical care, and victims of trafficking (Nethery et al. 2013, 97). However, the obligation of mandatory detention is on immigration officers while the police force has been issued with a contradictory Presidential instruction to avoid arresting asylum seekers for immigration violations. In practice, undocumented migrants including asylum seekers are generally detained if they are arrested while attempting to enter or leave the country, or if they give themselves up to immigration authorities in order to access assistance provided by IOM.

Refugees registered with UNHCR and the Indonesian Immigration Department are eligible to be released into community housing supported by IOM. However, the Immigration Department process requires refugees and asylum seekers who register with the Department to be held in immigration detention centres during the often lengthy process of UNHCR registration, refugee status determination and waiting for transfer to housing. Once registered, refugees remain in mandatory detention until an order is made for their release by the central office of the Immigration Department. In 2015, 730 people were released from immigration detention into IOM housing. In the same period, 744 refugees and asylum seekers turned themselves in to immigration detention in order to qualify for IOM assistance, as they were unable to provide for themselves in the community (Yonesta 2015).

UNHCR's Indonesia office cited a lack of staff and resources for status determination, bureaucratic procedures by the Immigration Department, and a shortage of community housing as factors contributing to lengthy detention of refugees and asylum seekers (UNHCR 2015b).

Australia has funded and lobbied for Indonesia to expand the capacity of immigration detention and to introduce more restrictive policies including the 2011 immigration law changes, contributing to an increase in the numbers of refugees and asylum seekers in detention (Nethery et al. 2013, 95–97). Funding to increase the capacity of immigration detention was provided through IOM and justified as part of an effort to bring facilities up to 'international human rights standards' (IOM 2014). However, reports of overcrowding continue as the detained population has increased, suggesting that increasing detention capacity is not in itself a solution for overcrowding (Global Detention Project 2016).

Migrants interviewed by Human Rights Watch (2013) who had been detained in Indonesia described appalling conditions, with insufficient food and poor hygiene. Children are held with unrelated adults and both children and adults are exposed to violence and abuse from guards. In February 2012, Taqi Naroye, a 28-year-old asylum seeker from Afghanistan was beaten to death by guards at the Pontiniak detention centre after he tried to escape. According to other detained migrants interviewed by Human Rights Watch (2013, 4) and journalists (Brown 2012), the beating and torture that killed Taqi Naroye was a common response by guards at the detention centre to migrants attempting to escape or disobeying orders.

Alternatives to Detention

While the dominant circuits of regional cooperation on migration border governance have been captured by advocates of strengthening carceral responses to irregular migration, there are also active regional networks of advocacy for alternatives to detention. UNHCR is an active advocate for policy change to avoid punitive migration sanctions being applied to asylum seekers, opposing criminalisation of asylum seekers in general and detention in particular. UNHCR has openly advocated for alternatives to detention for asylum seekers and has been critical of governments that have introduced mandatory or lengthy detention of asylum seekers, including Australia. However, UNHCR is somewhat constrained in its ability to criticise governments, since it needs to stay on good terms with states in the region in order to continue operating in their territory. UNHCR can draw on a certain amount of moral legitimacy from its mandate under the 1951 Refugee Convention and the 1967 Protocol, which are binding on signatories and establish peremptory norms of universal international law, including that of non-refoulement. However, the organisation lacks the capacity or leverage to enforce these norms on states that refuse to comply.

In the case of migrant workers, there is an even greater lack of institutional mandate and capacity on the part of international organisations to advocate against arbitrary detention. While the ILO has advocated for alternatives to detention for migrant workers with irregular status, particularly in the context of support for the Convention on the Rights All Migrant Workers, this is not the main focus of the organisation. The stance of the IOM is even more ambiguous, and although this organisation has argued for the expansion of opportunities for regular migration, it has also contributed to state efforts to expand the capacity of carceral border institutions, including detention facilities.

Support for expansion of alternatives to detention within migration border governance has primarily been sustained by regional networks of non-government organisations, in addition to some government institutions such as national human rights bodies. Such networks are able to lobby governments on the basis of existing national priorities, such as reducing expenditure on overcrowded detention facilities, and draw attention to policy alternatives and best practice from other states. For instance, in 2013 the Malaysian Human Rights Commission SUHAKAM convened a meeting on alternatives to detention with representatives from relevant government departments with responsibility for immigration enforcement and detention, in addition to members of NGOs and international organisations, including UNHCR, the International Committee of the Red Cross and the International Detention Coalition. Problems with overcrowding and extended periods of detention were raised in presentations by the Ministry of Immigration in addition to NGOs, contributing to a shared perspective on detention as a problem rather than a solution. The remainder of the sessions focused in detail on alternatives to detention, including presentations on the approaches taken by Hong Kong to reducing detention of asylum seekers (SUHAKUM 2013).

Non-state actors have also been influential in offering direct assistance to migrants, including refugees and asylum seekers and in conducting public advocacy and solidarity campaigns. In writing on the involvement of various activist and civil society groups in providing assistance to migrants crossing the US-Mexico border, Squire (2015) cautions of the dangers of adopting forms of humanitarianism based on pity, rather than solidarity. A stance of 'pitiful humanitarianism', while based on genuine sympathy and desire to help migrants, tends to reinforce the unequal power of the relationship between citizens and migrants with irregular status. Similarly, Boochani (2016c) describes his own work among fellow asylum seekers and refugees detained at Australia's Manus camp, along with that of others working in solidarity with refugees, as the production of hope in resistance to the effects of detention. But he rejects the reduction of detained refugees to objects of sympathy by 'Australian civil society', arguing that presenting refugees as the 'downtrodden' in 'need of care' reflects and repeats the oppressive 'logic of government propaganda' that strips refugees of individuality and political agency.

Conclusion

Migrants with irregular status, including asylum seekers and refugees, are subject to arbitrary detention across Southeast Asia and the Pacific. Despite the efforts of UNHCR, various NGO networks and national human rights institutions to advocate for alternatives to detention, the dominant processes of international cooperation between states have contributed to the expansion of the regional carceral network of migrant detention. International coordination between states and international organisations has contributed to this growth of the carceral network through direct support to increase enforcement and detention capacity and through the associated coordination of common techniques of interception, arrest, detention and deportation designed to prevent and deter irregular migration.

Notes

1. In addition to the lack of parliamentary authorisation for expenditure on offshore detention, a government audit found that DIBP management of more than two billion Australian dollars of spending had 'fallen well short of effective procurement practice' by failing to organise competitive tenders for contracts, properly check invoices, or authorise payments (ANAO 2017).
2. The Australian Senate Inquiry into the Serious Allegations of Abuse, Self-Harm and Neglect of Asylum Seekers in Relation to the Nauru Regional Processing Centre, and any like Allegations in Relation to the Manus Regional Processing Centre, was referred to the Senate Legal and Constitutional Affairs References Committee on 12 September 2016. http://www.aph.gov.au/Parliamentary_Business/Committees/Senate/Legal_and_Constitutional_Affairs/NauruandManusRPCs
3. The figures were provided by an international organisation on the condition the organisation not be identified (HRW 2014, 21).

Bibliography

ABC News. 2015. Reza Barati: Trial of Pair Accused of Killing Asylum Seeker Adjourned, Main Witness Fears for Life. *ABC News*, 25 September 2015. http://www.abc.net.au/news/2015-09-25/pair-accused-of-killing-asylum-seeker-appear-in-court/6804682

Amnesty International. 2016. *Island of Despair: Australia's "Processing" of Refugees on Nauru*. https://www.amnesty.org/download/Documents/ASA1249342016ENGLISH.PDF

ANAO—Australian National Audit Office. 2017. *Offshore Processing Centres in Nauru and Papua New Guinea: Procurement of Garrison Support and Welfare Services*.https://www.anao.gov.au/sites/g/files/net2446/f/ANAO_Report_2016-17_16.pdf

Aradau, Claudia. 2004. The Perverse Politics of Four-Letter Words: Risk and Pity in the Securitisation of Human Trafficking. *Millennium—Journal of International Studies* 33 (2): 251–277.

Boochani, Behrouz. 2016a. Australia, Exceptional in its Brutality. *Overland*, 25 April 2016. https://overland.org.au/2016/04/australia-exceptional-in-its-brutality/

———. 2016b. It's Hard for Me to Leave Manus Island without Justice: Behrouz Boochani on the US Refugee Deal. *The Guardian*, 13 November 2016. https://www.theguardian.com/australia-news/2016/nov/13/its-hard-for-me-to-leave-manus-island-without-justice-behrouz-boochani-on-the-us-refugee-deal

———. 2016c. A Cruel and Violent Political Strategy. *The Huffington Post*, 18 October 2016. http://www.huffingtonpost.com.au/behrouz-boochani/a-cruel-and-violent-political-strategy/

Brown, Matt. 2012. Asylum Seekers Allegedly Abused in Indonesia. *ABC Lateline*, 8 March 2012. http://www.abc.net.au/lateline/content/2012/s3449246.htm

Divakaran, P. 2016. Human Rights Commission of Malaysia Calls for Inquests Following Deaths at Immigration Detention Centres. *The Star (Malaysia)*, 3 September 2016. http://asianews.network/content/human-rights-commission-malaysia-calls-inquests-following-deaths-immigration-detention

Doty, Roxanne. 2011. Bare Life: Border-Crossing Deaths and Spaces of Moral Alibi. *Environment and Planning D: Society and Space 29*: 599–612.

Flynn, Michael. 2016. Sovereign Discomfort: Can Liberal Norms Lead to Increasing Immigration Detention? In *Immigration Detention, Risk and Human Rights*, ed. Maria João Guia, Robert Koulish, and Valsamis Mitsilegas. Cham: Springer.

Global Detention Project. 2015. Malaysia Immigration Detention Profile. https://www.globaldetentionproject.org/countries/asia-pacific/malaysia

———. 2016. Indonesia Immigration Detention Profile. https://www.global-detentionproject.org/countries/asia-pacific/indonesia

Hage, Ghassan. 2000. *White Nation: Fantasies of White Supremacy in a Multicultural Society*. New York: Routledge.

———. 2014. Continuity and Change in Australian Racism. *Journal of Intercultural Studies* 35 (3): 232–237.

HRLC (Human Rights Law Centre). 2015. High Court Set to Hear Challenge to Offshore Detention on Nauru—Nauru Announces Transition to 'Open Centre'. https://www.hrlc.org.au/news/high-court-set-to-hear-challenge-to-offshore-detention-on-nauru-nauru-announces-transition-to-open-centre

Human Rights Watch. 2013. *Barely Surviving: Detention, Abuse, and Neglect of Migrant Children in Indonesia*. https://www.hrw.org/sites/default/files/reports/indonesia0613webwcover.pdf

———. 2014. *Two Years With No Moon: Immigration Detention of Children in Thailand*. https://www.hrw.org/sites/default/files/reports/thailand0914_ForUpload_0.pdf

ICA (Immigration and Checkpoints Authority). 2017. Anti-Harbouring. https://www.ica.gov.sg/page.aspx?pageid=328

IDC—International Detention Coalition. 2016. *There are Alternatives: A Handbook for Preventing Unnecessary Immigration Detention* (revised edition). International Detention Coalition. http://idcoalition.org/publication/download/there-are-alternatives-revised-edition/

IOM—International Organisation for Migration. 2014. Factsheet: Immigration and Border Management. http://www.iom.or.id/sites/default/files/Factsheet%20-%20IBM.pdf.

Kingsley, Patrick, and Chris Stephen. 2016. Libyan Navy Admits Confrontation with Charity's Rescue Boat. *The Guardian*, 28 August 2016. https://www.theguardian.com/world/2016/aug/28/libyan-navy-admits-confrontation-charity-rescue-boat-msf

Mitropoulos, Angela. 2015. Archipelago of Risk: Uncertainty, Borders and Migration Detention Systems. *New Formations* 84 (85): 163–183.

———. 2016. On Borders / Race / Fascism / Labour / Precarity / Feminism / etc. *Base* 30 (1). http://www.basepublication.org/?p=107

MMN—Mekong Migration Network. 2014. The Precarious Status of Migrants in Thailand: Reflections on the Exodus of Cambodian Migrants and Lessons Learnt. http://www.mekongmigration.org/wp-content/uploads/2014/12/FINAL-REPORT-The-precarious-status-of-migrants-in-Thailand.pdf

Nethery, Amy. 2010. *Immigration Detention in Australia*. Doctoral Thesis, Deakin University. https://dro.deakin.edu.au/eserv/DU:30032385/nethery-immigrationdetention-2010A.pdf

Nethery, Amy, Brynna Rafferty-Brown, and Savitri Taylor. 2013. Exporting Detention: Australia-Funded Immigration Detention in Indonesia. *Journal of Refugee Studies* 26 (1): 88–109.

Peter, Zsombor, and Naren, Kuch. 2016. Maids Claim Fatal Abuse at Malaysian Depot. *The Cambodia Daily*, 15 August 2016. https://www.cambodiadaily.com/news/maids-claim-fatal-abuse-malaysian-depot-116653/

Pickering, Sharon. 2014. Floating Carceral Spaces: Border Enforcement and Gender on the High Seas. *Punishment & Society 16* (2): 187–205.

Pickering, Sharon, and Leanne Weber. 2011. *Globalization and Borders: Death at the Global Frontier*. Basingstoke, Hampshire: Palgrave Macmillan.

Rogers, Chris. 2016. The Christians Held in Thailand After Fleeing Pakistan. *BBC News*, 26 February 2016. www.bbc.com/news/magazine-35654804

Senate Select Committee on the Recent Allegations Relating to Conditions and Circumstances at the Regional Processing Centre in Nauru. 2015. *Taking Responsibility: Conditions and Circumstances at Australia's Regional Processing Centre in Nauru.*http://www.aph.gov.au/Parliamentary_Business/Committees/Senate/Regional_processing_Nauru/Regional_processing_Nauru/~/media/Committees/nauru_ctte/Final_Report/report.pdf

SPS—Singapore Prison Service. 2016. *Collaboration: Annual Report 2015.* http://www.sps.gov.sg/sites/default/files/SPSAnnual_lowres_revised.pdf

Squire, Vicki. 2015. *Post/Humanitarian Border Politics between Mexico and the US: People, Places, Things.* Basingstoke: Palgrave Macmillan.

SUHAKUM—Human Rights Commission of Malaysia. 2013. *Roundtable on Alternatives to Immigration Detention.* Kuala Lumpur: SUHAKUM.

Tlozek, Eric. 2015. Manus Island Detention Centre Staff Failing to Respect PNG Law, Flying Out to Escape Questioning, Police Say. *ABC News*, 28 September 2015. http://www.abc.net.au/news/2015-09-27/manus-island-police-detention-centre-staff-fail-to-respect-law/6807844

UNHRC (United Nations High Commission for Refugees). 1997. A v. Australia, Communication No. 560/1993, U.N. Doc. CCPR/C/59/D/560/1993. http://hrlibrary.umn.edu/undocs/html/vws560.html

UNHCR. 2007. Advisory Opinion on the Extraterritorial Application of Non-Refoulement Obligations under the 1951 Convention Relating to the Status of Refugees and its 1967 Protocol. 26 January 2007. http://www.refworld.org/docid/45f17a1a4.html

———. 2015a. National Action Plan—Malaysia. http://www.unhcr.org/5660000a9.pdf

———. 2015b. National Action Plan—Indonesia. http://www.unhcr.org/5666a2ea9.pdf

———. 2016a. Submission by The Office of the United Nations High Commissioner for Refugees. Inquiry into the Serious Allegations of Abuse, Self-Harm and Neglect of Asylum-Seekers in Relation to the Nauru Regional Processing Centre, and Any Like Allegations in Relation to the Manus Regional Processing Centre Referred to the Senate Legal and Constitutional

Affairs Committee. Submission 43. http://www.aph.gov.au/Parliamentary_Business/Committees/Senate/Legal_and_Constitutional_Affairs/NauruandManusRPCs/Submissions

———. 2016b. UNHCR Global Report 2015. http://www.unhcr.org/gr15/index.xml

———. 2016c. Mediterranean Death Toll Soars, 2016 is Deadliest Year Yet. http://www.unhcr.org/news/latest/2016/10/580f3e684/mediterranean-death-toll-soars-2016-deadliest-year.html

———. 2016d. Progress Report mid-2016. Beyond Detention: A Global Strategy to Support Governments to End the Detention of Asylum-seekers and Refugees—2014–2019. http://www.refworld.org/docid/57b850dba.html

UNOHCHR. 2017. International Covenant on Civil and Political Rights. http://www.ohchr.org/EN/ProfessionalInterest/Pages/CCPR.aspx

US State Department. 2015. Country Reports on Human Rights Practices for 2015: Thailand. Bureau of Democracy, Human Rights, and Labor. https://www.state.gov/j/drl/rls/hrrpt/humanrightsreport/index.htm?year=2015&dlid=252803

Vaughan-Williams, Nick. 2015. *Europe's Border Crisis: Biopolitical Security and Beyond*. Oxford: Oxford University Press.

Vaughan-Williams, Nick, and Adrian Little. 2016. Stopping Boats, Saving Lives, Securing Subjects: Humanitarian Borders in Europe and Australia. *European Journal of International Relations*: 1–24.

Yonesta, Febi. 2015. *Fact Sheet: Indonesia*. Jakarta: SUAKA.

CHAPTER 7

Producing Precarity

This chapter deals with regulatory frameworks and practices that contribute to the precarity of migrants' lives. The argument here is that precarious economic and social conditions for migrant workers and asylum seekers are neither accidental nor intrinsic to the process of migration, but rather are produced by a combination of punitive enforcement and systematic neglect in state regulation.

Some scholarship on labour precarity, especially in relation to developed economies, has tended to relate the concept to changes in forms of production and employment associated with post-Fordist or neo-liberal globalisation (e.g., Standing 2011). While such claims can draw valuable attention to the broader economic context of precarity, there is a danger of overemphasising the newness of precarious labour, or of assuming the phenomena is linked and limited to a particular stage of economic development. As Castles (2015) argues, the forms of labour precarity faced by migrant workers are part of a continuous history of labour market differentiation and segmentation produced and enforced through gendered and raced discrimination. The interaction of multiple forms of social discrimination with economic precarity has also been well described and theorised by intersectional feminist scholars (Crenshaw 1989; Yuval-Davis 2006).

Just as precarity has become a recognised term with a certain currency in academic and policy circles to describe the social effects of insecurity and uncertainty, 'resilience' has become used in some quarters to describe the capacity of individuals and communities to withstand conditions of

N. Henry, *Asylum, Work, and Precarity*, Critical Studies of the Asia-Pacific, DOI 10.1007/978-3-319-60567-8_7

insecurity and uncertainty. Even more than precarity though, resilience as a term of academic and policy art has functioned as an empty signifier (Laclau and Mouffe 1985), especially well suited to the projection of (neo-)liberal goals of state retrenchment (Joseph 2013), even as the term also finds favour in the academic niche of post-liberalism (Chandler 2014). Portraying communities as resilient to the collapse or withdrawal of public services, especially in disaster or crisis contexts, can operate as a moral alibi for the state to neglect the welfare and protection needs of vulnerable groups.

In *Precarious Life*, Butler argues for recognition of lived precarity and bodily vulnerability as an ethical practice within and against processes of extended extra-territorial sovereignty in the context of the war on terrorism, including state violence, torture and indefinite detention. Her argument is that the discursive framing of these sovereign practices have created categories of life which are denied the possibility of being mourned and as a consequence removed from consideration as political subjects. In this chapter, I suggest that the ethical and political imperative to recognise and resist the production of precarity that Butler draws attention to in the context of the war on terrorism is just as urgently applicable in the context of labour and asylum migration. Here too we find groups who are discursively framed as other and foreign to national populations, their existence and presence described routinely as illegal and undesirable, and who are exposed to risk and harm as a result, including through sovereign practices that exclude them from the protection of law or consideration as political subjects. Butler's theorisation of precarity is useful in the way it links the framing and production of precarity as a performative process, including through the ways that the production of precarity obscures its own existence and inhibits political recognition of vulnerable populations.

Precarity can be understood as the structural conditions and lived experience of a lack of security. Just as security takes a variety of forms or aspects, as described, for instance, in the literature on the necessary conditions and components of human security, so precarity is experienced as the result of intersecting vulnerabilities. As Banki (2013) points out, precarity does not necessarily denote an immediate harm or threat, but rather the state of vulnerability to a harm or threat that could strike at any time. Precarious labour, for instance, could be defined as a lack of security in the continuing availability and conditions of employment. Precarious workers lack protection against unemployment, and also face a lack of power to define the conditions of the work or protect themselves against exploitation and abuse. Precarity then, is not the fact of exploitation and abuse, but the vulnerability to it as a result of a structural lack of security. In this, precarity could be compared to Hobbes' description of the state of war in *Leviathan* (1996, 76):

> For war consisteth not in battle only, or the act of fighting, but in a tract of time, wherein the will to contend by battle is sufficiently known: and therefore the notion of time is to be considered in the nature of war, as it is in the nature of weather. For as the nature of foul weather lieth not in a shower or two of rain, but in an inclination thereto of many days together: so the nature of war consisteth not in actual fighting, but in the known disposition thereto during all the time there is no assurance to the contrary.

In the same way as precarious labour is structurally defined by the ever-present possibility of unemployment, precarious status for migrants who lack required documents is defined by the always imminent threat of detention and deportation. Precarity is a structural condition because it acts to define a whole field of life possibilities and power relations. A precarious worker can be more easily exploited because an employer can use the power to give or withhold work in order to bargain down other terms and conditions. A precarious migrant can be extorted for bribes, or otherwise exploited by any number of petty authority figures, because each holds the power to hand the migrant over to immigration authorities for detention or deportation. In the case of an undocumented migrant worker, who may also be an asylum seeker, an employer holds both these positions of unequal power and the migrant worker is doubly precarious.

Precarity is also a structural condition in a second sense, in that it is produced by the defining features of the social environment and power relations of the precarious subject. For migrant workers and asylum seekers, the precarity of their position is defined by the deliberate policy decisions and state actions that make up the migration border regime. Each dimension of vulnerability that produces migrant precarity is produced by a real and present threat underpinned by state violence or neglect. The vulnerability of migrants with irregular status is defined by the threat of arrest, detention and deportation, the arbitrary enforcement of the carceral immigration regime described in the previous chapter. The vulnerability of migrant workers is added to by the threat of total poverty that unemployment represents in conditions where the worker lacks access to social protection and welfare systems.

The precarity of asylum seekers and migrant workers also increases vulnerability to various forms of abuse, including sexual and gender-based violence. Migrants are vulnerable to coercion, including sexual harassment and assault, as a result of precarious employment and immigration status. Migrants with irregular status are also unlikely to be able to access protection from police or the justice system without putting themselves at risk of detention or deportation.

The intersectional nature of precarity is central to the concept and to the experience of the phenomenon. For asylum-seekers and refugees who lack what UNHCR calls a 'durable solution', including security of residence and livelihood as well as freedom from persecution, and for migrant workers who lack secure immigration and work-permit status, precarity is experienced as a multi-dimensional and intersectional exposure to constant risk. Central to this condition is what Banki (2013) defines as 'precarity of place', the danger of imminent removal or deportation, that prevents precarious refugees and other migrants from putting down roots and feeling secure in their lives. Exposure to some form of precarity of place, as a feeling of no longer being safe where one lives, is to some degree a universal aspect of the traumatic experience of becoming a refugee and is a common aspect of the experience of many migrant workers as well. When this precarity is extended through the operation of migration border regimes that prevent security of residence, in part through the constant threat of arbitrary removal, the re-traumatising effects of life under these conditions expose refugees and other migrants to serious psychological harm.

Previous chapters have focused on the mechanisms of overt control enabled by framing irregular migration as a security threat, from surveillance and screening mechanisms, to the carceral practices of migration enforcement and detention networks. As practices of state power in control of bodies, the physical features of these regimes of border control would fit within Foucault's early work on institutions of discipline and punishment. There would certainly be enough material to write on the panopticon of the border, or the penology of immigration detention. Nevertheless, as a set of disciplinary institutions, contemporary migration borders are in a state of constant flux aimed at influencing the movement of populations beyond the control of states, as well as to forestall and contain the agency of migrant populations within the territory of states. As such, the disciplinary functions of the migration border are caught up in what Deleuze (1992, 7) called in *Postscript on the Societies of Control* the 'crisis in institutions' accompanying the changing role of the state in governing processes of social, political and economic life that have exceeded traditional forms of regulation and discipline (see also Mitropoulos 2015).

Where Foucault's (2008) theory of governmentality as an approach to governance of populations emphasised concern with biopolitics, or forms of control over the care of the body and the necessities of life, Mbembe (2014) has described as 'necropolitics' the concomitant concern of contemporary states with control over the means and distribution of death. The production of precarity described in this chapter is a form of inversion of biopolitics, or withdrawal of care, that is aimed at the exploitation, control and governance of populations rather than their elimination. In producing precarity states withdraw and actively block access to the forms of care and protection necessary for security in contemporary life as a tactic in the control of populations. By the production of precarity, populations of asylum seekers and migrant workers are made more easily exploited through flexible labour arrangements, as well as less able to find settled or permanent forms of life, while the dangers and abuses suffered by irregular migrants are displayed as exemplary deterrents to others seeking to cross borders.

Asylum Seekers and Refugees

To be a refugee is already to be in a condition of precarity in relation to a well-founded fear of persecution. In addition to this originating precarity of persecution is the precarity of movement as a refugee, including the perils of migration with irregular status. In the territorial jurisdictions through which they pass on their journeys as well as that of their destination, asylum seekers face a further form of precarity of status as their claims for humanitarian protection remain undecided.

Delays in Status Determination

For asylum seekers, a major contributing factor to their precarious existence in transit countries is the lengthy delays in refugee status determination and the delay or unavailability of resettlement. In Southeast Asia, the main organisation responsible for status determination is the UNHCR, since the primary transit countries—Malaysia, Thailand and Indonesia—are not signatories to the refugee convention and do not conduct status determination. The problem for UNHCR Asia-Pacific is that they are substantially under-funded and as a result lack the capacity to manage status determination in a timely manner for the numbers of asylum-seekers in the region.

In the broad Asia-Pacific region of UNHCR operations, which includes Central Asia and Southwest Asia (the Middle-East), the final budget for approved operations in 2015 totalled 596 million US dollars, of which only 207 million dollars was contributed by donors, leaving nearly 65% of planned operations unfunded. As a result, the organisation was forced to make 'difficult decisions' to scale back operations and reduce staff. In particular, 'protection-related activities—including registration, monitoring and refugee status determination—were scaled down, causing some delays and backlogs' (UNHCR 2016, 77). The shortfall for Asia-Pacific operations was part of a global trend in which UNHCR budgets for operations to meet assessed needs doubled between 2010 and 2015 but were not met by equivalent growth in contributions, with the global UNHCR budget deficit increasing from 36% in 2010 to 49% in 2015 (UNHCR 2016, 20).

In Thailand, there were at least 10,000 asylum seekers and refugees living in urban areas without legal status or protection in 2016. This group are in addition to the refugees from Myanmar living in the camps on the Thai-Myanmar border, and the Rohingya asylum seekers in the South of Thailand. For the urban asylum seekers, the main purpose for being in Thailand is to gain access to UNHCR in the hope of being recognised as a refugee and resettled to a third country. However, without legal status in Thailand, these urban asylum seekers are in a highly precarious situation, vulnerable to arrest and detention at any time, and usually unable to access basic rights to health, education and employment. The precarity of their situation is exacerbated by extreme delays in the UNHCR process. It is common for asylum seekers to wait up to four years for their first appointment with UNHCR, and at least a further year for refugee status decisions. Appeals of rejected claims or to reopen closed cases take a similar length of time again, so that some refugees have waited eight to ten years for their status to be recognised by UNHCR (Interview with Asylum Access 2015).

While less extreme than the delays encountered in Thailand, asylum seekers in Indonesia and Malaysia also face lengthy delays in status determination as a result of a backlog of cases and a lack of capacity on the part of UNHCR. In 2015, asylum seekers in Indonesia were waiting up to 20 months for their first interview after registering with UNHCR, while waiting times of at least a year were reported in Malaysia (APRRN 2015; Matas 2015, 4).

In both Nauru and Papua New Guinea, asylum seekers transferred by the Australian government have faced extreme delays of three years or more in status determination. The delays were attributed in public statements by the Australian government to the need for Nauru and PNG to establish procedures and train personnel in refugee status determination. However, according to Human Rights Watch and Amnesty International, Australian immigration officials have conducted all refugee status determination interviews on Nauru, and many of those on Manus, 'purporting to act on behalf' of the governments of Nauru and Papua New Guinea (Human Rights Watch 2016, 11).

Lack of Protection Offered by Refugee Status

The lack of an integrated or well-functioning system of refugee status assessment and protection across the region of Southeast Asia and the Pacific means that large numbers of refugees and asylum seekers in the region face uncertain and precarious conditions for extended periods as they seek refugee status and asylum or resettlement.

For refugees from Myanmar in camps on the Thailand side of the border, precarious conditions of life are enforced under Thailand's designation of the camps as temporary shelters. Residents of the camps are not permitted to construct dwellings from permanent materials such as concrete, or even to use tarpaulins, but instead are required to purchase bamboo and thatch from contractors connected to the Thai military. Thatch roofs typically have to be replaced annually and, with dwellings packed close together, leave the camps susceptible to fire. Residents are also forbidden from raising livestock or planting crops, leaving them dependent on food aid provided by a consortium of NGOs. With the improvement of political conditions in central Myanmar from 2011 onwards, the focus of international aid efforts has shifted away from the border camps and UNHCR has ceased resettlement operations. However, by 2016 around 100,000 refugees remained in the camps with no immediate prospect of sustainable return to Myanmar. The home areas of some refugees remained active conflict zones, while others were covered only by temporary ceasefire arrangements. Moreover, after lengthy absences, many refugees were unsure that they would have homes or land to return to in their home villages. Members of the Karen relief committees interviewed in 2011 expressed hope that refugees would be able to begin to return home but emphasised that return should be voluntary and would require assistance with reintegration. This example illustrates that, just as peace is more than the absence of war, return and reintegration of refugees requires more than the cessation of the conflicts and persecution that resulted in displacement. The experience of refugees from Myanmar in Thailand for nearly three decades also shows that even where refugee status and recognition of protection needs affords some minimum of physical safety, it does not offer immunity from enforced precarity.

Conditions for urban refugees and asylum seekers in Thailand are even more precarious, with their legal status being equivalent to other migrants with irregular immigration status. For asylum seekers who have their refugee status recognised by UNHCR there is no guarantee of improvement in their situation. Of the 10,000 urban asylum seekers and refugees in Thailand in 2015, around 2000 had UNHCR refugee status. However, Thailand is not a signatory to international refugee conventions and UNHCR status gives no formal or guaranteed protection against arrest and detention under immigration law.

Similarly, for the asylum seekers transferred to Australian controlled detention centres in Nauru and Papua New Guinea, recognition of refugee status made little immediate difference to their living conditions or prospects. At the time that refugee status was determined for those on Nauru, a temporary permit was granted to stay on the island for five years, with no rights to travel. Likewise, asylum seekers accepted as refugees at the Manus centre were offered resettlement in Papua New Guinea. However, with limited opportunities for employment and frequent hostility from the local population, resettlement in PNG was received more as a threat than a desirable or safe option by those held at the Manus centre.

Prospects for resettlement are little better for asylum seekers and refugees waiting in Southeast Asia. In 2014, the Australian government announced it would no longer accept resettlement from Indonesia of refugees who registered as persons of concern to UNHCR after 1 July of that year. Despite the presence in Indonesia that year of 10,500 asylum-seekers and refugees awaiting resettlement, the Australian government reduced the resettlement quota from 600 to 450 per year. The purpose of this change was described by to the Minister responsible, Scott Morrison, as 'taking the sugar off the table', meaning that Australia was seeking to extend its policy of deterrence by eliminating the incentive for asylum seekers to travel to Indonesia as a transit country in order to seek resettlement in Australia. The move was criticised by the Indonesian Foreign Ministry, which voiced 'strong concern over Australia's unilateral policy' (Alford 2014; Martin 2014). For asylum seekers already in Indonesia and registered with the UNHCR, the change would mean even more extreme waiting periods for resettlement.

Australian governments have imposed various forms of temporary and precarious visa status on asylum seekers and refugees in the country. In 1999, the Howard Coalition government introduced measures that changed the treatment of refugees who had their protection claims recognised after they were released from detention. Rather than being granted residency with a pathway to citizenship, refugees would now be granted Temporary Protection Visas (TPVs) which were reviewed every three years, with limited access to settlement services and no rights to travel or apply for family reunion visas. From 1999 until the system was abolished by the Rudd Labour Government in 2008, 11,206 TPVs were issued, but 95% of holders were eventually granted permanent residency. TPVs were reintroduced by the Abbott Coalition government in 2013 (Spinks 2013) as part of a policy commitment not to grant permanent protection visas to asylum seekers who arrive by sea.

From July 2013, the Rudd Labor government introduced mandatory offshore detention for all asylum seekers and refugees arriving by sea after that date. The announcement of mandatory offshore detention on 19 July 2013 came as the government concluded a memorandum of understanding with the government of Papua New Guinea to establish a detention centre where asylum seekers would have their refugee status assessed (Karlsen and Phillips 2014). The agreement included a provision for those found to be refugees to be resettled in PNG, rather than Australia. On 3 August, a second memorandum was announced with the government of Nauru to establish a similar detention centre for women asylum seekers and family groups with children, including an arrangement for temporary resettlement of refugees on Nauru.

Refugees in Australia seeking to reunite their families face lengthy delays, bureaucratic difficulties and high costs in accessing visas and arranging travel. The Refugee Council of Australia (RCA 2016) reports that family reunion is the most commonly raised issue of concern in their consultations with people from a refugee background and community support organisations in Australia. The RCA reports a longstanding problem with excessive delays in processing applications for family reunion under the Special Humanitarian Programme. It is common for refugees to wait for several years for a decision. If an application has mistakes or incomplete documentation, it can be rejected entirely, forcing the applicant to start the process from scratch. Refugees have also complained that requirements for formal documentation of family relationships have been applied inflexibly in situations where such documents may not exist or have been lost in the process of displacement. Australia also requires that family members be registered as UNHCR refugees to qualify for resettlement, which may not be possible in situations where family members have remained in their home countries. If visas are granted, refugees in Australia are liable for the full cost of bringing family members to the country, including airfares, the cost of migration agents and lawyers, and resettlement costs. The Abbott and Turnbull Liberal governments have also used Ministerial discretion to discriminate against family reunion applications from permanently resettled refugees who originally arrived in Australia by boat, with these applications given lowest priority. Refugees who remain on Temporary Protection or Safe Haven Enterprise visas are not eligible to apply for family reunion.

Migrant Workers

The conditions of precarity for migrants are deliberately created and enforced by states as tools of migration border enforcement and instruments of economic discipline. Even states with the most complete control of migration borders, such as Singapore and Australia, cannot prevent visa holders from overstaying the length of their visa and becoming irregular migrants, but by denying irregular migrants access to housing, jobs and public services, the state seeks to prevent and deter irregular migrants by reducing the space in which it is possible to live without documentation. In the process of enforcing these conditions, the state turns private employers, property owners, teachers and medical staff into agents of the border and increasingly brings the regime of border enforcement into contact with everyday life throughout the population and the territory of the state.

Migrant workers on skilled temporary worker subclass 457 visas have been the subject of often emotive and exaggerated claims in Australian political discourse, with the term ‘457s’ becoming a commonly used pejorative term for migrant workers. In 2013, Labor Prime Minister Julia Gillard claimed that action was needed to protect ‘Aussie’ workers from competition with increasing numbers of temporary migrant workers (Kenny 2013). Subsequent legislation adjusting eligibility criteria and requiring employers to demonstrate efforts to hire local workers before hiring migrants were widely described as a ‘crackdown’ on the migrant labour visa category (Griffiths 2013). In 2016, Senator Jacquie Lambie wrongly claimed that the presence of 'over a million 457s' was depriving Australians of jobs (ABC News 2016a). In reality, the category makes up a relatively small number of migrant workers in Australia, with fewer than 100,000 primary visa holders and around 70,000 dependants with work rights in the country in June 2016, a decline on the previous year's numbers (DIBP 2016).

Australian trade unions have frequently portrayed the skilled temporary worker visa category as a threat to jobs and working conditions in Australia, based on claims that the scheme was being misused with 'widespread fraud and rorting of the system' (ACTU 2015). The claims have been repeated by Labor party politicians, both in government and opposition, accompanied by promises to 'crack down' on the scheme and limit numbers and criteria for migrant labour visas (Kenny 2013; Baxendale 2016). However, there is limited evidence for claims of misuse of the scheme by employers. Figures released by the Australian Fair Work Ombudsman in 2015 showed that regular workplace audits in the final quarter of 2014 had found migrant workers who appeared to be employed at lower pay or skill levels than that specified on their visa in approximately 20% of cases. Of the 516 workers covered by the audit, around 100 cases were referred to DIBP for further investigation, while in two cases employers were investigated for serious breaches of labour legislation (Toscano 2015). If this sample accurately represented wider trends, it would suggest that the vast majority of workers on 457 visas are employed at or above legal minimum conditions, while around 20% or approximately 20,000 workers in 2015 may be employed at conditions above the legal minimum but below those specified on their visas. This finding is also consistent with reports of exploitation and abuse of migrant workers suggesting the most vulnerable categories of workers are those on temporary working holiday visas, international students and those with irregular migration status (UNSW Human Rights Clinic 2015).

The most precarious conditions are faced by migrant workers with temporary or irregular immigration or work status that makes them dependant on employers to endorse a continuation of their visa, or not to report a violation of visa conditions. This includes working holiday visa holders, who need employers to sign off on three months of specified (largely horticultural) work in regional Australia to qualify for a renewal of their 12-month work visa, and international students who are limited to a maximum of 40 hours work per fortnight. These workers, for whom the inequality of the employment relationship is exacerbated by their precarious and limited immigration status, are at greater risk of exploitation and abuse and are less likely to make complaints for fear of retaliation by employers (Howe 2016).

Overall, abuse and exploitation of migrant workers in Australia is widespread, although not concentrated within the skilled temporary worker (subclass 457) visa category, as media and political attention would suggest. Workers on all categories of temporary visas made 1820 complaints to Australia's Fair Work Ombudsman (FWO) in the 2015–16 financial year, making up 13% of all requests for assistance. Complaints from migrant workers made up more than a third of enforcement actions taken by the FWO, including 76% of litigation, leading to the recovery of more than three million Australian dollars in lost wages and compensation. A significant number of complaints were filed by workers on working holiday (417 Class) visas, making up 45% of complaints and half of enforcement outcomes affecting migrant workers (FWO 2016).

Based on this data, in addition to public submissions and a survey of 4056 working holiday visa holders, the FWO released a 2016 report detailing widespread exploitation of these workers. Almost a third of those surveyed reported not being paid for some or all of their work, with more than a third paid less than the minimum wage. Significant numbers (14%) reported having to pay an agent or employer to secure work, while 6% were forced to pay employers to sign off their work as part of requirements to renew their visa. A majority of those surveyed were provided with accommodation as part of their employment, which was described as of a poor standard by 25% of respondents and in the case of 31% was paid for by deductions from employees' wages without their agreement (FWO 2016, 35–38).

A majority of international students in Australia do some amount of work to support themselves during their studies. Nyland et al. (2009) reported a small sample study of 200 international students at an Australian university that found 70% had undertaken paid employment during their studies. Of the 62 students who reported their wage rate, a majority, at least 36, were paid below the legal minimum wage. Students working in restaurants, where the legal minimum wage was at least $16.08 per hour, reported wage rates as low as $7 per hour.

In Malaysia, the most common complaint fielded by the Migrant Workers' Resource Centre is non-payment of salary. In some cases, this might mean employers delaying or refusing to pay the entire salary, but more common was refusal to pay workers their entitlements on top of the basic salary, such as overtime payments. The MWRC coordinator in Kuala Lumpur commented that while non-payment was the most common complaint from workers, interviews had revealed numerous other problems:

> When they come to us they say our salaries are not paid. But when you do an in-depth interview with them you realise they are surrounded by multiple problems that they don't realise.

Workers interviewed by MWRC Malaysia reported long hours of work, lack of payment for overtime, lack of a written contract or payslips, and overcrowded and unhygienic accommodation. Employers were also commonly holding workers' passports in violation of Malaysia's passport law:

> The employers want to hold the passports because they always say the workers will "run away" from employment. But nobody owns them, it's not that they are running away from a prison. When you use this term you are already putting it in your mind that they are slaves.

According to the MWRC coordinator, this perception that workers would 'run away' if employers did not hold their passports was even shared by many officials in the Home Ministry with responsibility for regulation of migrant labour. Although Malaysian law forbids employers from holding passports, the practice is widespread and the law was not being enforced.

Where contracts were provided to migrant workers in Malaysia, these were often used as part of a process of deceptive recruitment, to promise inflated wages that would not be paid. An organiser with the MTUC who had personally filed thousands of complaints on behalf of migrant workers showed binders full of contracts that had been provided to workers prior to departure for Malaysia, promising wages in excess of the legal minimum of 900 Ringgit per month, often as high as 1200 Ringgit. On arrival, workers would be required to sign substitute contracts held by the employer offering lower wages with deductions for accommodation and other expenses. According to an organiser with the Malaysian office of the Global Union Federation for construction workers IndustriALL, the practice of compulsory deductions for accommodation was only introduced after Malaysian law was changed to apply minimum wages to migrant workers. Before the change, migrants had been paid lower wages and required to stay in employer run dormitories as part of the practice of controlling workers.

Since the introduction of minimum wages, the controlled dormitories had been described as employer-provided private accommodation that workers were required to pay for out of their wages.

Other conditions in the contracts workers were required to sign included prohibitions on marrying Malaysians, participating in activities that could be interpreted as political or subversive or illegal, activities associated with trade unions, or causing social problems. Despite these provisions being outside of any legal restrictions, and contrary to legal rights of workers, employers were able to enforce the prohibitions with the threat of dismissal and deportation for non-compliance. Due to the fact migrant workers are not able to change employers on their existing work permit, if a worker is dismissed from their job they can be immediately sent back home.

The precarious status of both documented and undocumented migrant workers means they are vulnerable to demands for bribes by corrupt local officials. Workers interviewed by the MTUC as part of the organisation's complaints assistance process told staff they carry small amounts of money in different pockets stitched into their clothes, so they can pay bribes demanded by different local authorities without having all their money taken at once. Bribes are routinely demanded at street stops by RELA security volunteers, police, immigration and others. Police will typically demand 20 Ringgit, while immigration agents expect 40 Ringgit or higher. Workers who refused or were unable to pay risked being detained and deported, or beaten. The precarious legal and social status of migrant workers also leaves them vulnerable to violence and theft by local criminals and gangs who know that the workers are unlikely to seek help from the police.

In addition to vulnerability to violence, migrant workers are at increased risk of injury or death resulting from unsafe conditions in their workplaces. A large number of deaths of migrant workers in Malaysia go uninvestigated, and are not recorded in any government process or official statistics. An MTUC organiser who had personally dealt with a large number of such cases reported that families of migrants who were killed at work in Malaysia routinely had to pay bribes to hospital and morgue staff to have the bodies released for funerals. In one case, after the MTUC and Indonesian embassy staff intervened, staff at the hospital morgue agreed to reduce their demand for a bribe, but only from 4700 to 4200 Ringgit. The local police station demanded another bribe of 200 Ringgit to release the death certificate. Although no government agency was tracking work-related deaths in Malaysia, contacts at the Bangladesh embassy told MTUC staff they were dealing with an average of seven deaths per day of

Bangladeshi workers in Malaysia. Similar reports from the Nepal embassy suggested staff had processed over 300 deaths of Nepali workers in Malaysia in the first half of 2015. The understanding of embassy and trade union staff was that the majority of these deaths were work-related. MTUC staff also suggested that some deaths of migrant workers were suspicious, but had not been investigated as potential homicides. In one case, a migrant activist was found hanged in suspicious circumstances, but his death was recorded as suicide and his body sent home without further investigation.

A survey of Malaysian employers of migrant domestic workers found that a majority did not believe that workers should have the right to a weekly day off, or to overtime allowances for working more than 14 hours a day. 68% of employers believed domestic workers were sufficiently protected under existing Malaysian law. Despite this, 85% thought that employers should hold the passports of workers, in contravention of Malaysia's 1966 Passport Act (CARAM Asia 2010, 8, 43).

Migrant domestic workers in Malaysia are forbidden by law from becoming pregnant or getting married. If a domestic worker gets pregnant or marries, she may be immediately deported. According to a handbook for employers issued by the department of Labour, the employer is responsible for ensuring the worker does not marry. If the domestic worker 'runs away' from the employer's house, the employer may be fined 250 Ringgit. These rules and penalties create structural conditions that incentivise employers to restrict the freedom of movement and sexual and reproductive rights of women migrant workers employed in household labour.

Migrant workers in Thailand routinely face pay and conditions below legal minimum standards. Agricultural workers from Myanmar in the Northern Thai province of Tak commonly receive less than half the minimum wage of 300 Baht per day (Thin Lei Win 2014). Likewise, garment factory workers, typically female workers from Myanmar, working in Mae Sot and other towns on the Thai-Myanmar border, earn less than minimum wage, as do their male counterparts working in construction and agriculture. Interviews with migrant workers and organisers from informal trade union groups such as the Young Chi Oo workers' association and Joint Action Group in 2006, 2011 and 2013 revealed that while these wage rates had improved incrementally since 2006, when workers and trade union organisers reported standard wage rates as low as 60 baht per day, wages remained substantially below legal minimum rates and as low as 120 baht per day.

A 2006 study by the ILO found particularly heightened indicators of precarity for two groups of young migrant workers: female domestic workers and men working on fishing boats. 20% of migrants working in the fishing industry reported being forced to work, while 60% of domestic workers were not allowed to leave the premises and 8% reported being physically locked up by employers. Forty-five per cent of workers in the fishing industry and 82% of domestic workers reported working more than 12 hours a day (cited in Caballero-Antony 2008, 171).

Singapore has no minimum wage for workers on low-skilled work visas. Workers on skilled migrant visas ('S Pass' holders) qualify for a minimum wage of 2200 Singapore dollars per month, but low-skilled workers are paid substantially less than this, as little as 100 or 200 dollars per month after deductions for extremely basic accommodation. On the promise of significantly higher wages, migrant workers take on average debts of between 10,000 and 15,000 Singapore dollars to come to Singapore. For workers who manage to pay off these debts, it takes an average of 17 months working 15 hours every day before they are able to save any money for themselves or their families.

There is no financial support or safety net for migrant workers who are unable to work as a result of injury, or who arrive to find the jobs they were promised do not exist. An NGO working with migrant workers in Singapore, Transient Workers Count Too (TWC2) set up a food program to provide daily meals to 5–600 workers in these situations. Many of these workers eventually return home without managing to pay back the debts they incurred to get to Singapore. An organiser with TWC2 compared the situation for South Asian, particularly Bangladeshi, migrant workers in Singapore to that of their counterparts in the Gulf Arab States, where research has shown a majority of Bangladeshi workers return home financially worse off than they began, due to high-interest debts and chronic underpayment of wages (Rahman 2009).

Lack of Protection for Migrant Workers

Labour market institutions including trade union membership and collective bargaining, together with legislated standards such as minimum wages, are effective means of reducing precarity by improving wages and working conditions, reducing inequality and improving social cohesion (Betcherman 2012). Consequently, when particular groups such as migrant workers are excluded from these institutions the precarity of their working and social lives is exacerbated.

Labour Legislation and Minimum Standards

Migrant workers face difficulties accessing legal protection in the form of minimum wages and standards. In Malaysia and Thailand, flouting of minimum wages and other legislated standards including health and safety regulations is so common in industries where the workforce is predominantly composed of migrant workers, that there are effectively different standards for migrant workers than for permanent residents. Similar problems are widespread across the region of migrant workers lacking equivalent access to legal protection and minimum standards compared to the resident population.

In some industries, the remoteness or difficulty of access to the workplaces of migrants inhibits legal protection and regulation. This is the case for the fishing industry across the region, as well as for plantation workers in Malaysia. The dispersion of domestic workers in private homes also creates a challenge for regulation of minimum employment standards, which most states have not attempted to respond to. In effect, minimum standards for live-in domestic workers in Thailand, Malaysia and Singapore are defined only by criminal laws against the most extreme forms of physical abuse and by weakly enforced protection against non-payment of wages. Domestic workers in Malaysia and Singapore are classed as 'servants' and excluded from most provisions of the respective Employment Acts, including minimum wages, rights to rest days and holidays, maternity leave and notice or protection from dismissal (CARAM Asia 2010, 26–27).

In each of the countries of Southeast Asia and the Pacific, a lack of enforcement of legal minimum standards for migrant workers was linked to a lack of capacity in the inspection divisions of Ministries of Labour. In Thailand, labour inspectors lacked interpreters with Myanmar, Khmer, and Lao language skills, due to the Labour department's strict interpretation of public service rules prohibiting hiring non-Thai citizens. An ILO staff member interviewed in 2015 reported a conversation with a Thai labour inspector who had claimed to be able to tell whether Myanmar fishing workers were victims of trafficking or labour abuses by 'looking in their eyes' despite being unable to communicate with the workers.

In Malaysia, according to an official with the Malaysia Trade Union Confederation interviewed in 2015, the exacting requirements for correct paperwork in order for labour inspectors to enter a workplace had frequently thwarted attempts by trade union organisations to address illegal conditions of work. Labour inspectors required warrants to enter workplace and could be legally turned away by employers for any errors in specifying the name of the company and its address.

In other cases, the geographically remote or mobile locations of workplaces allowed employers to evade labour inspectors. According to officials of the All Malaysia Estates Staff Union, interviewed in 2015, conditions on plantations in the interior of the country are among the most exploitative and dangerous of any industry. Palm oil plantations in particular are known for harsh working conditions and remote locations and are staffed almost exclusively by migrant workers, many of them undocumented. Plantations are in difficult to access places and often near borders between the states of Malaysia. Labour inspectors in Malaysia only have jurisdiction for a particular state, so if workers cross state lines, the inspector loses jurisdiction. Isolated roads mean plantation managers can see inspectors coming and have time to send workers to hide in the jungle or in trucks across state lines.

Trade Union Membership

Trade union membership has been shown to be effective in increasing wages, reducing wage inequality and discrimination, and improving job security and other social benefits for members (Betcherman 2012, 27–34). Trade unions also provide political spaces for struggles against multiple social oppressions, including along lines of race, gender and sexuality, even as unequal power relations are reproduced within the structures of unions (see for instance Das Gupta 2008; Furnow et al. 2011; Ledwith and Colgan 2007). As collective political actors, trade unions build international coalitions on a range of social justice issues and in turn make use of these coalitions to promote union organising activities (Waterman and Timms 2005; Wills 2002). However, there are several factors that pose challenges for union organising of temporary migrant workers. Workers on temporary contracts or on sites where there is a high turnover of staff are more difficult for traditional trade unions to successfully organise and represent in collective bargaining. Migrant workers may face additional cultural and language barriers to membership where unions do not make sufficient efforts to overcome these differences. These difficulties can be compounded by government regulations and restrictions on unions, and by employers' use of a range of legal and extra-legal measures to deter unionisation. Holdcroft (2013, 43) cites 'triangular' employment relationships involving sub-contractors as a common factor preventing migrant workers from joining the same unions as their non-migrant co-workers, in addition to legislative restrictions and threats of retaliation by employers. In Malaysia, a trade union organiser showed me copies of employment contracts threatening dismissal for any workers who joined a union.

Such conditions are common, despite being illegal under Malaysian law and contrary to ILO conventions on freedom of association.

The ILO Committee on Freedom of Association (CFA) and Committee of Experts on the Application of Conventions and Recommendations (CEACR) have recognised that 'some forms of precariousness often deprive workers of access to freedom of association and collective bargaining rights or can dissuade them from trade union membership' (Vacotto 2013, 128). This is especially the case where workers are hired on temporary contracts by sub-contracting or labour hire firms, meaning that the workers have a different legal employer than permanent workers on the same sites and may not have the right to join the same union or collective contract as other employees (Holdcroft 2013, 43). Governments have obligations under ILO conventions to prevent anti-union discrimination, promote collective bargaining, and defend the rights to freely form and join trade unions and to take industrial action. However, ILO committees have upheld complaints in a wide range of cases where such rights and protections are undermined by the forms of precarious employment typically experienced by migrant workers, including the use of temporary insecure contracts and third-party labour outsourcing (Vacotto 2013, 129).

Under labour law in Thailand and Malaysia, any legally employed workers are eligible to join trade unions, but only citizens can be elected as union officials or delegates. This creates a serious restriction on union organising in industries where the workforce is predominantly or entirely composed of migrant workers. A further difficulty is introduced when migrant workers are employed by labour-hire outsourcing firms, as is increasingly the case in Malaysia. In these cases, migrant workers employed by a contracting firm may face difficulty joining the same union as directly employed workers and may consequently be excluded from collective bargaining unless unions make efforts to overcome barriers to multi-employer bargaining.

In 2003, when registration for work permits in Thailand was fully opened to migrant workers for the first time, local labour support groups on the Thai-Myanmar border made a concerted effort to organise workers to apply for both work permits and membership of Thai trade unions. Organisers with the Federation of Trade Unions of Burma, a network of clandestine workers' organisations operating in military-ruled Myanmar and operating as a labour support organisation for workers from Myanmar in Thailand, collected several hundred membership forms on behalf of a sympathetic Thai trade union. However, the membership drive proved unsuccessful because Thailand's Ministry of Labour would not accept registration of union branches without Thai citizen members as delegates.

In Malaysia, the MTUC trade union organisation had applied twice to register a legal association for migrant domestic workers, but had been turned down without explanation. On the second attempt, the MTUC had nominated domestic workers with Malaysian citizenship as the leaders of the association, but this was also rejected.

In Singapore, trade unions are closely linked to government and the largest association for migrant workers is state-run. The alignment of trade unions with state structures, combined with strict regulations on the activity of private associations, means that there are no significant efforts to independently organise migrant workers into unions. The largest association for migrant workers, HOME, is a state-run quasi-NGO that provides advocacy services and social activities for migrant workers. HOME also hosts the ILO-funded Migrant Workers' Resource Centre, filling a space that in Malaysia and Thailand is occupied by a national trade union centre.

In conditions where traditional trade union organising is made difficult or impossible by hostile regulations and structural conditions of precarity, trade unions and other labour support organisations are still able to act in solidarity with migrant workers by providing resources for community organising and advocacy. While there have been successful interventions in support of migrant workers by trade unions and labour support organisations in each of the destination countries in Southeast Asia and the Pacific, major challenges and difficulties remain, including continuing disinterest or hostility towards migrant workers from some among the members and leaders of traditional unions.

Profit from Precarity

Labour migration into and within Southeast Asia is financed by personal debt, typically advanced through informal credit connected to the recruitment chain. Workers borrow the costs of travel and the substantial fees and commissions they pay to recruitment agents against the promise of higher wages that will allow them to pay back their loans and save money to send home. This dynamic of labour migration is especially prevalent in Malaysia and Singapore, where a significant proportion of migrant labour comes from South Asia, with high recruitment costs financed by private loans. Although the same situation exists in Thailand, the relative ease of crossing borders for workers from Myanmar, Laos and Cambodia lowers the costs and hence the dependence on brokers.

In Malaysia and Singapore, it is common for employers to receive a kickback payment from recruitment agents when they hire new workers. Because immigration permits are issued in response to specific applications from employers, recruitment agents are willing to pay employers for the employment positions that they then on-sell to migrant workers. According to the Malaysian trade union federation, employers are able to make extra money from recruitment agents by agreeing to inflate the number of work permits they apply for, with the surplus workers then joining the irregular labour market.

The recruitment costs and government levies passed on to workers have the effect of putting a price on regular jobs, with the addition of a commission that is shared between employers and recruitment agents. This rent-seeking behaviour, financed by migrant workers' private debt, is so lucrative that at times it has eclipsed the profits to be made from productive migrant labour. According to interviews with staff of trade unions and labour support NGOs in 2015, unscrupulous agents in both Malaysia and Singapore have been known to exploit this opportunity by collecting fees from workers for non-existent jobs, who have then found themselves stranded at the airport or in substandard accommodation without income or employment.

In Singapore, the high monthly cost of government levies on employment of migrant workers, together with the potential to profit from employing new workers, creates the combined financial incentive to increase turnover of workers. In particular, it is more profitable for employers to lay off their workforce between busy periods and hire new workers when required. The combination of these financial incentives creates structural conditions of precarity by favouring high turnover, temporary and insecure work. According to a labour support organisation in Singapore, interviewed in 2015, in the cases where more established employers—such as large construction firms—wish to reduce staff turnover, it is common for workers to be charged a fee of around 4000 Singapore dollars to renew their work permit, despite the government fee for the renewal being only around 20 dollars. This fee is effectively covering the opportunity cost for the employer of choosing to forgo the recruitment fee kickback they could gain by continually churning their workforce.

In 2014, a Myanmar newspaper reported that Thai employers were concerned that improvements in the political situation in Myanmar would lead migrant workers to return home, depriving them of a cheap source of labour (Thin Lei Win 2014, 6). The article noted that workers from Myanmar typically receive less than the official Thai minimum wage and work in jobs and conditions that Thai nationals would refuse.[1]

Organising Against Precarity

In Singapore, employment law does not allow migrant workers on low-skill worker permits to join trade unions. In addition, state security laws limit freedom of speech and association and are applied particularly strictly to non-citizens, meaning that migrant workers are unable to formally organise in any kind of membership-based association. Even labour support organisations staffed by Singaporean and Western citizens were restricted in the kinds of events they could organise for migrant workers. No protests or marches were possible, but one organisation had held events such as poetry readings and theatre performances for audiences including migrant workers. Permits for these events had to applied for months in advance, with a full script of all speeches and performances to be included. Permits required participants not to deviate from vetted scripts and to avoid any comments on race, religion, or politics.

For some groups of migrant workers in Singapore, informal organising has been possible through social clubs. Two examples are the Indonesian Family Network (IFN) and the Filipino Family Network (FFN), comprising female migrants from Indonesia and the Philippines respectively who work in Singapore as domestic workers. IFN and FFN members are generally domestic workers who have a regular day off and arrange to meet in parks and other public spaces and organise social events. While the ostensible function of both organisations is social and non-political, members of the IFN and FFN support each other with personal problems, including employment disputes. The organisations also provide a conduit to Singaporean labour support organisations and media outlets who can advocate or intervene on behalf of domestic workers. However, a labour support organiser reported that no such organisations existed for male migrant workers, and suggested that such an organisation might be less likely to be tolerated by Singapore's police, who tend to treat groups of male foreign workers as a threat to public order. When migrant bus drivers organised a strike in 2013, many were deported and four were charged with criminal offences. Similarly, after the Little India riot of 2015, about 100 workers were deported and a few were criminally charged. Like many aspects of government policy in Singapore, the securitised policing of public order is structured around racialised profiling by nationality. In this context, police would be unlikely to grant permission for meetings or organisations of male migrant workers, even if the stated purpose was social and apolitical.

In Malaysia, the government has refused permission for migrant workers to form any legal associations. One association of Philippines workers, affiliated with the Migranté network, had been able to operate informally by registering with the Philippines government but organising workers in Malaysia, but the organisation had no official standing in Malaysia and was therefore in a precarious legal position. Another avenue for workers to seek support or assistance in filing legal complaints was to contact trade unions in their home countries who would then work together with the Malaysian trade union centre. The MTUC had ongoing working relationships with trade union centres in all the major origin countries of migrant workers, including Nepal and Bangladesh, with agreements to provide support to workers from these countries.

For the trade union supported MWRC and other labour support organisations in Malaysia such as Tenaganita, the main objective was to find ways of organising migrant workers, whether formally or informally. As the MWRC coordinator described the goal and purpose of autonomous organising:

> Only by organising the workers will you have leaders who are responsible to the workers themselves. Having advocacy is one thing, having good laws is one thing, but if the workers are not able to dialogue with the management of the company, everything goes down. So our main objective is to organise workers.

For some groups of workers, it was possible to organise informally in cooperation with religious organisations. This was especially fruitful in organising efforts among workers from the Philippines with the support of local leaders of the Catholic Church in Malaysia. However, according to the MWRC coordinator, this was not possible for some other groups, especially Hindu and Muslim female workers who were more likely to pray at home and not attend regular services. Domestic workers were also most difficult to organise in general due to their dispersal and isolation, effectively confined to the homes of their employers and often not allowed any independent time off work.

Despite difficulties in organising formal trade unions, migrant workers from Myanmar in Thailand have formed effective organisations for solidarity and mutual aid through community organising strategies, informal networking and formal cooperation with Thai and international NGOs. In the export-oriented garment industry around the border town of Mae Sot, the workforce of predominantly female garment workers maintain active social networks between factories, including through conversations at the local markets, Buddhist temple, and Baptist Church. Through these social networks, workers have contact with union organisers and organise collective social events, including for Karen New Year and religious holidays.

Community based organisations in Mae Sot such as the Yaung Chi Oo Workers Association maintain modest offices and a network of largely volunteer organisers who organise collective activities. In collaboration with the MAP foundation, organisers and members of Yaung Chi Oo run regular radio programs, information sessions on workers' rights, and legal clinics staffed by Thai lawyers. Organisers from the Federation of Trade Unions of Myanmar have also maintained a presence on the border since the organisation was founded, and have developed a successful school for the children of migrant workers. When workers have been laid off or locked out by their employers, organisers from these union networks and community organisations have helped with negotiations with employers and local authorities and worked with religious leaders to arrange shelter for the workers. This support is important, since the workers are vulnerable to arrest and deportation in any dispute with their employer or when their employment is terminated.

In Australia and New Zealand, formal trade union organising networks have rarely extended into communities of temporary migrant workers, although some unions have begun to organise around campaigns in particular industries. However, informal contacts between migrant workers and trade union activists have been significant in exposing and organising against the worst forms of precarious and abusive working conditions. In Australia, the systematic underpayment of migrant workers working for 7-Eleven franchises was exposed by workers, together with union activists and journalists, leading to both internal and government investigations and some workers receiving compensation. The National Union of Workers (NUW) has also made efforts to organise among temporary migrant workers in the agricultural and food processing sectors. While acknowledging the difficulties of organising a workforce that is transient and precariously employed, the union has had some high profile successes using a community organising approach to target the worst employers with legal cases and media attention. In New Zealand, First Union has formed a Union Network of Migrants (UNEMIG) to organise both temporary migrants and permanent residents from migrant communities across the various industries in which the union is active. The network has been effective in raising the profile of migrant workers and migrant issues in the existing work of the union, as well as highlighting particular cases of exploitation and immigration difficulties among migrant workers.

Conclusion

Temporary migrant workers and asylum seekers are exposed to conditions of precarity across the region of Southeast Asia and the Pacific. The vulnerability of these migrants to exploitation and abuse, and their lack of security in the face of threats of arrest, detention, and deportation, are forms of precarity produced by carceral border regimes together with the lack of equal access to legal freedoms and protections for migrants. The structures that produce precarity for temporary migrant workers and asylum seekers are more than legal, so that both undocumented migrants and those with regular status experience similarly precarious conditions. While regular status may offer some protection, and is usually sought by migrants when they have the opportunity, access to regular status is not enough to ensure security in the absence of other protections. Conditions for precarious migrants can be improved by self-determined community organising and relationships based on solidarity with existing institutions, including trade unions and NGOs. However, the underlying structures of precarity are based in the carceral border regimes that define migrants as populations of risk to be monitored and controlled, and as subaltern populations subject to reduced freedoms and protections, who are therefore marked as exploitable with impunity. To fundamentally alter the precarity of migrant lives across the region will require further-reaching challenges to the structures that produce precarity and the social actors that profit from it.

Notes

1. The article reported on reactions to the presentation of a research survey conducted by the IOM Country Mission in Thailand and the Asian Research Centre for Migration at Chulalongkorn University (2013).

Bibliography

ABC News. 2016a. Fact Check: Are there 'Over a Million 457s' in Australia? http://www.abc.net.au/news/2016-06-02/fact-check-are-there-over-a-million-457s-out-there/7463706

ACTU (Australian Council of Trade Unions). 2015. Government Must Do More to Stop Fraud and Rorting of 457 Visas. http://www.actu.org.au/actumedia/media-releases/2015/government-must-do-more-to-stop-fraud-and-rorting-of-457-visas

Alford, Peter. 2014. Indonesia Calls in Envoy over Morrison Shift on Refugee Resettlement. *The Australian*, 22 November 2014. http://www.theaustralian.com.au/national-affairs/immigration/indonesia-calls-in-envoy-over-morrison-shift-on-refugee-resettlement/news-story/297d5a4fdb2fca93024e05fb897d9a67

APRRN (Asia Pacific Refugee Rights Network). 2015. Indonesia Country Briefing. http://www.aprrn.info/1//pdf/Combined_NZ.pdf

Banki, Susan. 2013. Precarity of Place: A Complement to the Growing Precariat Literature. *Global Discourse 3* (3–4): 450–463.

Baxendale, Rachel. 2016. Bill Shorten's Stance on Foreign Workers Breathtaking Hypocrisy: PM. *The Australian*. http://www.theaustralian.com.au/national-affairs/capital-circle/bill-shortens-stance-on-foreign-workers-breathtaking-hypocrisy-pm/news-story/d7d9632d9f0136664301 99f995b5318d

Betcherman, Gordon. 2012. Labor Market Institutions: A Review of the Literature. Background paper to the World Development Report 2013. *World Bank Group*. https://www.researchgate.net/publication/255724718_Labor_Market_Institutions_A_Review_of_the_Literature

Caballero-Antony, Mely. 2008. Reflections on Managing Migration in Southeast Asia: Mitigating the Unintended Consequences of Securitisation. In *Security and Migration in Asia: The Dynamics of Securitisation*, ed. Melissa G. Curley and Wong Siu-lun. Oxon: Routledge.

CARAM Asia. 2010. *Malaysia vs Hong Kong: Employers' Perception and Attitudes Towards Foreign Domestic Workers*. Kuala Lumpur: CARAM Asia.

Castles, Stephen. 2015. Migration, Precarious Work, and Rights: Historical and Current Perspectives. In *Migration, Precarity, and Global Governance: Challenges and Opportunities for Labour*, ed. Carl-Ulrik Schierup, Ronaldo Munck, Branka Likic-Brboric, and Anders Neergaard, 46–67. Oxford: Oxford University Press.

Chandler, David. 2014. Beyond Neoliberalism: Resilience, the New Art of Governing Complexity. *Resilience 2* (1): 47–63.

Crenshaw, Kimberlé. 1989. Demarginalizing the Intersection of Race and Sex: A Black Feminist Critique of Antidiscrimination Doctrine, Feminist Theory and Antiracist Politics. *University of Chicago Legal Forum*. 138–167.

Das Gupta, Tanya. 2008. Racism/Anti-Racism, Precarious Employment, and Unions. In *Daily Struggles: The Deepening Racialization and Feminization of Poverty in Canada*, ed. Siu-ming Kwok and Maria A. Wallis, 143–157. Toronto: Canadian Scholars' Press.

Deleuze, Gilles. 1992. Postscript on the Societies of Control. *October* 59: 3–7.

DIBP (Department of Immigration and Border Protection). 2016. Subclass 457 Quarterly Report: Quarter Ending at 30 June 2016. https://www.border.gov.au/ReportsandPublications/Documents/statistics/457-quarterly-report-30-06-2016.pdf

Foucault, Michel. 2008. *The Birth of Biopolitics: Lectures at the Collège de France, 1978–1979*. Basingstoke: Palgrave Macmillan.

Furnow, Mary Margaret, Suzanne Franzway, and Valentine M. Moghadam. 2011. Introduction: Globalization and Women's Social Rights. In *Making Globalization Work for Women: The Role of Social Rights and Trade Union Leadership*, ed. Valentine M. Moghadam, Mary Margaret Fonow, and Suzanne Franzway. Albany: SUNY Press.

FWO (Fair Work Ombudsman). 2016. Inquiry into the Wages and Conditions of People Working Under the 417 Working Holiday Visa Program. https://www.fairwork.gov.au/ArticleDocuments/763/417-visa-inquiry-report.pdf.aspx

Griffiths, Emma. 2013. Labor Strikes Compromise 457 Visa Crackdown Deal with Crossbench MPs. *ABC News*, 26 June 2013. http://www.abc.net.au/news/2013-06-26/labor-strikes-compromise-457-visa-deal-with-crossbench-mps/4782722

Hobbes, Thomas. 1996. *Leviathan*. Oxford: Oxford University Press.

Holdcroft, Jenny. 2013. Implications for Union Work of the Trend Towards Precarization of Work. *International Journal of Labour Research* 5 (1): 41–58.

Howe, Joanna. 2016. Examining a Temporary Migrant Worker's Ability to Make a Complaint of Sexual Harassment. *Adelaide Law School Research Paper No. 2016-25*. https://papers.ssrn.com/sol3/Delivery.cfm?abstractid=2821351

Human Rights Watch. 2016. *Submission to the Senate Legal and Constitutional Affairs Committee on its Inquiry into Abuse, Self-harm, and Neglect of Refugees and Asylum Seekers on Nauru and Manus Island*. Inquiry into the Serious Allegations of Abuse, Self-Harm and Neglect of Asylum-Seekers in Relation to the Nauru Regional Processing Centre, and Any Like Allegations in Relation to the Manus Regional Processing Centre Referred to the Senate Legal and Constitutional Affairs Committee. Submission 22. http://www.aph.gov.au/Parliamentary_Business/Committees/Senate/Legal_and_Constitutional_Affairs/NauruandManusRPCs/Submissions

IOM Country Mission in Thailand and the Asian Research Center for Migration, Chulalongkorn University. 2013. Assessing Potential Changes in the Migration Patterns of Myanmar Migrants and their Impacts on Thailand. http://th.iom.int/index.php/migration-resources/func-download/201/chk,61c1a7e0a53f61289109191a7914141a/no_html,1/

Joseph, Jonathan. 2013. Resilience as Embedded Neoliberalism: A Governmentality Approach. *Resilience 1* (1): 38–52.

Karlsen, Elibritt, and Janet Phillips. 2014. Developments in Australian Refugee Law and Policy (2012 to August 2013). Parliamentary Library of Australia. http://www.aph.gov.au/About_Parliament/Parliamentary_Departments/Parliamentary_Library/pubs/rp/rp1415/RefugeeLawPolicy

Kenny, Mark. 2013. Labor Taps Resentment on 457 Visas. *The Age*, 14 March 2013. http://www.theage.com.au/federal-politics/political-news/labor-taps-resentment-on-457-visas-20130313-2g0so

Laclau, Ernesto, and Chantal Mouffe. 1985. *Hegemony and Socialist Strategy: Towards a Radical Democratic Politics*. New York: Verso.

Ledwith, Sue, and Fiona Colgan. 2007. Tackling Gender, Diversity and Trade Union Democracy: A Worldwide Project? In *Gender, Diversity and Trade Unions: International Perspectives*, ed. Fiona Colgan and Sue Ledwith, 1–27. Abingdon: Routledge.

Martin, Lisa. 2014. We're Taking the Sugar Off Table: Morrison. *Sydney Morning Herald*, 19 November 2014. http://www.smh.com.au//breaking-news-national/were-taking-the-sugar-off-table-morrison-20141119-3kndk.html

Matas, David. 2015. Sri Lankan Tamil Refugees: Malaysia February 2015. http://www.i-tran.ca/I-TRAN%20FINAL%20REPORT%20%20MALAYSIA%202015.pdf

Mbembe, Achille. 2014. Necropolitics. In *Foucault in an Age of Terror: Essays on Biopolitics and the Defence of Society*, ed. Stephen Morton and Stephen Bygrave, 152–182. Basingstoke: Palgrave Macmillan.

Mitropoulos, Angela. 2015. Archipelago of Risk: Uncertainty, Borders and Migration Detention Systems. *New Formations* 84 (85): 163–183.

Nyland, Chris, Helen Forbes-Mewett, Simon Marginson, Gaby Ramia, Erlenawati Sawir, and Sharon Smith. 2009. International Student-Workers in Australia: A New Vulnerable Workforce. *Journal of Education and Work* 22 (1): 1–14.

Rahman, Mizanur. 2009. *In Quest of Golden Deer: Bangladeshi Transient Migrants Overseas*. Saarbrucken: VDM Verlag.

RCA (Refugee Council of Australia). 2016. Addressing The Pain of Separation for Refugee Families. http://www.refugeecouncil.org.au/wpcontent/uploads/2016/11/RCOA-Report-Family-Reunion-11-16-WEB.pdf

Spinks, Harriet. 2013. A Return to Temporary Protection Visas? *Australian Parliamentary Library*. http://www.aph.gov.au/About_Parliament/Parliamentary_Departments/Parliamentary_Library/FlagPost/2013/November/A_return_to_Temporary_Protection_Visas

Standing, Guy. 2011. *The Precariat: The New Dangerous Class*. London: Bloomsbury Academic.

Thin Lei Win. 2014. Most Burmese Migrants in Thailand Want to Go Home, But Not Yet. *Myanmar Business Today*, 2–8 January 2014, P6, 10.

Toscano, Nick. 2015. One in Five Migrant Workers on 457 Visas could be Underpaid or Incorrectly Employed. *The Sydney Morning Herald*, 29 May 2015. http://www.smh.com.au/national/one-in-five-migrant-workers-on-457-visas-could-be-underpaid-or-incorrectly-employed-20150529-ghcmxr.html

UNHCR. 2016. UNHCR Global Report 2015. http://www.unhcr.org/gr15/index.xml

UNSW Human Rights Clinic. 2015. *Temporary Migrant Workers in Australia*. University of New South Wales.

Vacotto, Beatriz. 2013. Precarious Work and the Exercise of Freedom of Association and Collective Bargaining: Current ILO Jurisprudence. *International Journal of Labour Research* 5 (1): 117–132.

Waterman, Peter, and Jill Timms. 2005. Trade Union Internationalism and a Global Civil Society in the Making. In *Global Civil Society 2004–5*, ed. Helmut Anheier, Marlies Glasius, and Mary Kaldor, 175–202. Thousand Oaks, CA: Sage.

Wills, Jane. 2002. Bargaining for the Space to Organize in the Global Economy: A Review of the Accor-IUF Trade Union Rights Agreement. *Review of International Political Economy* 9 (4): 675–700.

Yuval-Davis, Nira. 2006. Intersectionality and Feminist Politics. *European Journal of Women's Studies 1* (3): 193–209.

CHAPTER 8

Conclusion

Migration border regimes across the region of Southeast Asia and the Pacific have been transformed by the institutional framing of irregular migration as a criminal and security threat. Despite the efforts of states to prevent and deter irregular migration, the economic demand for migrant labour continues to outstrip the capacity of formal channels of migration, and the protection needs of asylum seekers from inside and outside the region continue to exceed the extremely limited places in formal resettlement programs. Irregular migration is produced by the same drivers as regular migration in combination with restrictions on opportunities to travel, work, and access protection by regular means. Carceral regimes of migration control cannot prevent irregular migration; they can only displace it and make migrant lives more precarious in the process.

The Failures of Carceral and Restrictive Border Regimes

Carceral and restrictive approaches to migration border control, of the kind increasingly implemented across the region of Southeast Asia and the Pacific, fail to meet their stated security objectives because they largely create the problems they purport to solve. At the cost of widespread and severe human suffering, restrictive migration borders allow states to partially displace populations defined as undesirable onto neighbouring

N. Henry, *Asylum, Work, and Precarity*, Critical Studies of the Asia-Pacific, DOI 10.1007/978-3-319-60567-8_8

states. This is a zero-sum approach to border management, where if one state gains another necessarily loses, and when considered from a regional perspective is worse than pointless.

Labour Migration

Across Southeast Asia and the Pacific, the richest economies depend on migrant workers for essential labour, while the economies of middle-income states rely heavily on remittances from migrants. It may seem contradictory then that states and regional organisations put such priority and spend such resources on preventing migrants from travelling for work, and that national policies across the region make the lives of migrant workers so difficult and precarious. I have argued that this apparent contradiction is a result of coordinated border regimes that are just open enough to allow for both regular and irregular movement and employment of migrant workers, while restrictive enough to keep those workers in the status of temporary precarity in which they are able to be most effectively exploited for their labour at the lowest cost.

When Thailand's military rulers attempted a total crackdown on migrant workers with irregular status in 2013, they were quickly confronted with the economic reality of Thailand's dependence on migrant labour and were forced to reverse their policy. The One-Stop Service Centres that were then opened across Thailand's border regions and industrial zones created a process for large numbers of migrant workers to achieve regularisation of their migration and work status. However, in the absence of broader reforms, regular status for migrant workers has not been enough to substantially reduce the precarity of workers' lives. Although work permits give the right to remain in Thailand, this right is temporary and conditional, and workers remain subject to arbitrary detention and deportation if they change jobs or are in dispute with their employers. The absence of political will or institutional capacity to effectively enforce minimum labour standards, combined with restrictions on the ability of migrant workers to form independent trade unions, means that migrant workers in Thailand remain in precarious conditions similar to those across the region. This is, not coincidentally, the situation that best suits the owners of industries that employ migrant workers. The opportunity to acquire regular status does, however, represent a partial improvement in the situation of migrant workers and makes organising for further improvements more possible.

The production of precarity for migrant workers by the combination of carceral border regimes and systemic neglect of protection mechanisms serves powerful interests, maintaining the exploitability and temporary status of migrant workers. The exposure of migrant workers to severe exploitation as a result of the precarity of their situation means there will always be some who perceive labour migration as undermining the conditions of other workers. Where labour migration is misrecognised as the cause of precarity and exploitation, popular support emerges for restrictions on migration and increasingly arbitrary forms of carceral border enforcement. But rather than being solutions, these measures are the foundation of the problem of migrant exploitation, by creating migrant workers as an exploitable category of precarious and unprotected workers. The alternative is to go beyond the demands of employers for continued access to migrant workers by ensuring that migrants have access to the same rights and protections as other workers, including access to regular and secure migration and work status.

Asylum

When former Australian Prime Minister Tony Abbott gave the second annual Margaret Thatcher Lecture to a Conservative Party audience in London in 2015, shortly after his removal as leader, he used the opportunity to urge Europe to follow the example his government had set by turning back asylum seekers (Clarke 2015). He claimed that turning back boats at sea, denying asylum seekers entry at borders, and setting up detention camps for those who could not be immediately returned, were the only ways 'to prevent a tide of humanity surging through Europe'. Abbott said that people smuggling was a global problem that only Australia had managed to solve. By following his government's lead, Abbott argued, other countries could solve the problem too.

However, from a regional perspective, the extreme carceral regime introduced to deter asylum seekers by successive Australian governments, and escalated by Abbott, solved no problems and created several new ones. It did nothing of course to reduce the well-founded fears of persecution driving movement of asylum seekers in the region, including from Myanmar and Sri Lanka. Preventing refugees and asylum seekers in the region from reaching Australia has done nothing to solve the causes of their displacement or to provide solutions; it has simply displaced the problem onto other states. When viewed from a regional perspective, it becomes obvious that if other states follow Australia's example by seeking to displace refugees and asylum seekers onto each other, then no state will be better off and the only result will be greater suffering for displaced people.

This was the result in May 2015, when the Thai military cracked down on migrant smuggling routes, leading to several thousand people being abandoned at sea by their smugglers. The passengers, a mix of migrant workers from Bangladesh and Rohingya asylum seekers from Myanmar, had been en route to Malaysia, but were left to drift and were repeatedly pushed back to sea by the military border agencies of Malaysia, Thailand and Indonesia. Thousands were rescued by fishing communities in Aceh, Indonesia, and others were eventually brought ashore in Malaysia, but not before hundreds died. The crisis was initially produced by a securitised response to migrant smuggling and was exacerbated by restrictive border regimes that prioritised deterrence measures to push back boats rather than rescue, disembark and protect the occupants.

As states externalise border controls beyond the immediate frontiers of their territories and increasingly enter into cooperative border control mechanisms with other states, a regional perspective becomes necessary to fully understand the processes and effects of migration border regimes. Regional organisations are emerging as significant sources of change in border regimes, alongside bilateral processes of inter-state cooperation, although the key dynamic of change in Southeast Asia and the Pacific continues to be the selective adoption by states of techniques of border management, along with opportunities for capacity building offered by regional cooperation.

The dynamics of selective adoption partially explain the unintended effects of liberal humanitarian approaches that promote the enforcement of formal channels of migration alongside protection mechanisms. The non-binding nature of cooperation and regional commitments in Southeast Asia and the Pacific has allowed states to access support for building the carceral capacity of border regimes without adopting the mechanisms of protection that are typically intended as part of the liberal humanitarian package of formal migration management.

While Australian leaders have claimed success in 'stopping the boats', the crackdown on movement of asylum seekers by sea has done nothing to reduce the population of displaced people in the region of Southeast Asia and the Pacific, who still need protection. Carceral border regimes of the type introduced by Australia and extended throughout the region of Southeast Asia and the Pacific can have some impact in preventing asylum seekers from reaching particular states, but they cannot solve the underlying causes of forced displacement.

Contributions to Research

Defining the region of interest for this book as Southeast Asia and the Pacific proved productive because it allowed for the integrated study of both source and destination countries of migration, as well as the institutional processes that connect their border regimes. The insights gained from this regional perspective could usefully provoke further comparison with similar studies of migration and border regimes in the trans-Mediterranean region (Vaughan-Williams 2015; Crawley et al. 2016) and in the Americas (Duany 2011; Rodriguez 2010; Squire 2015).

In describing border regimes as political spaces, I introduce the Deleuzian concept of the fold to describe transformations of migration border regimes based on the strategic introduction of functional ambiguity and obscurity to the political space of the border. With specific reference to the developments in Australia's extended border regime in response to asylum seekers, I argue that the space of the border has been subject to folds of location, legality, logistics, and legibility. This concept of border regimes as folded political space contributes to the spatial theory of critical border studies and responds to the call by Parker and Vaughan-Williams (2009) for new concepts of the political topology of borders.

My argument that institutional framing as trafficking and smuggling has driven the securitisation and criminalisation of irregular migration contributes most immediately to research on migration border regimes and is also relevant to the broader literature on regime formation and processes of institutional change in international relations. The concept of institutional framing adds to Entman's (1993) definition by emphasising the selection and definition of policy problems and governance approaches through which the jurisdiction, mandate and management techniques of organisations are contested and established.

The main findings of this book contribute to research on migration border regimes by showing how states coordinate carceral border regimes through the transfer of techniques and capacities of enforcement, with the assistance of regional and international organisations. Through the extension of screening mechanisms based on risk-profiling and arbitrary enforcement enabled by the expansion of carceral border institutions, states channel migration to enable some movements and frustrate others. Combined with systemic neglect of protection mechanisms, the growth of carceral borders produces precarious populations of migrants vulnerable to exploitation and abuse. This argument contributes to the emerging literature on precarity by studying the causes of precarity for migrant populations across case studies including both high-income and middle-income states. I integrate a concern with conditions for workers, focused on by most studies on precarity, with analysis of the distinct forms of precarity faced by asylum seekers and refugees that Banki (2013) draws attention to.

Contrary to research and policy approaches that cast irregular migration in terms of trafficking in persons and migrant smuggling and propose solutions based on criminalisation and securitisation, I argue that carceral and restrictive approaches to migration border governance cause the problems they claim to solve.

Ways Forward

The institutional framing of irregular migration around counter-trafficking and counter-smuggling programs has promoted the securitisation and criminalisation of migration border regimes. These approaches have failed to improve outcomes for migrants or to reduce the phenomenon of irregular migration. The process of building alternatives to carceral and restrictive migration borders needs to start with reframing our view of the problem around the needs of migrants, rather than perceived threats to borders. Migrants need access to safe regular modes of travel, protection from persecution and protection of minimum labour standards, including the freedom to form and join trade unions. These are all expectations that holders of Western passports take for granted, but they are undermined for other migrants by restrictive border regimes and arbitrary enforcement of migration rules.

To assess the protection needs of displaced people in the region, UNHCR has called for all states to adopt status determination processes and protection mechanisms for refugees. While this would ideally be done as part of a state signing up to the 1951 Convention on the Status of Refugees and the 1967 Protocol, there are existing models for states to adopt protection mechanisms without signing up to the Convention. Along these lines, the procedures adopted in Hong Kong have been promoted by UNHCR in Southeast Asia and have received some interest from policy makers in Thailand.

States in the region should be pressured to adopt a presumption of liberty and alternatives to detention in the process of assessing the status of asylum seekers. No one should be detained for seeking asylum. If an asylum seeker is detained on other grounds, including claims of security risk, they must have access to information about the reasons for their detention, access to legal representation and advocacy, and the right to challenge their detention.

Refugees and asylum seekers should have access to secure status in every country, including the legal right to work. Where refugees and asylum seekers lack recognised documents, this would require states to issue identity documents as part of status determination, or to recognise documents issued by UNHCR for the purpose of issuing work permits. Arrangements should be coordinated between states in the region so that refugees and asylum seekers can travel for work. For instance, Rohingya asylum seekers should be able to register for documents in Myanmar or Bangladesh that would allow them to work in Malaysia without relying on smugglers to make the journey. Resettlement coordinated by UNHCR should be expanded for the most vulnerable refugees, with increased quotas for resettlement in Australia and New Zealand.

For migrant workers, the process of applying for regular migration and work status must be made much easier and more affordable, to reduce the dominance of recruitment agents and the scale of private debt driving existing systems of labour migration in the region.

To ensure regular status comes with tangible benefits, workers must be able to rely on labour institutions to protect their legal rights and minimum conditions. To achieve this would require major changes in the institutional cultures and capacities of government labour institutions across the region, to shift from the informal tolerance of severe exploitation in industries staffed by migrant workers to an approach that treats migrants as worthy of protection and dignity at work.

Migrant workers must have the unrestricted right to form and join trade unions, and to take part in industrial action, with protection against retaliation by employers. Workers must also have the right to change employers and to seek alternative employment if they lose their jobs.

Freedom and dignity for migrant workers and asylum seekers will only be achieved to the extent that they have access to freedom of movement. Where the freedom to move and to remain within the territory of states is restricted, whether on the basis of citizenship or employment status, this creates categories of migrants who can be exploited on the basis of their precarious status, and it creates categories of asylum seekers whose enforced precarity is defined by their inability either to move or to settle and begin new lives. As Southeast Asia and the Pacific develops as an integrated economic region with the ASEAN Economic Community at its core, those of us with Western passports or the qualifications for skilled work already have access to unprecedented freedom to live and work in the country of our choice. We are already witnessing the dramatic development of an integrated market and production base across the region, based on the free movement of goods, services and investment. For the region to offer freedom, security and opportunity for all will require an equally dramatic expansion of freedom of movement for people.

Bibliography

Banki, Susan. 2013. Precarity of Place: A Complement to the Growing Precariat Literature. *Global Discourse 3* (3–4): 450–463.

Clarke, Melissa. 2015. Tony Abbott tells European Leaders to Turn Back Asylum Seekers or Risk 'Catastrophic Error'. *ABC News*. http://www.abc.net.au/news/2015-10-28/tony-abbott-urges-european-leaders-to-turn-back-asylum-seekers/6890886

Crawley, Heaven, Franck Düvell, Katharine Jones, Simon McMahon, and Nando Sigona. 2016. Destination Europe? Understanding the Dynamics and Drivers of Mediterranean Migration in 2015. *Unravelling the Mediterranean Migration Crisis (MEDMIG) Final Report*, November 2016. http://www.medmig.info/wp-content/uploads/2016/12/research-brief-destination-europe.pdf

Duany, Jorge. 2011. *Blurred Borders: Transnational Migration between the Hispanic Caribbean and the United States*. Chapel Hill: University of North Carolina Press.

Entman, Robert M. 1993. Framing: Toward Clarification of a Fractured Paradigm. *Journal of Communication* 43 (4): 51–58.

Rodriguez, Cristina. 2010. Building Capacity for the Transnational Regulation of Migration. *Columbia Law Review Sidebar 110*: 1–11.

Squire, Vicki. 2015. *Post/Humanitarian Border Politics between Mexico and the US: People, Places, Things*. Basingstoke: Palgrave Macmillan.

Vaughan-Williams, Nick. 2009. The Generalised Bio-political Border? Re-conceptualising the Limits of Sovereign Power. *Review of International Studies* 35 (4): 729–749.

———. 2015. *Europe's Border Crisis: Biopolitical Security and Beyond*. Oxford: Oxford University Press.

Bibliography

ABC News. 2015. Reza Barati: Trial of Pair Accused of Killing Asylum Seeker Adjourned, Main Witness Fears for Life. *ABC News*, 25 September 2015. http://www.abc.net.au/news/2015-09-25/pair-accused-of-killing-asylum-seeker-appear-in-court/6804682

———. 2016a. Fact Check: Are there 'Over a Million 457s' in Australia? http://www.abc.net.au/news/2016-06-02/fact-check-are-there-over-a-million-457s-out-there/7463706

———. 2016b. Fact Check: Would Paying People Smugglers to Turn Back Boats be Illegal? http://www.abc.net.au/news/2015-07-07/fact-check-paying-people-smugglers-to-turn-back-boats-illegal/6566184

ACTU—Australian Council of Trade Unions. 2015. Government Must Do More to Stop Fraud and Rorting of 457 Visas. http://www.actu.org.au/actu-media/media-releases/2015/government-must-do-more-to-stop-fraud-and-rorting-of-457-visas

Ah Lek, Pook. 2016. The Dilemma of having Foreign Workers in Malaysia. *The Straits Times*, 17 September 2016. http://www.straitstimes.com/opinion/the-dilemma-of-having-foreign-workers-in-malaysia

AHRC—Australian Human Rights Commission. 2016. Pathways to Protection: A Human Rights-based Response to the Flight of Asylum Seekers by Sea. https://www.humanrights.gov.au/sites/default/files/20160913_Pathways_to_Protection.pdf

Alford, Peter. 2014. Indonesia Calls in Envoy over Morrison Shift on Refugee Resettlement. *The Australian*, 22 November 2014. http://www.theaustralian.com.au/national-affairs/immigration/indonesia-calls-in-envoy-over-morrison-shift-on-refugee-resettlement/news-story/297d5a4fdb2fca93024e05fb897d9a67

N. Henry, *Asylum, Work, and Precarity*, Critical Studies of the Asia-Pacific, DOI 10.1007/978-3-319-60567-8

Ambrosini, Maurizio. 2016. Why Irregular Migrants Arrive and Remain: The Role of Intermediaries. *Journal of Ethnic and Migration Studies.* http://www.tandfonline.com/doi/pdf/10.1080/1369183X.2016.1260442

Amnesty International. 2016a. Norway: The Human Cost of 'Crushing' the Market: Criminalization of Sex Work in Norway. https://www.amnesty.org/en/documents/eur36/4034/2016/en/

———. 2016b. *By Hook or By Crook: Australia's Abuse of Asylum-Seekers at Sea.* https://www.amnesty.org.nz/sites/default/files/By_Hook_or_by_Crook_Australias_abuse_of_asylum_seekers_at_sea.pdf

———. 2016c. *Island of Despair: Australia's "Processing" of Refugees on Nauru.* https://www.amnesty.org/download/Documents/ASA1249342016ENGLISH.PDF

ANAO—Australian National Audit Office. 2017. *Offshore Processing Centres in Nauru and Papua New Guinea: Procurement of Garrison Support and Welfare Services.* https://www.anao.gov.au/sites/g/files/net2446/f/ANAO_Report_2016-17_16.pdf

Andrijasevic, Rutvica, and William Walters. 2010. The International Organization for Migration and the International Government of Borders. *Environment and Planning D: Society and Space 28* (6): 977–999.

APRRN—Asia Pacific Refugee Rights Network. 2015. *Indonesia Country Briefing.* http://www.aprrn.info/1//pdf/Combined_NZ.pdf

Aradau, Claudia. 2004. The Perverse Politics of Four-Letter Words: Risk and Pity in the Securitisation of Human Trafficking. *Millennium—Journal of International Studies* 33 (2): 251–277.

Arendt, Hannah. 1995. *Men in Dark Times.* New York: Harvest.

ASEAN—Association of Southeast Asian Nations Secretariat. 2015. *ASEAN Integration Report 2015.* ASEAN. http://www.miti.gov.my/miti/resources/ASEAN_Integration_Report_20151.pdf?mid=431

Attorney General of Australia. 2015. Portfolio Budget Statement: Australian Security Intelligence Organisation. https://www.ag.gov.au/Publications/Budgets/Budget2015-16/Documents/Portfolio-budget-statements/PBS-ASIO-2015-16.pdf

Australian Department of Defence. 2016. Operation Resolute. http://www.defence.gov.au/operations/BorderProtection/

Bali Process—Regional Support Office. 2016. Regional Cooperation Framework. www.baliprocess.net/regional-cooperation-framework

Banki, Susan. 2013. Precarity of Place: A Complement to the Growing Precariat Literature. *Global Discourse 3* (3–4): 450–463.

Barthes, Roland. 2012. *How to Live Together: Novelistic Simulations of Some Everyday Spaces.* New York: Columbia University Press.

Battistella, Graziano. 2007. Migration without Borders: A Long Way to Go in the Asian Region. In *Migration Without Borders: Essays on the Free Movement of People*, ed. Antoine Pécoud and Paul de Guchteneire. New York: Berghahn.

Baxendale, Rachel. 2016. Bill Shorten's Stance on Foreign Workers Breathtaking Hypocrisy: PM. *The Australian*. http://www.theaustralian.com.au/national-affairs/capital-circle/bill-shortens-stance-on-foreign-workers-breathtaking-hypocrisy-pm/news-story/d7d9632d9f0136664301 99f995b5318d
Bernstein, Elizabeth. 2012. Carceral Politics as Gender Justice? The "Traffic in Women" and Neoliberal Circuits of Crime, Sex, and Rights. *Theory and Society 41* (3): 233–259.
Betcherman, Gordon. 2012. Labor Market Institutions: A Review of the Literature. Background paper to the World Development Report 2013. *World Bank Group*. https://www.researchgate.net/publication/255724718_Labor_Market_Institutions_A_Review_of_the_Literature
Betts, Alexander. 2009. *Protection by Persuasion: International Cooperation in the Refugee Regime*. Cornell University Press.
Bhabha, Homi K. 2004. *The Location of Culture*. Abingdon: Routledge.
Boochani, Behrouz. 2016a. Australia, Exceptional in its Brutality. *Overland*, 25 April 2016. https://overland.org.au/2016/04/australia-exceptional-in-its-brutality/
———. 2016b. It's Hard for Me to Leave Manus Island without Justice: Behrouz Boochani on the US Refugee Deal. *The Guardian*, 13 November 2016. https://www.theguardian.com/australia-news/2016/nov/13/its-hard-for-me-to-leave-manus-island-without-justice-behrouz-boochani-on-the-us-refugee-deal
———. 2016c. A Cruel and Violent Political Strategy. *The Huffington Post*, 18 October 2016. http://www.huffingtonpost.com.au/behrouz-boochani/a-cruel-and-violent-political-strategy/
The Border Consortium. 2016. Refugee and IDP Camp Populations. December 2016. http://www.theborderconsortium.org/media/76787/2016-12-dec-map-tbc-unhcr.pdf
The Borneo Post. 2014. New Policy to Limit Recruitment of Foreign Workers. *The Borneo Post*, 27 May 2014. http://www.theborneopost.com/2014/05/27/new-policy-to-limit-recruitment-of-foreign-workers/
Broome, André, and Leonard Seabrooke. 2015. Shaping Policy Curves: Cognitive Authority in Transnational Capacity Building. *Public Administration 93* (4): 956–972.
Brown, Matt. 2012. Asylum Seekers Allegedly Abused in Indonesia. *ABC Lateline*, 8 March 2012. http://www.abc.net.au/lateline/content/2012/s3449246.htm
Brundige, Elizabeth, Winter King, Priyneha Vahali, Stephen Vladeck, and Xiang Yuan. 2004. Indonesian Human Rights Abuses in West Papua: Application of the Law of Genocide to the History of Indonesian Control. A paper prepared for the Indonesia Human Rights Network by the Allard K. Lowenstein International Human Rights Clinic Yale Law School. http://www.g-a-l.info/Yale%20Report%20on%20West%20Papuah%20rights.pdf

Burton-Bradley, Robert. 2016. 'We are Living Like a Dog': Explosion in Malaysians Seeking Asylum in Australia. *SBS World News*, 22 November 2016. http://www.sbs.com.au/news/article/2016/11/21/we-are-living-dog-explosion-malaysians-seeking-asylum-australia

Buss, Doris, and Didi Herman. 2003. *Globalizing Family Values: The Christian Right in International Politics*. Minneapolis: University of Minnesota Press.

Bustamante, Jorge. 2011. Report of the Special Rapporteur on the Human Rights of Migrants. Human Rights Council A/HRC/17/33. https://documents-dds-ny.un.org/doc/UNDOC/GEN/G11/121/83/PDF/G1112183.pdf

Caballero-Antony, Mely. 2008. Reflections on Managing Migration in Southeast Asia: Mitigating the Unintended Consequences of Securitisation. In *Security and Migration in Asia: The Dynamics of Securitisation*, ed. Melissa G. Curley and Wong Siu-lun. Oxon: Routledge.

Caouette, Dominique, and Denis Cote. 2011. Ripe for A New Asian Multilateralism? Asean and Contemporary Regional Dynamics. *European journal of East Asian studies 10* (1): 5–36.

CARAM Asia. 2010. *Malaysia vs Hong Kong: Employers' Perception and Attitudes Towards Foreign Domestic Workers*. Kuala Lumpur: CARAM Asia.

Cardno. 2016a. http://www.cardno.com/en-au/AboutUs/Pages/Home.aspx

———. 2016b. http://www.cardno.com/en-au/Projects/Pages/Labour-Mobility-Assistance-Program-(LMAP).aspx

Castells, Manuel. 2010. *The Network Society*. Hoboken: Wiley.

Castles, Stephen. 2013. The Forces Driving Global Migration. *Journal of Intercultural Studies 34* (2): 122–140.

———. 2015. Migration, Precarious Work, and Rights: Historical and Current Perspectives. In *Migration, Precarity, and Global Governance: Challenges and Opportunities for Labour*, ed. Carl-Ulrik Schierup, Ronaldo Munck, Branka Likic-Brboric, and Anders Neergaard, 46–67. Oxford: Oxford University Press.

Castles, Stephen, and S. Loughna. 2005. Trends in Asylum Migration to Industrialized Countries, 1990–2001. In *Poverty, International Migration and Asylum*, ed. G. Burjas and J. Crisp. New York: Palgrave Macmillan.

Chandler, David. 2014. Beyond Neoliberalism: Resilience, the New Art of Governing Complexity. *Resilience 2* (1): 47–63.

Charnysh, Volha, Paulette Lloyd, and Beth A. Simmons. 2015. Frames and Consensus Formation in International Relations: The Case of Trafficking in Persons. *European Journal of International Relations 21* (2): 323–351.

Clarke, Melissa. 2015. Tony Abbott tells European Leaders to Turn Back Asylum Seekers or Risk 'Catastrophic Error'. *ABC News*. http://www.abc.net.au/news/2015-10-28/tony-abbott-urges-european-leaders-to-turn-back-asylum-seekers/6890886

Clemens, Michael. 2014. Does Development Reduce Migration? *CGD Working Paper 359*. Washington, DC: Center for Global Development. http://www.cgdev.org/publication/does-development-reduce-migration-working-paper-359

Cohen, Eliot A. 1996. A Revolution in Warfare. *Foreign Affairs 75* (2): 37–54.
Commission on Filipinos Overseas. 2014. *2014 CFO Compendium of Statistics.* http://cfo.gov.ph/images/pdf/pdf-migration/2014-CFO-Statistical-Compendium.pdf
Crawley, Heaven, Franck Düvell, Katharine Jones, Simon McMahon, and Nando Sigona. 2016. Destination Europe? Understanding the Dynamics and Drivers of Mediterranean Migration in 2015. *Unravelling the Mediterranean Migration Crisis (MEDMIG) Final Report*, November 2016. http://www.medmig.info/wp-content/uploads/2016/12/research-brief-destination-europe.pdf
Crenshaw, Kimberlé. 1989. Demarginalizing the Intersection of Race and Sex: A Black Feminist Critique of Antidiscrimination Doctrine, Feminist Theory and Antiracist Politics. *University of Chicago Legal Forum.* 138–167.
Cronin, Kathryn. 1999. Controlling Immigration: Australian Legislation and Practice. *Reform 19* (75): 6–9.
Das Gupta, Tanya. 2008. Racism/Anti-Racism, Precarious Employment, and Unions. In *Daily Struggles: The Deepening Racialization and Feminization of Poverty in Canada*, ed. Siu-ming Kwok and Maria A. Wallis, 143–157. Toronto: Canadian Scholars' Press.
Dauvergne, Catherine. 2005. *Humanitarianism, Identity, and Nation: Migration Laws of Australia and Canada.* Vancouver: UBC Press.
Deleuze, Gilles. 1992. Postscript on the Societies of Control. *October* 59: 3–7.
Detienne, Marcel. 2002. *The Writing of Orpheus: Greek Myth in Cultural Context.* Trans. Janet Lloyd. Baltimore: Johns Hopkins University Press.
Devetak, Richard. 2004. In Fear of Refugees: The Politics of Border Protection in Australia. *The International Journal of Human Rights* 8 (1): 101–109.
DIBP—Department of Immigration and Border Protection. 2013. Asylum Trends—Australia 2012–13. https://www.immi.gov.au/media/publications/statistics/immigration-update/asylum-trends-aus-2012-13.pdf
DIBP. 2014a. FOI Release to Sean Parnell on Movement Alert List. https://www.border.gov.au/AccessandAccountability/Documents/FOI/FA140100764.pdf
———. 2014b. Asylum Statistics—Australia: Quarterly Tables—June Quarter 2014.
———. 2015a. *Strategy 2020.* https://www.border.gov.au/CorporateInformation/Documents/strategy-2020.pdf
———. 2015b. Border Technology Strategy. Presentation to DIBP Industry Summit. https://www.border.gov.au/Engagingwithindustry/Documents/industry-summit/border-technology-strategy.pdf
———. 2016a. Movement Alert List Factsheet. https://www.border.gov.au/about/corporate/information/fact-sheets/77mal
———. 2016b. ABF Assists Malaysian Maritime Enforcement Agency in Maritime Security Operation. Australian Border Force Press Release. 29 June 2016. http://newsroom.border.gov.au/releases/b504bc51-9d8e-47bb-a7c1-d62caf14a85a

———. 2016c. Subclass 457 Quarterly Report: Quarter Ending at 30 June 2016. https://www.border.gov.au/ReportsandPublications/Documents/statistics/457-quarterly-report-30-06-2016.pdf

Divakaran, P. 2016. Human Rights Commission of Malaysia Calls for Inquests Following Deaths at Immigration Detention Centres. *The Star (Malaysia)*, 3 September2016.http://asianews.network/content/human-rights-commission-malaysia-calls-inquests-following-deaths-immigration-detention

Doezema, Jo. 2010. *Sex Slaves and Discourse Masters: The Construction of Trafficking*. London; New York: Zed Books.

Doherty, Ben. 2012. We Live in Fear Every Day. *The Age*, 24 July 2012. http://www.theage.com.au/world/we-live-in-fear-every-day-20120723-22koc.html

———. 2016. Asylum Seeker Forcibly Returned by Australia says his Refugee Claim was Ignored. *The Guardian*, 17 May 2016. https://www.theguardian.com/australia-news/2016/may/18/asylum-seeker-forcibly-returned-by-australia-says-his-refugee-claim-was-ignored

Doty, Roxanne. 2011. Bare Life: Border-Crossing Deaths and Spaces of Moral Alibi. *Environment and Planning D: Society and Space 29*: 599–612.

Duany, Jorge. 2011. *Blurred Borders: Transnational Migration between the Hispanic Caribbean and the United States*. Chapel Hill: University of North Carolina Press.

Dutton, Peter. 2015. Stronger Regional Maritime Security. Minister for Immigration and Border Protection Press Release. 27 February 2015. http://www.minister.border.gov.au/peterdutton/2015/Pages/stronger-regional-maritime-security.aspx

Emmers, Ralf, Beth K. Greener, and Nicholas Thomas. 2008. Securitising Human Trafficking in the Asia-Pacific: Regional Organisations and Response Strategies. In *Security and Migration in Asia: The Dynamics of Securitisation*, ed. Melissa G. Curley and Wong Siu-lun. Oxon: Routledge.

Empower. 2012. Recommendations Regarding Trafficking from Sex Workers of Empower. http://www.empowerfoundation.org/sexy_en.php?id=6

Entman, Robert M. 1993. Framing: Toward Clarification of a Fractured Paradigm. *Journal of Communication* 43 (4): 51–58.

Fassin, Didier. 2012. *Humanitarian Reason: A Moral History of the Present*. Berkeley: University of California Press.

Finnemore, Martha, and Kathryn Sikkink. 1998. International Norm Dynamics and Political Change. *International Organization* 52 (04): 887–917.

Firth, Stewart. 2007. Pacific Islands Trade, Labor, and Security in an Era of Globalization. *The Contemporary Pacific 19* (1): 111–134.

Flynn, Michael. 2016. Sovereign Discomfort: Can Liberal Norms Lead to Increasing Immigration Detention? In *Immigration Detention, Risk and Human Rights*, ed. Maria João Guia, Robert Koulish, and Valsamis Mitsilegas. Cham: Springer.

Forss, Kim. 2012. Working Against Trafficking through the Multilateral System—A Study of Coordination between UN Agencies at Global, Regional and National Levels. Commissioned by the Ministry for Foreign Affairs, Sweden. http://un-act.org/wp-content/uploads/2016/01/Coordination20Anti-Trafficking20Report1.pdf

Foucualt, Michel. 2008. *The Birth of Biopolitics: Lectures at the Collège de France, 1978–1979*. Basingstoke: Palgrave Macmillan.

Furnow, Mary Margaret, Suzanne Franzway, and Valentine M. Moghadam. 2011. Introduction: Globalization and Women's Social Rights. In *Making Globalization Work for Women: The Role of Social Rights and Trade Union Leadership*, ed. Valentine M. Moghadam, Mary Margaret Fonow, and Suzanne Franzway. Albany: SUNY Press.

GAATW—Global Alliance Against Traffic in Women, Foundation Against Trafficking in Women, and International Human Rights Law Group. 1999. Human Rights Standards for the Treatment of Trafficked Persons. http://www.hrlawgroup.org/resources/content/IHRLGTraffickin_tsStandards.pdf

GAATW. 2014. Criminalising Clients Endangers Sex Workers and Creates Barriers to Exiting Sex Work: Lessons Learned from the Anti-Trafficking Industry. Brief to the Senate Legal and Constitutional Affairs Committee on Bill C-36: Protection of Communities and Exploited Persons Act Submitted 8 September 2014 by the Global Alliance against Traffic in Women, International Secretariat (GAATW-IS) and Global Alliance Against Traffic in Women—Canada (GAATW-Canada). http://www.gaatw.org/advocacy/Bill_C-36-GAATW_brief.pdf

———. 2016a. The Early Years. http://gaatw.org/about-us/history/156-about-us/history/440-the-early-years

———. 2016b. GAATW-IS Statement on Amnesty International's Policy on Sex Work. http://gaatw.org/events-and-news/68-gaatw-news/847-gaatw-is-statement-on-amnesty-international-s-policy-on-sex-work

Gallagher, Anne. 2006. Human Rights and Human Trafficking in Thailand: A Shadow TIP Report. In *Trafficking and the Global Sex Industry*, ed. Karen Beeks and Delila Amir, 139–163. Lanham, MD: Lexington Books.

———. 2016. Unravelling the 2016 Global Slavery Index. *Open Democracy*, 28 June 2016. https://www.opendemocracy.net/anne-gallagher/unravelling-2016-global-slavery-index

Gallagher, Anne, and Surtees, Rebecca. 2012. Measuring the Success of Counter Trafficking Interventions in the Criminal Justice Sector: Who Decides—and How? *Anti-Trafficking Review 1*: 10–30.

Ghosh, Bimal, ed. 2000. *Managing Migration: Time for a New International Regime?* Oxford: Oxford University Press.

———. 2005. Managing Migration: Whither the Missing Regime? UNESCO. http://unesdoc.unesco.org/images/0013/001391/139149e.pdf

Global Commission on International Migration. 2005. *Migration in an Interconnected World: New Directions for Action*. http://www.iom.int/jahia/webdav/site/myjahiasite/shared/shared/mainsite/policy_and_research/gcim/GCIM_Report_Complete.pdf

Global Detention Project. 2015. Malaysia Immigration Detention Profile. https://www.globaldetentionproject.org/countries/asia-pacific/malaysia

———. 2016. Indonesia Immigration Detention Profile. https://www.globaldetentionproject.org/countries/asia-pacific/indonesia

Gregory, Derek. 2004. *The Colonial Present: Afghanistan, Palestine, Iraq*. Malden: Blackwell.

Griffiths, Emma. 2013. Labor Strikes Compromise 457 Visa Crackdown Deal with Crossbench MPs. *ABC News*, 26 June 2013. http://www.abc.net.au/news/2013-06-26/labor-strikes-compromise-457-visa-deal-with-crossbench-mps/4782722

Grundy-Warr, Carl, and Elaine Wong Siew Yin. 2002. Geographies of Displacement: The Karenni and the Shan Across The Myanmar-Thailand Border. *Singapore Journal of Tropical Geography* 23 (1): 93–122.

Haas, Ernst B. 1980. Why Collaborate? Issue-Linkage and International Regimes. *World Politics 32* (3): 357–405.

de Haas, Hein. 2010. Migration Transitions: A Theoretical and Empirical Inquiry into the Developmental Drivers of International Migration. *International Migration Institute Working Paper 24*. https://heindehaas.files.wordpress.com/2015/05/de-haas-2010-migration-transitions-imi-wp-24.pdf

Hage, Ghassan. 2000. *White Nation: Fantasies of White Supremacy in a Multicultural Society*. New York: Routledge.

———. 2014. Continuity and Change in Australian Racism. *Journal of Intercultural Studies 35* (3): 232–237.

Hasham, Nicole. 2016. Blow to Australia's $55 Million Cambodia Deal as Two More Refugees Quit. *Sydney Morning Herald*, 8 March 2016. http://www.smh.com.au/federal-politics/political-news/blow-to-australias-55-million-cambodia-deal-as-two-more-refugees-reportedly-leave-20160308-gnda8q.html

Hirschman, Albert O. 1978. Exit, Voice, and the State. *World Politics 31* (1): 90–107.

Hobbes, Thomas. 1996. *Leviathan*. Oxford: Oxford University Press.

Holdcroft, Jenny. 2013. Implications for Union Work of the Trend Towards Precarization of Work. *International Journal of Labour Research 5* (1): 41–58.

Hollifield, James F. 2000. Migration and the 'New' International Order: The Missing Regime. In *Managing Migration: Time for a New International Regime?* ed. Bimal Ghosh. Oxford: Oxford University Press.

Howe, Joanna. 2016. Examining a Temporary Migrant Worker's Ability to Make a Complaint of Sexual Harassment. *Adelaide Law School Research Paper No. 2016-25*. https://papers.ssrn.com/sol3/Delivery.cfm?abstractid=2821351

Hughes, Steve. 2002. Coming in from the Cold: Labour, the ILO, and the International Labour Standards Regime. In *Global Governance: Critical Perspectives*, ed. Rorden Wilkinson and Steve Hughes, 155–171. London: Routledge.

Huguet, Jerrold. 2014. Introduction. In *Thailand Migration Report*, ed. Jerrold Huguet, xix–xxi. Bangkok: United Nations Thematic Working Group on Migration in Thailand.

Human Rights Watch. 2013. *Barely Surviving: Detention, Abuse, and Neglect of Migrant Children in Indonesia*. https://www.hrw.org/sites/default/files/reports/indonesia0613webwcover.pdf

———. 2014. *Two Years With No Moon: Immigration Detention of Children in Thailand*. https://www.hrw.org/sites/default/files/reports/thailand0914_ForUpload_0.pdf

———. 2016. *Submission to the Senate Legal and Constitutional Affairs Committee on its Inquiry into Abuse, Self-harm, and Neglect of Refugees and Asylum Seekers on Nauru and Manus Island*. Inquiry into the Serious Allegations of Abuse, Self-Harm and Neglect of Asylum-Seekers in Relation to the Nauru Regional Processing Centre, and Any Like Allegations in Relation to the Manus Regional Processing Centre Referred to the Senate Legal and Constitutional Affairs Committee. Submission 22. http://www.aph.gov.au/Parliamentary_Business/Committees/Senate/Legal_and_Constitutional_Affairs/NauruandManusRPCs/Submissions

Hyndman, Jennifer, and Alison Mountz. 2008. Another Brick in the Wall? Neo-Refoulement and the Externalization of Asylum by Australia and Europe. *Government and Opposition* 43 (2): 249–269.

ICA (Immigration and Checkpoints Authority). 2017. Anti-Harbouring. https://www.ica.gov.sg/page.aspx?pageid=328

IDC—International Detention Coalition. 2016. *There are Alternatives: A Handbook for Preventing Unnecessary Immigration Detention* (revised edition). International Detention Coalition. http://idcoalition.org/publication/download/there-are-alternatives-revised-edition/

ILO—International Labour Organisation. 2012. ILO Global Estimate of Forced Labour: Results and Methodology. http://www.ilo.org/wcmsp5/groups/public/@ed_norm/@declaration/documents/publication/wcms_182004.pdf

ILO. 2015. Analytical Report on the International Labour Migration Statistics Database in ASEAN

Immigration and Refugee Board of Canada. 2013. Responses to Information Requests (August 2011–January 2013). Ottawa: Research Directorate, Immigration and Refugee Board of Canada. https://www.justice.gov/sites/default/files/eoir/legacy/2014/03/06/LKA104245.E.pdf

IOM Country Mission in Thailand and the Asian Research Center for Migration, Chulalongkorn University. 2013. Assessing Potential Changes in the Migration

Patterns of Myanmar Migrants and their Impacts on Thailand. http://th.iom.int/index.php/migration-resources/func-download/201/chk,61c1a7e0a53f61289109191a7914141a/no_html,1/

IOM—International Organisation for Migration. 2014. Factsheet: Immigration and Border Management. http://www.iom.or.id/sites/default/files/Factsheet%20-%20IBM.pdf.

IOM. 2016. https://www.iom.int/news/iom-assists-7000-victims-human-trafficking-globally-2015

Joly, Danièle. 2002. Introduction. In *Global Changes in Asylum Regimes*, ed. Danièle Joly. Palgrave Macmillan.

Joseph, Jonathan. 2013. Resilience as Embedded Neoliberalism: A Governmentality Approach. *Resilience 1* (1): 38–52.

Karlsen, Elibritt, and Janet Phillips. 2014. Developments in Australian Refugee Law and Policy (2012 to August 2013). Parliamentary Library of Australia. http://www.aph.gov.au/About_Parliament/Parliamentary_Departments/Parliamentary_Library/pubs/rp/rp1415/RefugeeLawPolicy

Kaur, Amarjit. 2014. Managing Labour Migration in Malaysia: Guest Worker Programs and the Regularisation of Irregular Labour Migrants as a Policy Instrument. *Asian Studies Review 38* (3): 345–366.

Kelley, Judith G., and Beth A. Simmons. 2014. Politics by Number: Indicators as Social Pressure in International Relations. *American Journal of Political Science* 59 (1): 55–70.

Kenny, Mark. 2013. Labor Taps Resentment on 457 Visas. *The Age*, 14 March 2013. http://www.theage.com.au/federal-politics/political-news/labor-taps-resentment-on-457-visas-20130313-2g0so

Kingsley, Patrick, and Chris Stephen. 2016. Libyan Navy Admits Confrontation with Charity's Rescue Boat. *The Guardian*, 28 August 2016. https://www.theguardian.com/world/2016/aug/28/libyan-navy-admits-confrontation-charity-rescue-boat-msf

Koser, Khalid. 2010. Responding to Boat Arrivals in Australia: Time for a Reality Check. *Lowy Institute for International Policy*. http://m.lowyinstitute.org/files/pubfiles/Koser,_Responding_web.pdf

Laclau, Ernesto, and Chantal Mouffe. 1985. *Hegemony and Socialist Strategy: Towards a Radical Democratic Politics*. New York: Verso.

Landry, Rachel. 2016. The 'Humanitarian Smuggling' of Refugees: Criminal Offence or Moral Obligation? *Oxford University Refugee Studies Centre Working Paper Series No. 119*.

Ledwith, Sue, and Fiona Colgan. 2007. Tackling Gender, Diversity and Trade Union Democracy: A Worldwide Project? In *Gender, Diversity and Trade Unions: International Perspectives*, ed. Fiona Colgan and Sue Ledwith, 1–27. Abingdon: Routledge.

Leidholdt, Dorchen A. 2003. Prostitution and Trafficking in Women: An Intimate Relationship. In *Prostitution, Trafficking and Traumatic Stress*, ed. Melissa Farley. Hoboken: Routledge.

Lewis, Daniel Ray, Nuarpear Lekfuangfu, Irena Vojackova-Sollorano, Federico Soda, and Claudia Natali. 2010. *Forecasting Migration Flows: The Relationships among Economic Development, Demographic Change and Migration in the Greater Mekong Subregion*. IOM.

Makaremi, Chowra. 2009. Governing Borders in France: From Extraterritorial to Humanitarian Confinement. *Canadian Journal of Law and Society 24* (3): 411–432.

Maley, William. 2001. Security, People-Smuggling, and Australia's New Afghan Refugees. *Australian Journal of International Affairs* 55 (3): 351–370. doi:10.1080/10357710120095216.

March, James G., and Johan P. Olsen. 1998. The Institutional Dynamics of International Political Orders. *International Organization 52*: 943–969.

Martin, Phillip. 2007. The Economic Contribution of Migrant Workers to Thailand: Towards Policy Development. *ILO Sub-regional Office for East Asia*. http://natlex.ilo.ch/wcmsp5/groups/public/---asia/---ro-bangkok/documents/publication/wcms_098230.pdf

Martin, Lisa. 2014. We're Taking the Sugar Off Table: Morrison. *Sydney Morning Herald*, 19 November 2014. http://www.smh.com.au//breaking-news-national/were-taking-the-sugar-off-table-morrison-20141119-3kndk.html

Matas, David. 2015. Sri Lankan Tamil Refugees: Malaysia February 2015. http://www.i-tran.ca/I-TRAN%20FINAL%20REPORT%20%20MALAYSIA%202015.pdf

Mbembe, Achille. 2014. Necropolitics. In *Foucault in an Age of Terror: Essays on Biopolitics and the Defence of Society*, ed. Stephen Morton and Stephen Bygrave, 152–182. Basingstoke: Palgrave Macmillan.

McAdam, Jane. 2011. Swimming against the Tide: Why a Climate Change Displacement Treaty is Not the Answer. *International Journal of Refugee Law 23* (1): 2–27.

McAulife, Marie. 2013. Seeking the Views of Irregular Migrants: Decision Making, Drivers and Migration Journeys. *Irregular Migration Research Program Occasional Paper Series 05/2013*, Department of Immigration and Border Protection. https://www.border.gov.au/ReportsandPublications/Documents/research/views-irregular-migrant-decision-drivers-journey.pdf

McNamara, Karen Elizabeth, and Chris Gibson. 2009. 'We Do Not Want to Leave Our Land': Pacific Ambassadors at the United Nations Resist the Category of 'Climate Refugees'. *Geoforum 40* (3): 475–483.

Medhora, Shalailah. 2015. 'Nope, Nope, Nope': Tony Abbott says Australia will Take no Rohingya Refugees. *The Guardian*, 21 May 2015. https://www.theguardian.com/world/2015/may/21/nope-nope-nope-tony-abbott-says-australia-will-take-no-rohingya-refugees

Ministry of Foreign Affairs of the People's Republic of China. 2014. *China's Relationship with United Nations High Commissioner for Refugees (UNHCR)*. Statement by the Permanent Mission of the People's Republic of China to the United Nations Office at Geneva and Other International Organizations in Switzerland. Accessed 5 January 2016. http://www.fmprc.gov.cn/ce/cegv/eng/rqrd/jblc/t85094.htm

Ministry of Immigration of Malaysia, Information Technology and Records Section. 2015. Statistik pekerja asing aktif mengikut sektor dan warganegara dari 1 januari 2015 sehinga 31 Oktober 2015 [Statistics on Foreign Workers by Sector and Citizenship from January 1, 2015 until October 31, 2015]. Copy of Unpublished Statistics Provided to the Author by Malaysia Trade Union Congress.

Ministry of Manpower, Singapore. 2016a. Foreign Workforce Numbers. http://www.mom.gov.sg/documents-and-publications/foreign-workforce-numbers

———. 2016b. Work Passes and Permits. http://www.mom.gov.sg/passes-and-permits

———. 2016c. Sector-Specific Rules for Work Permit. http://www.mom.gov.sg/passes-and-permits/work-permit-for-foreign-worker/sector-specific-rules

Mitropoulos, Angela. 2012. *Contract and Contagion: From Biopolitics to Oikonomia*. New York: Minor Compositions.

———. 2015. Archipelago of Risk: Uncertainty, Borders and Migration Detention Systems. *New Formations* 84 (85): 163–183.

———. 2016. On Borders / Race / Fascism / Labour / Precarity / Feminism / etc. *Base* 30 (1). http://www.basepublication.org/?p=107

MMN—Mekong Migration Network. 2014. The Precarious Status of Migrants in Thailand: Reflections on the Exodus of Cambodian Migrants and Lessons Learnt. http://www.mekongmigration.org/wp-content/uploads/2014/12/FINAL-REPORT-The-precarious-status-of-migrants-in-Thailand.pdf

Morrisson, Scott. 2014. A New Force Protecting Australia's Borders. Address to the Lowy Institute for International Policy, Sydney. Friday, 9 May 2014. https://www.lowyinstitute.org/news-and-media/multimedia/audio/podcast-future-border-protection-scott-morrison-mp

National Economic and Social Development Board. 2011. *The Eleventh National Economic and Social Development Plan (2012–2016)*. Bangkok: Office of the Prime Minister.

Nethery, Amy. 2010. *Immigration Detention in Australia*. Doctoral Thesis, Deakin University. https://dro.deakin.edu.au/eserv/DU:30032385/nethery-immigrationdetention-2010A.pdf

Neumayer, Eric. 2004. Asylum Destination Choice: What Makes Some West European Countries More Attractive than Others? *European Union Politics* 5 (2): 156–180.

New York Times Editorial Board. 2015. Australia's Brutal Treatment of Migrants. *New York Times*. A30 of Print Edition. 3 September 2015. http://www.nytimes.com/2015/09/03/opinion/australias-brutal-treatment-of-migrants.html

Nyland, Chris, Helen Forbes-Mewett, Simon Marginson, Gaby Ramia, Erlenawati Sawir, and Sharon Smith. 2009. International Student-Workers in Australia: A New Vulnerable Workforce. *Journal of Education and Work* 22 (1): 1–14.

Ooi, Giok Ling. 2005. The Role of the Developmental State and Interethnic Relations in Singapore. *Asian Ethnicity 6* (2): 109–120.

Parker, Noel, Nick Vaughan-Williams, et al. 2009. Lines in the Sand? Towards an Agenda for Critical Border Studies. *Geopolitics 14* (3): 582–587.

Parliament of Australia. 2013. Migration Amendment (Unauthorised Maritime Arrivals and Other Measures) Act 2013. https://www.comlaw.gov.au/Details/C2013A00035

Peter, Zsombor, and Naren, Kuch. 2016. Maids Claim Fatal Abuse at Malaysian Depot. *The Cambodia Daily*, 15 August 2016. https://www.cambodiadaily.com/news/maids-claim-fatal-abuse-malaysian-depot-116653/

Phillips, Lawrence. 2000. British Slavery after Abolition: The Pacific Trade. *Race and Class 41* (3): 13–27.

Pickering, Sharon. 2014. Floating Carceral Spaces: Border Enforcement and Gender on the High Seas. *Punishment & Society 16* (2): 187–205.

Pickering, Sharon, and Leanne Weber. 2011. *Globalization and Borders: Death at the Global Frontier*. Basingstoke, Hampshire: Palgrave Macmillan.

———. 2013. Policing Transversal Borders. In *The Borders of Punishment. Migration, Citizenship, and Social Exclusion*, ed. Katja Franko Aas and Mary Bosworth, 93–110. Oxford: Oxford University Press.

Pilz, Kerstin. 2005. *Mapping Complexity: Literature and Science in the Works of Italo Calvino*. Leicester: Troubador.

Pongsawat, Pitch. 2007. Border Partial Citizenship, Border Towns, and Thai-Myanmar Cross-Border Development: Case Studies at the Thai Border Towns. Doctoral dissertation in City and Regional Planning, University of California, Berkeley.

Quirk, Joel, and André Broome. 2015. The Politics of Numbers: The Global Slavery Index and the Marketplace of Activism. 10 March 2015. https://www.opendemocracy.net/beyondslavery/joel-quirk-andré-broome/politics-of-numbers-global-slavery-index-and-marketplace-of-ac

Radio New Zealand. 2017. Pacific Concern Relayed at UN over West Papua Abuses. *Radio New Zealand News*, 2 March 2017. http://www.radionz.co.nz/international/pacific-news/325717/pacific-concern-relayed-at-un-over-west-papua-abuses

Rahman, Mizanur. 2009. *In Quest of Golden Deer: Bangladeshi Transient Migrants Overseas*. Saarbrucken: VDM Verlag.

Rajaram, Prem Kumar, and Carl Grundy-Warr, eds. 2007. *Borderscapes: Hidden Geographies and Politics at Territory's Edge*. Vol. 29. Minneapolis: University of Minnesota Press.

Rebgetz, Louisa. 2016. Inadequate Care, Communication Failures in Lead-up to Asylum Seeker's Death, Court Hears. *ABC News*, 10 June 2016. http://www.abc.net.au/news/2016-06-10/khazaei-coronial-inquest-inadequate-care-in-lead-up-to-death/7501106

Reid-Henry, S.M. 2014. Humanitarianism as Liberal Diagnostic: Humanitarian Reason and the Political Rationalities of the Liberal Will-to-Care. *Transactions of the Institute of British Geographers 39*: 418–431.

Reus-Smit, Christian. 1997. The Constitutional Structure of International Society and the Nature of Fundamental Institutions. *International Organization* 51 (4): 555–589.

RISE—Refugees, Survivors and Ex-Detainees. 2015. Twitter Post, 3 September 2015. https://twitter.com/riserefugee/status/639597818559098880

Roberts, George. 2015. Indonesian Police Documents detail Boat Turn-back and Alleged Payments to People Smuggling Crew. *ABC News*, 17 June 2015. http://www.abc.net.au/news/2015-06-17/indonesian-documents-detail-boat-turnback-and-alleged-payments/6551472

Robinson, Gwen. 2013. Anti-Muslim Violence Spreads in Myanmar. *Financial Times*, 25 March. http://www.ft.com/cms/s/0/5fdec778-9553-11e2-a4fa-00144feabdc0.html

Robinson, Duncan. 2016. EU Border Force Accuses Charities of Collusion with Migrant Smugglers. *Financial Times*, 15 December 2016. https://www.ft.com/content/3e6b6450-c1f7-11e6-9bca-2b93a6856354

Robinson, Vaughan, and Segrott, Jeremy. 2002. Understanding the Decision-Making of Asylum Seekers. Home Office Research Study 243. UK Home Office Research, Development and Statistics Directorate. https://www.researchgate.net/profile/Jeremy_Segrott/publication/248205716_Understanding_the_Decision-Making_of_Asylum-Seekers/links/00b49537f535421143000000.pdf

Rodenhäuser, Tilman. 2014. Another Brick in the Wall: Carrier Sanctions and the Privatization of Immigration Control. *International Journal of Refugee Law 26* (2): 223–247.

Rodriguez, Cristina. 2010. Building Capacity for the Transnational Regulation of Migration. *Columbia Law Review Sidebar 110*: 1–11.

Rogers, Chris. 2016. The Christians Held in Thailand After Fleeing Pakistan. *BBC News*, 26 February 2016. www.bbc.com/news/magazine-35654804

RSO—Regional Support Office to the Bali Process. 2013. Concept Note: Meeting under RSO Auspices on "Mapping Disembarkation Options: Towards Strengthening Cooperation in Managing Irregular Movements by Sea". http://www.baliprocess.net/regional-support-office/movements-by-sea/

RSO. 2014a. Policy Guide on Criminalizing Trafficking in Persons.
———. 2014b. Policy Guide on Criminalizing Migrant Smuggling.
———. 2014c. RSO Forward Work Plan 2015–17. http://www.baliprocess.net/files/Forward%20Work%20Plan%202015-2017.pdf
——— 2016. Bali Process Strategy for Cooperation: Update. http://www.baliprocess.net/UserFiles/baliprocess/File/BP%20Strategy%20-%20Presented%20to%20SOM%20March%202016.pdf
Ruggie, John G. 1982. International Regimes, Transactions, and Change: Embedded Liberalism in the Postwar Economic Order. *International Organization 36* (2): 379–415.
Sampson, Robyn. 2015. Mandatory, Non-Reviewable, Indefinite: Immigration Detention in Australia. In *Immigration Detention: The Migration of a Policy and Its Human Impact*, ed. Amy Nethery and Stephanie J. Silverman, 104–114. Oxon: Routledge.
Sampson, Robyn C., Sandra M. Gifford, and Savitri Taylor. 2016. The Myth of Transit: The Making of a Life by Asylum Seekers and Refugees in Indonesia. *Journal of Ethnic and Migration Studies* 42 (7): 1135–1152.
Schloenhardt, Andreas. 2008. Illegal Migration and Migrant Smuggling in the Asia-Pacific: Balancing Regional Security and Human Rights. In *Security and Migration in Asia: The Dynamics of Securitisation*, ed. Melissa G. Curley and Wong Siu-lun. Oxon: Routledge.
Sekretariat Kabinet Republik Indonesia. 2017. President Jokowi Signs Presidential Regulation on Handling of Refugees from Abroad. 16 January 2017. http://setkab.go.id/en/president-jokowi-signs-presidential-regulation-on-handling-of-refugees-from-abroad/
Senate Select Committee on the Recent Allegations Relating to Conditions and Circumstances at the Regional Processing Centre in Nauru. 2015. *Taking Responsibility: Conditions and Circumstances at Australia's Regional Processing Centre in Nauru.* http://www.aph.gov.au/Parliamentary_Business/Committees/Senate/Regional_processing_Nauru/Regional_processing_Nauru/~/media/Committees/nauru_ctte/Final_Report/report.pdf
Sending, Ole Jacob, and Iver B. Neumann. 2006. Governance to Governmentality: Analyzing NGOs, States, and Power. *International Studies Quarterly* 50 (3): 651–672.
Shih, Elena. 2014. Globalising Rehabilitative Regimes: Framing the Moral Economy of Vocational Training in After-Trafficking Work. In *Human Trafficking in Asia: Forcing Issues*, ed. Sallie Yea, 64–77. Oxon: Routledge.
Shwegu Thitsar. 2014. Cheated Seafarers Speak Out: 'It's Simply Human Trafficking. *Myanmar Times*, 27 October 2014. http://www.mmtimes.com/index.php/national-news/12077-cheated-seafarers-speak-out-it-s-simply-human-trafficking.html

Sigona, Nando, and Jennifer Allsopp. 2016. Mind the Gap: Why are Unaccompanied Children Disappearing in their Thousands? *Open Democracy*. https://www.opendemocracy.net/5050/nando-sigona-and-jennifer-allsopp/mind-gap-why-are-unaccompanied-children-disappearing-in-thous

Spinks, Harriet. 2013. A Return to Temporary Protection Visas? *Australian Parliamentary Library*. http://www.aph.gov.au/About_Parliament/Parliamentary_Departments/Parliamentary_Library/FlagPost/2013/November/A_return_to_Temporary_Protection_Visas

SPS—Singapore Prison Service. 2016. *Collaboration: Annual Report 2015*. http://www.sps.gov.sg/sites/default/files/SPSAnnual_lowres_revised.pdf

Squire, Vicki, ed. 2010. *The Contested Politics of Mobility: Borderzones and Irregularity*. London: Routledge.

———. 2015. *Post/Humanitarian Border Politics between Mexico and the US: People, Places, Things*. Basingstoke: Palgrave Macmillan.

Stasiulis, Daiva, and Nira Yuval-Davis, eds. 1995. *Unsettling Settler Societies: Articulations of Gender, Race, Ethnicity and Class*. Thousand Oaks, CA: Sage.

Stewart, Cameron. 2004. Put Out of Business. *Weekend Australian*, 21 August 2004.

SUHAKUM—Human Rights Commission of Malaysia. 2013. *Roundtable on Alternatives to Immigration Detention*. Kuala Lumpur: SUHAKUM.

The Sun Daily. 2015. No Indication of Second Wave of 'Boat People' at the Moment, says MMEA. 13 November 2015. http://www.thesundaily.my/news/1610306

———. 2016a. MMEA Probes Possibility of Terrorists Entering M'sia through National Waters. 16 January 2016. http://www.thesundaily.my/news/1667889

———. 2016b. Curbing Movement of Terrorists New Focus of Ops Redback. 25 October 2016. http://www.thesundaily.my/news/2015537

Taylor, Savitri. 2008. Offshore Barriers to Asylum Seeker Movement: The Exercise of Power without Responsibility? In *Forced Migration, Human Rights and Security*, ed. Jane McAdam. Portland, OR: Hart Publishing.

Thin Lei Win. 2014. Most Burmese Migrants in Thailand Want to Go Home, But Not Yet. *Myanmar Business Today*, 2–8 January 2014, P6, 10.

Thompson, Geoff, Joel Tozer, and Wayne Harley. 2016. Manus Island: 'Pathetic' Bureaucratic Response Blamed for Asylum Seeker Hamid Khazaei's Death. *ABC News*, 26 April 2016. http://www.abc.net.au/news/2016-04-25/manus-island-blunder-blamed-for-asylum-seeker-death/7355858

Tlozek, Eric. 2015. Manus Island Detention Centre Staff Failing to Respect PNG Law, Flying Out to Escape Questioning, Police Say. *ABC News*, 28 September 2015. http://www.abc.net.au/news/2015-09-27/manus-island-police-detention-centre-staff-fail-to-respect-law/6807844

Toscano, Nick. 2015. One in Five Migrant Workers on 457 Visas could be Underpaid or Incorrectly Employed. *The Sydney Morning Herald*, 29 May 2015.

http://www.smh.com.au/national/one-in-five-migrant-workers-on-457-visas-could-be-underpaid-or-incorrectly-employed-20150529-ghcmxr.html
UN. 2000. Protocol to Prevent, Suppress and Punish Trafficking in Persons, Especially Women and Children, Supplementing the United Nations Convention Against Transnational Organized Crime. United Nations.
UN-ACT. 2004. Memorandum of Understanding on Cooperation Against Trafficking in Persons in the Greater Mekong Sub-Region. http://un-act.org/publication/view/2004-commit-mou/
———. 2016a. The Bangkok Declaration on Irregular Migration. http://un-act.org/publication/view/the-bangkok-declaration-on-irregular-migration-1999/
———. 2016b. Coordinating and Innovating Counter-Trafficking. http://un-act.org/wp-content/uploads/2016/04/UN-ACT-Brochure.pdf
UNDESA (United Nations Department of Economic and Social Affairs) Population Division. 2013. Trends in International Migrant Stock: The 2013 Revision (United Nations Database, POP/DB/MIG/Stock/Rev. 2013). http://esa.un.org/unmigration/migrantstocks2013.htm?mtotals
UNDESA. 2016. International Migration Report 2015. ST/ESA/SER.A/375. http://www.un.org/en/development/desa/population/migration/publications/migrationreport/docs/MigrationReport2015_Highlights.pdf
UNHRC (United Nations High Commission for Refugees). 1997. A v. Australia, Communication No. 560/1993, U.N. Doc. CCPR/C/59/D/560/1993. http://hrlibrary.umn.edu/undocs/html/vws560.html
UNHCR. 2007a. Vietnamese Refugees Well Settled in China, Await Citizenship. http://www.unhcr.org/464302994.html
———. 2007b. Advisory Opinion on the Extraterritorial Application of Non-Refoulement Obligations under the 1951 Convention Relating to the Status of Refugees and its 1967 Protocol. 26 January 2007. http://www.refworld.org/docid/45f17a1a4.html
———. 2015a. *2015 UNHCR Country Operations Profile—Myanmar*. http://www.unhcr.org/pages/49e4877d6.html#
———. 2015b. *Bay of Bengal and Andaman Sea Initiative*. http://www.unhcr.org/557040af9.html
———. 2015c. South-East Asia: Mixed Maritime Movements, April–June 2015.
———. 2015d. National Action Plan—Malaysia. http://www.unhcr.org/5660000a9.pdf
———. 2015e. National Action Plan—Indonesia. http://www.unhcr.org/5666a2ea9.pdf
———. 2016a. Submission by The Office of the United Nations High Commissioner for Refugees. Inquiry into the Serious Allegations of Abuse, Self-Harm and Neglect of Asylum-Seekers in Relation to the Nauru Regional Processing Centre, and Any Like Allegations in Relation to the Manus Regional

Processing Centre Referred to the Senate Legal and Constitutional Affairs Committee. Submission 43. http://www.aph.gov.au/Parliamentary_Business/Committees/Senate/Legal_and_Constitutional_Affairs/NauruandManusRPCs/Submissions

———. 2016b. UNHCR Global Report 2015. http://www.unhcr.org/gr15/index.xml

———. 2016c. Mediterranean Death Toll Soars, 2016 is Deadliest Year Yet. http://www.unhcr.org/news/latest/2016/10/580f3e684/mediterranean-death-toll-soars-2016-deadliest-year.html

———. 2016d. Progress Report mid-2016. Beyond Detention: A Global Strategy to Support Governments to End the Detention of Asylum-seekers and Refugees—2014–2019. http://www.refworld.org/docid/57b850dba.html

———. 2017. Population Statistics—Persons of Concern. http://popstats.unhcr.org/en/persons_of_concern

UNODC. 2014. Global Report on Trafficking in Persons. https://www.unodc.org/documents/data-and-analysis/glotip/GLOTIP_2014_full_report.pdf

———. 2015. Issue Paper on 'The Concept of "Exploitation" in the Trafficking in Persons Protocol'. http://un-act.org/wp-content/uploads/2015/06/The-Concept-of-Exploitation-in-the-Trafficking-in-Persons-Protocol.pdf

UNOHCHR. 2017. International Covenant on Civil and Political Rights. http://www.ohchr.org/EN/ProfessionalInterest/Pages/CCPR.aspx

UNSW Human Rights Clinic. 2015. *Temporary Migrant Workers in Australia.* University of New South Wales.

US State Department. 2005. Trafficking Victims Protection Reauthorization Act of 2005. http://www.state.gov/j/tip/laws/61106.htm

———. 2015. Country Reports on Human Rights Practices for 2015: Thailand. Bureau of Democracy, Human Rights, and Labor. https://www.state.gov/j/drl/rls/hrrpt/humanrightsreport/index.htm?year=2015&dlid=252803

Vacotto, Beatriz. 2013. Precarious Work and the Exercise of Freedom of Association and Collective Bargaining: Current ILO Jurisprudence. *International Journal of Labour Research* 5 (1): 117–132.

Vaughan-Williams, Nick. 2009. The Generalised Bio-political Border? Re-conceptualising the Limits of Sovereign Power. *Review of International Studies* 35 (4): 729–749.

———. 2015. *Europe's Border Crisis: Biopolitical Security and Beyond.* Oxford: Oxford University Press.

Vaughan-Williams, Nick, and Adrian Little. 2016. Stopping Boats, Saving Lives, Securing Subjects: Humanitarian Borders in Europe and Australia. *European Journal of International Relations*: 1–24.

Verma, Sanmati. 2015. Why Were Most of the Anti-Reclaim Protestors White? *New Matilda.* https://newmatilda.com/2015/04/19/why-were-most-anti-reclaim-protestors-white/

Waever, Ole. 1995. Securitisation and De-securitisation. In *On Security*, ed. Ronnie D. Lipschultz, 46–86. New York: Columbia University Press.
Walia, Harsha. 2013. *Undoing Border Imperialism*. Oakland: AK Press.
Waterman, Peter, and Jill Timms. 2005. Trade Union Internationalism and a Global Civil Society in the Making. In *Global Civil Society 2004–5*, ed. Helmut Anheier, Marlies Glasius, and Mary Kaldor, 175–202. Thousand Oaks, CA: Sage.
Weber, Leanne. 2007. Policing the Virtual Border: Punitive Preemption in Australian Offshore Migration Control. *Social Justice 34*: 77–93.
Weiss, Thomas, and Ramesh Thakur. 2010. *Global Governance and the UN: An Unfinished Journey*. Bloomington: University of Indiana Press.
Williams, Angela. 2008. Turning the Tide: Recognizing Climate Change Refugees in International Law. *Law & Policy 30* (4): 502–529.
Wills, Jane. 2002. Bargaining for the Space to Organize in the Global Economy: A Review of the Accor-IUF Trade Union Rights Agreement. *Review of International Political Economy* 9 (4): 675–700.
Wilson, Lauren. 2013. Senate Passes Amendment to Excise Mainland from Migration Zone. *The Australian*, 16 May 2013.
World Bank. 2016. *Migration and Remittances Factbook 2016*. http://www.worldbank.org/en/research/brief/migration-and-remittances
Xinhua. 2009. Malaysia, Australia to Jointly Curb Human Trafficking. 26 August 2009. http://news.xinhuanet.com/english/2009-08/26/content_11949076.htm
Yonesta, Febi. 2015. *Fact Sheet: Indonesia*. Jakarta: SUAKA.
Yuval-Davis, Nira. 2006. Intersectionality and Feminist Politics. *European Journal of Women's Studies 1* (3): 193–209.

Index[1]

[1] Note: Page numbers followed by "n" refers to notes.

N. Henry, *Asylum, Work, and Precarity*, Critical Studies of the Asia-Pacific, DOI 10.1007/978-3-319-60567-8

The manufacturer's authorised representative in the EU is Springer Nature Customer Service Centre GmbH, Europaplatz 3, 69115 Heidelberg, Germany. If you have any concerns regarding our products, please contact ProductSafety@springernature.com

Printed and bound by CPI Group (UK) Ltd, Croydon, CR0 4YY
30/09/2026
02225565-0007